FYODOR DOSTOEVSKY—THE GATHERING STORM (1846–1847)

A volume in the

NIU Series in Slavic, East European, and Eurasian Studies
Edited by Christine D. Worobec

For a list of books in the series, visit our website at cornellpress.cornell.edu.

FYODOR DOSTOEVSKY—THE GATHERING STORM (1846–1847)

A Life in Letters, Memoirs, and Criticism

Thomas Gaiton Marullo

NORTHERN ILLINOIS UNIVERSITY PRESS
AN IMPRINT OF CORNELL UNIVERSITY PRESS
Ithaca and London

Copyright © 2020 by Cornell University

All rights reserved. Except for brief quotations in a review, this book, or parts thereof, must not be reproduced in any form without permission in writing from the publisher. For information, address Cornell University Press, Sage House, 512 East State Street, Ithaca, New York 14850. Visit our website at cornellpress.cornell.edu.

First published 2020 by Cornell University Press

Library of Congress Cataloging-in-Publication Data

Names: Marullo, Thomas Gaiton, author.
Title: Fyodor Dostoevsky : the gathering storm (1846–1847) : a life in letters, memoirs, and criticism / Thomas Gaiton Marullo.
Description: Ithaca [New York] : Northern Illinois University Press, an imprint of Cornell University Press, 2020. | Series: NIU Series in Slavic, East European, and Eurasian Studies | Includes bibliographical references and index.
Identifiers: LCCN 2020003014 (print) | LCCN 2020003015 (ebook) | ISBN 9781501751851 (cloth) | ISBN 9781501751868 (epub) | ISBN 9781501751875 (pdf)
Subjects: LCSH: Dostoyevsky, Fyodor, 1821–1881. | Dostoyevsky, Fyodor, 1821–1881—Correspondence. | Authors, Russian—19th century—Biography.
Classification: LCC PG3328 .M384 2020 (print) | LCC PG3328 (ebook) | DDC 891.73/3 [B] —dc23
LC record available at https://lccn.loc.gov/2020003014
LC ebook record available at https://lccn.loc.gov/2020003015

*For Jeff Brooks,
colleague and friend*

Contents

Note on the First Volume ix
Preface xi

Introduction   1

I. Pride before the Fall: Belinsky and the Aftermath of *Poor Folk*   29

II. Havens from the Storms: The Vielgorskys, Beketovs, and Maykovs   85

III. The Psycho-Spiritual Turn: *The Double*, "Mr. Prokharchin," "The Landlady," and "A Novel in Nine Letters"   137

Conclusion   203

Directory of Prominent Names 207
Notes 215
Source Notes 233
Index 243

Note on the First Volume

Fyodor Dostoevsky—In the Beginning (1821–1845): A Life in Letters, Memoirs, and Criticism, the first in a three-volume study of the writer's early life and work, focuses on the images and ideas, and on the people, places, and events, that influenced Dostoevsky in the first twenty-four years of his life. It renders the writer in a new and seminal way: a diary-portrait of Dostoevsky drawn from letters, memoirs, and criticism of the writer, as well as the witness and testimony of family and friends, readers and reviewers, observers and participants as he stepped forward into existence.

Each of the three parts of *Fyodor Dostoevsky—In the Beginning* includes a wide selection of excerpts from primary sources, arranged chronologically and thematically. Prominent sources include the memoirs or notes of Dostoevsky's brother Andrei, his daughter Lyubov, and his friend and roommate Alexander Rizemkampf; letters between Dostoevsky's parents, between Dostoevsky and his older brother Mikhail, and between both siblings and their father; and quotations from Orest Miller and Nikolai Strakhov's 1883 biography of Dostoevsky and from Dostoevsky's own *Diary of a Writer*.

An important aspect of *Fyodor Dostoevsky—In the Beginning* is the debunking of clichés and misinformation, particularly about the writer's family, such as time-honored assertions that Dostoevsky's father was murdered by the serfs, and that he was so at odds with his sons Fyodor and Mikhail over money and vocation that they wished him dead. Indeed, from the pantomime villain of legend, Dostoevsky's father emerges from the study of primary materials as a caring and solicitous parent to his children and as a tender and loving spouse to his wife.

The first part, "All in the Family," considers Dostoevsky's early formation and schooling—his time in city and country, and his ties to his family, particularly his parents. The second part, "To Petersburg," features Dostoevsky's early days in Russia's imperial city, his years at the Main Engineering Academy, and the death of his father. The third part, "Darkness before Dawn," deals with the writer's youthful struggles and strivings, culminating in the success of *Poor Folk*. Each section is introduced by a brief essay on select people and events in the young writer's life.

Fyodor Dostoevsky—In the Beginning seeks to shed light on many dark and unexplored corners of the young writer's life. More important, it strives to render a clear and cohesive picture of the early years of one of the world's greatest writers.

Preface

Scholars and students of nineteenth-century Russian literature see the foremost prose practitioners of the period as pursuing a simple if straightforward path to greatness. Evidence for such a view abounds. Between 1820 and 1900, foremost indigenous writers of novels and novellas, short stories, and tales seemed to climb the ladder of success in dizzying, lockstep fashion. Alexander Pushkin progressed from *Tales of Belkin* (1831) to *Eugene Onegin* (1833) to *Queen of Spades* (1834) and *Captain's Daughter* (1836). Nikolai Gogol advanced from *Evenings on a Farm Near Dikanka* (1831–32) to *Arabesques* and *Mirgorod* (1835), "The Nose" (1835–1836), "The Overcoat" (1842), and *Dead Souls* (1842). Also writing works in rapidly ascendant succession was Ivan Turgenev with *Diary of a Superfluous Man* (1850), *Notes of a Huntsman* (1852), *Rudin* (1857), *Asya* (1858), *A Nest of Gentlefolk* (1859), *On the Eve* (1860), *First Love* (1860), and *Fathers and Sons* (1862). Even more destined for upward literary mobility was Leo Tolstoy, first with *Childhood* (1852), *Adolescence* (1854), and *Youth* (1856); then with *Family Happiness* (1859) and *The Cossacks* (1863); next with *War and Peace* (1869) and *Anna Karenina* (1878); and finally with *The Death of Ivan Ilyich* (1886), *The Kreutzer Sonata* (1889), and *Resurrection* (1899).

In charting the steady rise of nineteenth-century Russian writers to greatness, scholars and students of the national written expression note a grand exception: Fyodor Dostoevsky. They are correct to do so. As quickly as Pushkin, Gogol, Turgenev, and Tolstoy ascended to fortune and fame, so did Dostoevsky, Icarus-like, crash and burn when he approached metaphorical suns.

For followers and admirers of Russian literature, Dostoevsky's failure to scale literary heights safely and soundly was especially tragic given two facts. His first literary venture, *Poor Folk* (1845), caused a sensation that far outstripped the fictional debuts of Pushkin, Gogol, Turgenev, and Tolstoy. Also, Dostoevsky had to wait almost twenty years before he reached his literary stride with *Notes from the Underground* (1864) and, at long last, achieved steady and lasting renown with *Crime and Punishment* (1866), *The Idiot* (1869), *Devils* (1872), and *The Brothers Karamazov* (1880). Most assuredly, Dostoevsky did not follow the seemingly simple and straightforward path of Pushkin, Gogol, Turgenev, and Tolstoy. Indeed, it is a measure of the ongoing fascination with the writer and his works that he did not.

Students and scholars of Russian literature agree, though, that the ins and outs, ups and downs, and zigs and zags that mark Dostoevsky's path in the years between *Poor Folk* and *Notes from the Underground* were crucial to his personal and literary growth. They assert rightly that Dostoevsky could not have written *Notes* and subsequent works without the people, places, and events that had let him experience and understand life in ways that none of his literary confreres could or would.

In their studies of Dostoevsky between 1846 and 1864, personal and professional enthusiasts of Russian literature reveal a key flaw. They do not discuss adequately these people, places, and events that influenced Dostoevsky in this period. Not unlike their investigations into the first twenty-four years of the young writer's life, they pass or rush over this material or absorb it into larger, overriding movements and trends.

In so doing, scholars and students of Russian literature miss the many small and momentary, accidental, and incidental issues, images, and ideas that entered into Dostoevsky's mind, heart, and soul, and that served as stimuli and seedbeds for his mature fiction and thought. They also fail to realize the ultimate paradox of investigations into the writer: only by sweating the small stuff can one gain a complete and integral understanding of Dostoevsky's literature and life.

Fyodor Dostoevsky—The Gathering Storm (1846–1847): A Life in Letters, Memoirs, and Criticism, the second of what will be a three-volume study on the writer's early years, rushes in where others feared or failed to tread. Like its predecessor, *Fyodor Dostoevsky—In the Beginning (1821–1845)*, it focuses on the prosaics that shaped Dostoevsky and his writing, taken from the letters, memoirs, and criticism of the young writer, as well as from the witness and testimony of family and friends, readers and reviewers, and participants and players who stepped into Dostoevsky's life in the first two years after *Poor Folk*.

With this second volume also, I again note several things. First, I have sought the fullest picture of Dostoevsky in 1846 and 1847, via an exhaustive search and study of all published materials on the writer. No stone has been left unturned in my quest. Second, I have arranged citations both chronologically and from the vantage points of ten, twenty, thirty, even forty years later, interlacing the voices of both the young and the mature Dostoevsky with those of individuals who knew him personally or from his writings, literary and otherwise. In so doing, I seek to inform all the individuals in my study with an artistic and modern allure, presenting them as many-faceted, engaged, and self-determining beings, as well as spontaneous and multiple selves who dialogue about people, places, and events in 1846 and 1847, and who, in a seminal way, show maturity and growth, dualism and conflict, physically, socially, and spiritually. Third, I have given equal opportunity and freedom to all the actors in this tale. Truths and lies, facts and fictions—intimate and disturbing, outrageous and far-fetched—enter the narrative, with notes that provide correctives, counterarguments, and/or pertinent information to set the record straight on Dostoevsky's thoughts, emotions, and actions at this time. Fourth, I have again rejected the still strong urge to measure the people and events of Dostoevsky's first two years after *Poor Folk* against the characters and events of both his early and his mature fiction. Any references to the writer's oeuvre are from the speakers alone.

As I did in *Fyodor Dostoevsky—In the Beginning*, I seek in *Fyodor Dostoevsky—The Gathering Storm* to extend the map of Dostoevsky's physical and spiritual terrain as he moved, tentatively, into the socio-literary life of his time. Again, with this second volume, my purpose is not only to plot the coordinates of Dostoevsky's passage to greatness in the first two years after *Poor Folk* but also to call attention to the many people, places, and events that helped or deterred him in his journey forward.

If in *Fyodor Dostoevsky—In the Beginning* I showed how Dostoevsky moved in upward spirals—he had known a loving family, received an excellent education, launched a promising career, and scored a runaway hit with *Poor Folk*—I demonstrate in *Fyodor Dostoevsky—The Gathering Storm* how Dostoevsky, sadly, advanced along slippery slopes. In what would be recurring patterns in the young writer's existence, and not unlike his playing with time in his later fiction in which moments become eternities, not only did the events and experiences of the young writer in the first two years after *Poor Folk* remain etched, acid-like, in his consciousness throughout his life but also, perhaps more important, they portended troubles and tribulations that would beset him and his characters in the next three decades or so of his time on earth. In 1846 and 1847, Dostoevsky experienced frustration and anger, doubt and despair, loneliness and isolation in both literature and life. The failures of his second, third, fourth, and fifth works—*The Double*, "Mr. Prokharchin," "The Landlady," and "A Novel in Nine Letters"—threatened oblivion, even extinction as a writer. His difficulties with Vissarion Belinsky, Nikolai Nekrasov, Ivan Turgenev, Ivan Panaev, and other members of the Russian literary world cast him as a loser and a buffoon for all to mock and scorn.

In retrospect, the triumph of *Poor Folk* was for Dostoevsky a curse, not a blessing. Given the young writer's temperament, it might have been better if he had started his literary career with a whimper, not a bang. Caught between the success of his first work and the failures of his following four pieces, Dostoevsky "split" into warring halves. On the one hand, he was an "extraordinary" being, a lord and master above everyone and everything. On the other hand, he was an "underground" man, a louse and mouse below everyone and everything. Indeed, the personal and professional crises that beset Dostoevsky in 1846 and 1847 so shattered the young writer that they moved him to catastrophe two years later: his implication in the Petrashevsky affair, a plot to overthrow the government, and his subsequent decade-long exile in Siberia.

The dark clouds that hung over Dostoevsky in 1846 and 1847, though, had two silver linings. The first is that the young writer found solace and support in three new families: the Vielgorskys, the Beketovs, and the Maykovs. The second and more important, perhaps, is that Dostoevsky, even in fictional failure, was portending literary success. In his stories he was finding himself as a thinker and an artist, probing human weakness and sin in ways that no one else in Russian or world literature could or would. In his literary laboratory were men, women, and children who, like himself, split into conflicting selves, inhabited multiple realities, and perhaps most important, declared war on themselves and others with murderous glee. Like a mad scientist, Dostoevsky was creating Russian Frankensteins who, within twenty years, would say more about human debasement and deformity than anyone else would care or dare to admit.

Indeed, it can be argued that without the physical and metaphysical trials, travails, and traumas that took root during the first two years after *Poor Folk* and later, Dostoevsky might not have created "extraordinary" qua "underground" men, women, and children who enthrall if unnerve readers and reviewers in the first decades of the twenty-first century in much the same way they did in the last decades of the nineteenth. In a dramatic way, for both himself and others, Dostoevsky embodied the adage "no pain, no gain."

As was the case with the previous volume, *Fyodor Dostoevsky—The Gathering Storm* consists of a preface, an introduction, three parts, a conclusion, endnotes, a directory of names, and notes on sources. The first part, "Pride before the Fall," focuses on Dostoevsky's increasingly tense ties with Vissarion Belinsky, Nikolai Nekrasov, Ivan Turgenev, Ivan Panaev, and other figures of the Russian literary world. The second part, "Havens from the Storms," deals with the reception, often negative, from writers and critics in response not only to the success of *Poor Folk* but also to the failures that followed quickly. The third part, "The Psycho-Spiritual Turn," centers on Dostoevsky's final break with Belinsky and his circle, as well as his increasing struggles to stay afloat, internally and externally.

Furthermore, each section is introduced by a brief essay on select people, issues, and events in Dostoevsky's life at this time. The preface to "Pride before the Fall" is a piece on the writer's tortuous tie to Belinsky, a stance of love and hate that haunted him throughout his life. A sketch on the Vielgorskys, Maykovs, and Beketovs, three families who proved to be Dostoevsky's salvation in this period, heads "Havens from the Storms"; and a unifying analysis of *The Double*, "Mr. Prokharchin," "The Landlady," and "A Novel in Nine Letters" introduces "The Psycho-Spiritual Turn."

For their assistance in *Fyodor Dostoevsky—The Gathering Storm*, I wish to express my deep gratitude to Joseph Lenkart, Annabella Irvine, and especially Jan Adamczyk of the Slavic Reference Service at the University of Illinois, who, with exceptional diligence, endless patience, and exemplary grace and good cheer, found answers to the myriad, complicated, and often outrageous questions that I asked regarding the young Dostoevsky; and who, as has always been the case in my now forty-five-year association with the group, ended their responses with offers of further assistance. If there are heroes and heroines in the academy of Russian studies in America today, it is they. I also thank Bethany Wasik, Karen Hwa, Sarah Noell, Richanna Patrick, Michael Morris, and especially Amanda Heller, the copyeditor of this volume, at Cornell University Press for the exceptional attention and expertise they gave to my book.

Here at Notre Dame, I thank Thomas Merluzzi and Alison Rice, past and present directors of the Institute for Scholarship in the Liberal Arts, for their continued support; Nita Hashil of Interlibrary Loan for supplying materials for research, especially from libraries and institutions in Russia; Randy Yoho and Matthew Pollard, who kept my computers in good working order; and Cheryl Reed, who transformed my chaotic files into a professional document.

It is with special gratitude and warmth that I salute my research assistants Maria Hieber, Ana Miravete, Katherine Mansourova, Charles Sedore, and especially Joshua O'Brien, whom, during his four years as a student at Notre Dame and the two summers after graduation, I drove to the brink and beyond with endless queries on pages and dates; obscure questions on people, places, and events; and torturous searches through newspapers, journals, books, and cyberspace for citations and claims. Truly, and as was the case with *Fyodor Dostoevsky—In the Beginning*, *Fyodor Dostoevsky—The Gathering Storm* would never have seen the light of day without him.

I also acknowledge my wife, Gloria Gibbs Marullo, for forty-one years of unstinting encouragement and support, and my cats, Benedict Joseph,

Francis Xavier, and Agnes Mary, for unconditional warmth and love. (For readers of my scholarly adventures, Bernadette Marie and Bridget Josephine passed from this life at age nineteen and eighteen, respectively, and now watch down on me from heaven.)

With *Fyodor Dostoevsky—The Gathering Storm*, four individuals deserve special acclaim and applause: Irwin Weil, Department of Slavic Languages and Literatures, Northwestern University; Kathleen Parthé, Department of Modern Languages and Cultures, University of Rochester; Jeff Brooks, Department of History, Johns Hopkins University; and Amy Farranto, senior acquisitions editor, Northern Illinois University Press. With painstaking care and concern, they read the manuscript, offered counsel and advice, and cheered me on in my work. I am particularly grateful to Kathleen Parthé for editing the entire study; and to Jeff Brooks for sending email after email, often on a daily basis, with ideas and suggestions to improve my work. A special and affectionate note of thanks is due to Amy Farranto, who oversaw the publication of what is now our third book together with exemplary energy and expertise, graciousness and aplomb. Indeed, if *Fyodor Dostoevsky—The Gathering Storm* qualifies as a work of readable scholarship, it is in no small measure because of the efforts of all four individuals on my behalf.

Finally, it is with special gratitude that I again acknowledge Jeff Brooks for his assistance not only in this work but also in many of my previous studies. He has been a devoted friend and colleague, a gentleman and a scholar, and it is with deep admiration and affection for him as a person and a professional that I dedicate *Fyodor Dostoevsky—The Gathering Storm* to him.

May he and all who have accompanied me in this venture know only happiness, health, and peace.

FYODOR DOSTOEVSKY—THE GATHERING STORM (1846–1847)

Introduction

In early 1846, the young Dostoevsky was the toast of the town. The applause was deafening. Everyone wanted to meet the new writer who, with the publication of *Poor Folk*, was hailed as a savior, a prophet, and an idol whom God had chosen to lead Russian literature from alleged deserts to promised lands. It was a measure of the angst and concern for the fate and future of the national written expression that readers, writers, and reviewers embraced Dostoevsky with such excitement and joy. All wanted to meet the young man, to shake his hand, to talk with him, to introduce him to society, and, most important, to claim him as a colleague, teacher, and friend.

With bated breath, readers, writers, and reviewers waited to see what Dostoevsky would do next. They wondered: Would he write a second *Poor Folk*? Would he, à la Charles Dickens, Victor Hugo, or Honoré de Balzac, pursue the trials and travails of urban denizens? Would he, like Pushkin, Mikhail Lermontov, and Gogol censure inertia and injustice, as well as sanction freedom and change? Would he emulate the Decembrists and challenge Nicholas I and "orthodoxy, autocracy, and nationality," which since 1833 had defined the very foundation of the Russian state?

Two individuals were particularly taken with Dostoevsky. One was Vissarion Belinsky; the other, Nikolai Nekrasov. Both men had been educated in the school of hard knocks. Neither of them had known security and love in their early years. Belinsky's father, Grigory Nikiforovich Belinsky, was a rural doctor who so angered patients with his drunkenness, atheism, and enthusiasm for Voltaire that he feared violence against his person. His equally unstable mother fueled fires. The young Belinsky was subjected not only to violent quarrels between the two but also to abuse at their hands. Formal education was minimal, the lad having been expelled from Moscow University in 1832 for alleged ill health and limited intelligence, but in truth because he had not taken a single examination in his three years at the school. A tragedy, titled *Dmitri Kalinin* and written by Belinsky as a student, captured his frame of mind: a noble soul is driven to suicide by an inscrutable and unjust fate.

Nekrasov fared even worse. The son of a poor and equally violent gentryman, he had been disowned by his father for seeking admission to the university in St. Petersburg. For the next three years, Nekrasov fended off poverty and starvation in the city by begging, tutoring, and writing.

It speaks greatly to the minds, hearts, and souls of both men that despite such setbacks, they were, in 1846 and 1847, key figures in the Russian literary world. At thirty-seven years old, Belinsky had a string of successes to his name. He had turned *The Fatherland Notes* into the leading publication of the day. He was also the foremost champion qua interpreter of Pushkin, Lermontov, and Gogol. A decade younger than Belinsky, Nekrasov had won acclaim for writing poems about Russian provincial life, for publishing *The Physiology of Petersburg* (1845) and *The Petersburg Miscellany* (1846), and, in 1847, for purchasing *The Contemporary* and attracting Belinsky to its ranks.

Although earlier in their careers both Belinsky and Nekrasov were romantics, they were, by 1846 and 1847, staunch realists, as well as avid proponents of progressivism in Russian literature and life. In their view, writers should address political and social ills, and move their country westward, toward democracy and liberalism. Both men took heart that the national written expression, after an embarrassingly slow start, was approaching universal prominence and respect. They were particularly thrilled with what came to be known as the "Petersburg tradition" in Russian literature: fiction about "little" men and women who lived and loved, worked and died, often tragically, in the imperial city. With pride—and, in truth, relief—they pointed to Pushkin's "The Bronze Horseman" (1833); to Gogol's "Nevsky Prospekt" and "The Nose"; and to the so-called "physiological sketches" that appeared in newspapers and journals, almanacs, and anthologies throughout the northern metropolis.

Both Belinsky and Nekrasov realized, though, that when measured against the fiction of western Europe, Russian literature had a long way to go. Nothing in the national written expression could compare with the novels of

Dickens, Balzac, and Hugo. Pieces on native urban life were scarce, short, sour, and ended in madness and death. Heroes and heroines—Pushkin's Yevgeny and Gogol's Akaky and Kovalyov, Pirogov and Piskaryov come to mind—spoke and acted little. More often than not, they moved to type and daguerreotype, into cartoon and cardboard characters, with strings pulled, puppet-like, by their creators.

Both Belinsky and Nekrasov had an additional if not more pressing cause for worry. No one, it seemed, was on hand to carry on their goals for literature and life. Pushkin had died in 1837, Gogol had left fiction and, worse, in 1847 was writing *Selected Passages from Correspondence to Friends*, a bizarre collection of homilies, exhortations, and personal confessions, often of a conservative, even reactionary bent.

Understandable, therefore, was the excitement—and again relief—of both Belinsky and Nekrasov, as well as of writers, readers, and reviewers of Russian literature, over Dostoevsky and *Poor Folk*. At long last they had an indigenous novel of urban life, with flesh-and-blood characters who talked about their unhappy lives in a credible and realistic way. Dostoevsky, they believed, was the answer to their prayers. He was the hope, if not the salvation, of Russia and its literature.

They were in for the shock of their lives. On both counts—the writer and his writing—Dostoevsky failed miserably.

Physically, he could not have made a worse impression. If Russian readers, writers, and reviewers were expecting a strapping Goliath, they got a sickly David. The writer of *Poor Folk* was frail and pale. His clothes were worn and poorly fitting. His surroundings were monastically spartan. Visitors sat on the one dilapidated chair in his home.

Dostoevsky did little to help the situation. When admirers oohed and aahed over *Poor Folk*, he became embarrassed and confused. Conversations were sporadic and brief. Others often did the talking. Also, Dostoevsky kept his cards close to his vest, answering questions in sporadic and evasive ways.

Ironically, personal discomfort only increased public allure. As would be the case with the eccentrics of Dostoevsky's mature fiction—Prince Myshkin of *The Idiot* is a pertinent example—and as in his own time as a student at the Main Engineering Academy in St. Petersburg, Dostoevsky impressed others as somber and strange, but also as attuned to truths of this and other worlds.

Willingly, devotees of *Poor Folk* cut its creator a great deal of slack. Despite the disappointment, if not the shock, of initial encounters, they found—or, more accurately, persuaded themselves to find—Dostoevsky worthy to present in public, if only for their own honor and glory: they were groupies with a genius in tow.

Or so they thought. If Dostoevsky failed in private, he fared even worse in public. Invitations to homes and gatherings were greeted with unease, even fear. It was only after repeated entreaties and threats that Dostoevsky showed himself to the world. To friends and followers, the public Dostoevsky was like an erupting volcano. His body shook and shuddered; his face was stormy and dark. The writer of *Poor Folk* also did not accept people at face value or with good intentions. Rather, he sensed threats and agendas from all. Anxiety and paranoia raised their heads. Before, during, and after meetings, Dostoevsky asked attendees to repeat what they and others had said. Not unlike his fictional clerks, he often eluded scrutiny in nooks and corners and behind screens.

At first glance, Dostoevsky's angst over the beau monde belies the facts. He was hardly déclassé. The writer of *Poor Folk* was a bona fide aristocrat who, as a child, adolescent, and youth, had known only stability and love from parents, teachers, and friends. Values of industry and culture encouraged virtues of confidence and self-respect. Unlike many of the higher-ups he reportedly feared, Dostoevsky was superbly educated in both the sciences and the arts. He was better read in classical and contemporary literature than any of his peers. Furthermore, Dostoevsky was comfortable and convivial with all types and castes. He was particularly enterprising with editors, publishers, and booksellers. With potential patrons, too, Dostoevsky had everything to gain and nothing to lose, particularly with wolves at his door. Reasons for reticence are lacking.

Plausible if problematic reasons for Dostoevsky's standoffishness are fourfold. Most obviously, the young man—having come to St. Petersburg from Moscow less than a decade previously, and by education and training a draftsman and engineer—was shy, if not uncomfortable, with larger-than-life individuals like Belinsky and Nekrasov, as well as with the intellectual and cultural society of the imperial city. He feared, rightly, that he would be seen as little more than a local yokel who would amuse the literati without joining their ranks.

Another apparent reason for Dostoevsky's aloofness—and a characteristic that new acquaintances also noted in the young writer—was pride. They had every reason to do so. If Dostoevsky did not look or act like a genius, he had no trouble seeing himself as one. The success of *Poor Folk* had gone to his head. A legend in his own mind, Dostoevsky had become insufferable. The bragging and boasting were nonstop. The young writer was heir to Lord Byron, Pushkin, and Gogol. He laid claim to a brilliant and lucrative future. By his own (generous) count, he had been cited in articles and reviews thirty-five times in the first three months of 1846 alone. Heady, even intoxicated, with the success of *Poor Folk*, Dostoevsky had even greater hopes for *The Double*. In his view, his second work was ten times better than his first one. It was a worthy successor to Gogol's *Dead Souls*, if not a vanquishing challenger.

Such braggadocio, of course, brought to bear still a third reason for Dostoevsky's remoteness from people: his insecurity as a writer. He was having great difficulty with *The Double*. He also would have grave doubts over "Mr. Prokharchin," "The Landlady," and "A Novel in Nine Letters." Understandably, the young writer wondered if he had had beginner's luck with *Poor Folk*, if he were a flash-in-the-pan sensation who would exit the national written expression as quickly as he had entered it.

Given his uneasiness with high society, his pride over *Poor Folk*, and his doubts about his next four works, Dostoevsky soon alienated everyone. More seriously, he clashed with the very people who not only had introduced him to the Russian literary world but also could and would have advanced his career as a writer. Akin to his fictional down-and-outers who revere and then rebel against patrons and benefactors, Dostoevsky bit hands that fed him. His behavior was often scandalous. Arguably, Dostoevsky was the only person in Russia who told Belinsky to keep still. He fought with Turgenev, Panaev, and Nekrasov. He bolted from parties and gatherings; he shunned confreres in public places. Anything could raise his temper and fists. Whispers and winks provoked sound and fury. Sallies and ribbings triggered war and revenge. Dostoevsky had people walking on eggshells to the point where they rejoiced at his exit or absence. Purposely Belinsky eschewed conversation and contact with the young writer, thereby infuriating his obstreperous protégé by being seemingly callous and cold.

Truth be told, Dostoevsky was only partially responsible for the difficulties. Readers, writers, and reviewers in the Russian literary world drove him wild. With Dostoevsky, Belinsky and Nekrasov overstepped bounds. Having championed *Poor Folk*—wrongly—as sociopolitical exposé, they demanded that new works by the writer be similarly reproachful and accusatory. Men of principle, but also ideologues—not for nothing was Belinsky called "frenzied"—the two brooked no compromise. Mirroring the tortuous ties between man-gods and disciples in Dostoevsky's mature novels, Belinsky and Nekrasov saw Dostoevsky as their creature and captive. Neither man valued Dostoevsky for who he was or for what he was trying to be—or write. Rather, Belinsky and Nekrasov sought to remake Dostoevsky in their own image and likeness, to use him for their own ends, and to bend him to their political, social, and economic wills and worldviews. Whatever the cost, Dostoevsky would be their herald for a progressive, democratic Russia.

It was a recipe for disaster.

Dostoevsky again failed to live up to expectations. Part of the problem was that the young writer, in thrall to editors, publishers, and booksellers, was forced to meet deadlines, to write hurriedly, and, by his own admission, to rush images, issues, and ideas. More seriously, perhaps, Dostoevsky continued to do in his twenty-fifth and twenty-six years of life what he had done in his previous twenty-four. In a move that would have thrilled his headstrong father, Mikhail, he went his own way as an artist and a man.

Despite the cosmopolitan formation of his early years, Dostoevsky was alien or indifferent to sociopolitical discussions. Not once in 1846 and 1847—in oral or written form, or in the witness and testimony of companions and colleagues—did Dostoevsky comment on the burning images, issues, and ideas of the day. He held his tongue on Hegelianism, Fourierism, socialism, and communism. Meetings with Mikhail Petrashevsky, the radical *intelligent* who, in 1849, would bring the young writer to ruin, were sporadic and brief. It was only in *Diary of a Writer*, written from 1873 to 1876, that Dostoevsky addressed the controversy between Westernizers and Slavophiles. The next four works of his literary career—*The Double* and "Mr. Prokharchin" in 1846, "The Landlady" and "A Novel in Nine Letters" in 1847—showed that Dostoevsky heard a different drummer, one who sounded beats from pounding minds and hearts, not prattling forums and public squares.

From the beginning of his fictional foray, Dostoevsky opposed the idea that writers should address civic ills. Rather, he looked internally for causes of human suffering, to unearth in his characters the reasons for their distress. If Belinsky and Nekrasov sought political, social, and economic integration in Russia and the world, Dostoevsky looked to psychological and spiritual disintegration in corners and "depths." If they talked about autocracy, serfdom, and censorship, he discussed schizophrenia, deviancy, and execution of self and others. If they believed that humankind was poor in spirit, he insisted that society was even sicker in body and mind. As conflicted and confused as the young Dostoevsky might have been about everyone and everything in his life, nothing would deter him from his quest to find out what made people tick—and explode.

Predictably, Belinsky and company were furious over what they saw as personal and fictional perfidy. Dostoevsky, they charged, was cultivating thistles and thorns. He was brandishing wooden swords and spears. It was again symptomatic of their misplaced and overblown faith in the young writer that they responded so violently to the four works after *Poor Folk*. The abuse was unending, Nekrasov, Turgenev, Ivan Panaev, and Dmitri Grigorovich leading the way. In their view, Dostoevsky was yesterday's news. He was a traitor, a fop, and a fraud.

In the literary uproar over Dostoevsky in 1846 and 1847, two things are clear. The first is that fans turned foes were remarkably candid about their earlier enthusiasm for the young writer. Unlike the false friends in Dostoevsky's oeuvre who applauded alleged geniuses in surreptitious tête-à-têtes—the specious ovations of the musician B. for Yefimov in *Netochka Nezvanova*, and of Pyotr Verkhovensky for Nikolai Stavrogin in *Devils* are pertinent examples—Dostoevsky's disenchanted followers acknowledged publicly that it was they who had made the man. Confessions came fast and furious. It was Belinsky and company who had proclaimed Dostoevsky a genius. Even more stridently, it was they who had raised the writer to a savior, idol, and god. Powerful literary figures had put Dostoevsky on a pedestal, carried him throughout the city, and demanded that he be worshiped by all. Gladly had they suffered Dostoevsky's failings and flaws to proclaim him the great hope of Russian literature.

Now, with metaphorical egg on their faces, former devotees were as upset with themselves as they were with Dostoevsky over what they now saw as their illusions and delusions about the young writer. Some blamed Belinsky for the fiasco. With Dostoevsky, they said, the critic had extolled a talent that in fact had never existed. Others cried foul, charging that they—sincere, disinterested, and well meaning—had been duped by a master manipulator.

Other emotions fueled the fire. Even as members of the Belinsky circle applauded Dostoevsky's *Poor Folk*, they also envied—and resented—the success of the piece. No one in the group could claim an initial work that had caused the sensation that *Poor Folk* did. Belinsky and company were now seized with schadenfreude. As quickly as their god had ascended into heaven, equally swiftly had he descended into hell.

The anger of Belinsky and company was understandable. A native Russian literature was the sole means by which citizens could discuss the "damned questions." National written expression was also proof that Russians were viable and visionary, that they were moving toward progress and democracy, and that they were contributing to human culture and civilization.

In Dostoevsky, Belinsky and company believed, Russians had their Dickens, Hugo, and Balzac. With the young writer, national literature was alive and well. What Pushkin had done with *Eugene Onegin* in 1833, Lermontov with *A Hero of Our Time* in 1840, and Gogol with *Dead Souls* in 1842, Dostoevsky did with *Poor Folk* in 1845. Like gamblers at a roulette wheel, Belinsky and company staked all their hopes and dreams on the young writer; and when they lost their bets on subsequent works in 1846 and 1847, they were even more furious and fuming than Dostoevsky himself. Portraits of a schizophrenic clerk, a churlish miser, scheming cardsharps, and a head-in-the-clouds intellectual in a ménage à trois with a young maiden and her father, husband, or lover (it is not clear whom) only reinforced stereotypes of Russia and Russians as backward, barbaric, and perverse. Very possibly, Belinsky and company fretted, Russian literature was regressing altogether. Instead of Dickens, Hugo, or Balzac, they had at best a pale imitation of E. T. A. Hoffmann.

Revenge was swift and sweet. For Belinsky and company, the idol and god had shrunk suddenly. He was now "little" as well as ill, physically and mentally. The young writer spoke in strained tones. He fainted before large crowds. His face seemingly disappeared; his body faded into shadows. He had one foot in the grave, the other on a cabbage leaf.

In truth, the former apostles found Dostoevsky loathsome. He obsessed over glory and fame. He demanded adoration and praise. He waved letters from fans, imagined more than real. He insisted that borders surround *Poor Folk* and *The Double* in anthologies and journals to distinguish them from other works. He himself did no wrong. Everyone and everything else had caused his troubles. Rumors titillated and teased, as Dostoevsky's detractors claimed that he was no Casanova but captive to a siren who directed his every move, a socialite who transfixed him with her beauty, and a sibyl who proclaimed him the sun, moon, and stars.

The members of the Belinsky circle also accused Dostoevsky of having multiple faces, personae, and masks. He feigned happiness and humility. He played people like harps. He weaseled his way into social and literary ranks. Privately, local literati derided him. Grigorovich and Panaev spread stories that Dostoevsky was castigating everyone as heartless, insignificant, and jealous, convinced that chance had made him an eagle but had left others grounded, flopping and floundering. Publicly, fellow writers taunted him. Turgenev drove Dostoevsky to the brink. Privately, they went in for the kill with poems and prose that mocked the writer as once the toast of sultans and sovereigns but now a mournful knight scorned by all. Gogol was still king, Turgenev and company proclaimed, but Dostoevsky was only a jester, a knave.

A second issue in the ruckus over Dostoevsky during the first two years after *Poor Folk* was that former admirers conceded that they too had demonstrated shortcomings as lovers of the Russian word. A truism of the national written expression has been that literary circles in Moscow and St. Petersburg served as havens for Russian intellectuals and writers in the 1840s, as places where, behind closed doors, people could discuss political, social, and aesthetic images, issues, and ideas in a free and safe way. No doubt this was so, but contemporaries of Dostoevsky in 1846 and 1847 tell a different story about these cliques, particularly about the members of the Belinsky circle.

If Nekrasov, Panaev, and others are to be believed, the individuals who had gathered about the famous critic were as imperfect as—if not more so than—the object of their scorn. In fact, a case can be made that Nekrasov and others, because of who and what they were, bore partial responsibility for driving the admittedly difficult young man into more radical and dangerous groups, and ultimately into disaster: his involvement, in 1849, with the Petrashevsky affair and his decade-long exile to Siberia.

The lampoons that Nekrasov, Panaev, Turgenev, and others wrote about Dostoevsky reveal as much about themselves as they do their subject. If in public Nekrasov and company appeared solid and serious in politics and art, they were in private like everyone else: mortals with weaknesses that were trivial, motives that were petty, and emotions that were base.

A particular failing of the members of the Belinsky circle was that, like the great critic himself, they also crossed lines, personally and professionally. Mock concerns for body and soul, specious appeals to justice and enlightenment, irksome bursts of mischief and boredom, and naked attempts at despotism and power play were the catalysts by which members of the Belinsky circle curbed everyone around them. Newcomers felt insulted, not instructed; chastised, not cherished; pained, not pleased. With Dostoevsky a prime example, the members of the Belinsky circle often chased out more adherents than they attracted.

As conceded by Nekrasov, Panaev, Turgenev, and others, still another problem with the members of the Belinsky circle was that they looked to votaries as lackeys and minions to do their bidding, not to discuss literature or art. Writers and retainers existed in a symbiosis—a literary ecosystem, so to speak—in which parasites, for a tie to the Russian literary world, did everything and anything to safeguard the peace and happiness of their hosts. If in theory Nekrasov and company objected to serfdom as a sociopolitical evil, they in practice had little problem with exacting servitude from their followers. Master was to man as oppressor was to oppressed. Unrelenting and cruel were the insults and humiliations to which the members of the Belinsky circle subjected their vassals and valets. Devotees were for them *Untermenschen*: dimwitted and dull, with large heads and small minds. They were fictional "little men" come to life. Heads drooped, faces paled, and bodies sagged. Utterances were monosyllabic; voices were gasping and low.

To be sure, the flunkeys and attendants who served the members of the Belinsky circle got what they deserved. Not unlike the fixations of Belinsky, Turgenev, Panaev, Nekrasov, and others on Dostoevsky, their obsession as groupies—their mania to see and be seen with Russian literati-glitterati—caused them not only to tolerate abuse but also to welcome it. In a sense, the servants of the Belinsky circle were the real villains in the story of Dostoevsky in 1846 and 1847. Scraping and bowing to Belinsky and company, they made a bad situation worse—especially for the young writer.

The domestic footmen of the Belinsky circle were literary in name only. They cared little for intellectual and aesthetic concerns. They rarely picked up a book, much less a pen. Beyond engaging writers, they did little other than eat, sleep, and receive the world with apathy and indifference. What these individuals lacked in substance, they made up for in style. The only art they pursued was that of posturing and pose. Consciously and unconsciously, the have-nots of the Belinsky circle parodied the haves. As rendered by Nekrasov in his spoof *The Stone Heart*, their names said it all. There was The Poet in Soul and The Noble Personality. There was The Artistic Nature and The Practical Head. There was The Library and The Newspaper. There was Sputnik, The Element of Good Breeding, and The All-Around (and Also Embracing) Nature.

The attendants to the Belinsky circle kept the writers in the group in good working order. With no other purpose in life, they did their job well. For their literary guests, they ran literary hotels. Star boarders were surrounded with laughter and good cheer; stroked with flattering and fawning; titillated with gossip and news; and regaled with jam, tea, pretzels, books, pillows, money, and cigars. To their lettered clients, also, the maître d' qua managers of the Belinsky circle offered maximum security and comfort. Parroting views and opinions, often conflicting or diametrically opposed, was one service. Helping with correspondence and engaging editors, publishers, and booksellers was a second. Parading as writers and critics extolling geniuses was a third. Nothing fazed the hospitallers of the Belinsky circle. They saw and understood everything. They embraced and relished everyone.

The writers of the Belinsky circle obliged with gusto. Outwardly they proclaimed the moral and aesthetic sensitivities of their sidekicks, but inwardly they looked to more pragmatic virtues. They ran their attendants ragged, seeing them as creditors who supplied funds; caterers who furnished truffles and champagne; and clerks who, like Gogol's Akaky Akakievich, copied manuscripts or who, like Dostoevsky's Devushkin or Golyadkin, suffered insults and injuries. Anything could trigger hazings and dressing-downs, sneers and jeers: a dinner that was not up to snuff, a book that was delivered late, a request that wives or children attend a gathering. Even as the members of the Belinsky circle championed idealistic youth, they did not hesitate to dine at the expense of a boyish sponsor before being ejected by an outraged parent footing the bill. Even as they penned stories about tender marriage and love, they did not waver in salivating over tales of followers in marital distress, of wives beating husbands, even seeking out victims with black eyes with faux-solace and support. The members of the Belinsky circle championed liberalism and democracy, but they did not tolerate images and ideas other than their own. They extolled harmony and peace, but they did not think twice about unleashing adherents on enemies and rivals.

The antics of Nekrasov, Panaev, Turgenev, and others exacerbated the tension and bad feeling between Dostoevsky and the Russian literary world. Already nervous and high-strung, the writer of one success and four failures struggled with demons from both without and within. Dostoevsky began to withdraw from Belinsky and his circle, but he was hardly quiet in his retreat. Seething with anger and bile, the young writer charged subversion and spite. Everyone was laughing at him, he believed, both to his face and behind his back. Not unlike the heroes of his fiction, he was at war with the world.

Critics rubbed salt into wounds. Although reviewers received Dostoevsky's *Poor Folk* along party lines—fiery liberals took on passionate conservatives—members of both camps took Dostoevsky to task for what they saw as the shortcomings of the work.

All agreed that as a writer, Dostoevsky lacked discipline. *Poor Folk*, they charged, was a molehill, not a mountain. It suffered from aimless creativity: pages of trifles. Details were numerous and repetitive, extraneous and tiresome. Language was prolix and long-winded, mawkish and sentimental. Images and ideas smacked of Lermontov, Gogol, and Hryhory Kvitka. Hero and heroine were types and daguerreotypes. To see the clerk Poprishchin in Gogol's *Diary of a Madman*, one critic sniffed, was to see them all. For reviewers of all colors and stripes, the writer of *Poor Folk* ran a distant second to the author of *Dead Souls*. He was Gogol writ small.

Ironically, in their censure of *Poor Folk*, liberal and conservative critics came close to understanding Dostoevsky's motives for the work. Unlike Belinsky or Nekrasov, they were not taken in by the faux pathos and bathos of the narrative. The pictures of poverty in the piece, they maintained, were random and added little to the story. Reviewers also did not see Makar Devushkin and Varvara Dobroselova as insulted and injured. Rather, they indicted hero and heroine as users and abusers with agendas, grudges, and ends.

For both liberal and conservative critics, Makar Devushkin was a loser who deserved life's blows. He was not Gogol's hapless Akaky Akakievich but an individual who could advance in life. For all his aloofness, Makar was also seen by reviewers as an avid social animal. He was consumed by ambition, as well as by the rumors and gossip about him. Furthermore, Makar suffered from wounded pride, taking umbrage at Akaky Akakievich, to whom, he sensed, he was too close for comfort. Varvara caused even greater anger and consternation in that heroine regarded hero as a slave, not a savior. Particularly irksome to critics were the final scenes of *Poor Folk*, in which Varvara not only told Makar of her upcoming marriage in a cold, offhand way but also, even more callously, tormented him with orders for her upcoming wedding to another.

Reviewers were not immune either to the sexual darkness of the work. They noted how Makar called Varvara "little mother" and bore the name Lovelace. They also recorded how Varvara, foreshadowing the heroine in *A Gentle Creature* (1876), opted for a monster for a mate who more than met his match. Even as critics moaned and groaned over hero and heroine—Varvara recalled Shakespeare's Desdemona, one said—they remarked that the two assuaged searing fear and angst with sentimental tenderness and concern.

Reviewers were even more united in their condemnation of *The Double*. Conservative critics were particularly gleeful, rejoicing that they had been right about the so-called genius all along. Dostoevsky had regressed as a writer, both "right" and "left" groups said. The initial blunders of his first work had become enduring mistakes and inadequacies in the second. Dostoevsky, they continued, had grown even more verbose, sterile, and boring. Indeed, the faults and failings of *The Double* were so great that one critic wondered if Dostoevsky had penned an inferior piece to amuse himself at public expense.

What Dostoevsky had done in *The Double*, liberal and conservative reviewers went on to charge, was pathological, nightmarish, and corpse-like. With his second work, they added, Dostoevsky was eating Gogol's dust, his latest effort being no more than a parody of the great writer. Anyone who read *The Double*, critics agreed, merged with the hero and became diminished and destroyed. In their view also, it would have been easier on everyone if author had accompanied hero to the madhouse on the first page of the work, not on the last. Throw in "Mr. Prokharchin," liberal and conservative reviewers concluded, and a former talent like Dostoevsky had to face a bitter truth: he had only stepped out in the clothing of an artist. He had a tragic sense, but only from under piles of manure.

The failures of Dostoevsky's "Mr. Prokharchin," "The Landlady," and "A Novel in Nine Letters" only deepened the anger, confusion, and dismay over the young writer. Dostoevsky, critics agreed, had turned inward. He had retreated from civic realism to gothic romanticism. He had forsaken social exposé for schlock sensationalism. He had repudiated enlightened politics for specious psychology. He had replaced men and women in urban "corners" and "depths" with madmen, misers, and mystics from dark and demented worlds. Like jackals around wounded prey, "left" and "right" reviewers linked arms with members of the Belinsky circle in seeing Dostoevsky as smoke, not fire.

A particularly troubling feature in the darkening assessments of Dostoevsky was the problematic stance of Belinsky toward his former protégé. If memoirists in 1846 and 1847 attested to the great critic's initial praise of *Poor Folk* in private, they also noted his subsequent if almost immediate doubt about the young writer and his works in public. More than anyone else in his circle, Belinsky had had his fill of Dostoevsky's shenanigans. He was particularly incensed that Dostoevsky had rejected him as a mentor, and that the would-be genius wanted success without sweat. He also had grave reservations about Dostoevsky's well-being, wondering, accurately and loudly, if the young writer's instability would get the better of his literature and life. Belinsky loved and valued Dostoevsky; but he also pitied and grieved for the young man, fearing, again presciently, that he would waste or even scotch his talent in self-deception and destruction.

Given Belinsky's growing misgivings about Dostoevsky, it is not surprising that in his articles and reviews, he damned his charge's latest works, and even *Poor Folk*, with faint praise. Platitudes and clichés were the order of the day. The success of *Poor Folk*, Belinsky maintained, was beyond a doubt. It was poetic and creative, humorous and simple, sensitive and tragic. In his first work, Belinsky continued, Dostoevsky shook the souls of readers; he forced them to laugh through tears.

Poor Folk, though, failed in key criteria that Belinsky held dear for art. It did not spring from a knowledge of life. It did not break free from the melodrama of French novelists. Belinsky fretted that if only Dostoevsky had cut *Poor Folk* by 10 percent and rid his piece of repetitions and redundancies, his debut in fiction would have been beyond artistic reproach.

Even worse, perhaps, Belinsky missed Dostoevsky's intentions for the piece. Wrongly he proclaimed Makar Devushkin a model of humanity and Varvara Dobroselova a paragon of virtue. Equally off the mark was Belinsky's avowal that with Varenka, Makar was a knight in shining armor who sought to rescue an imperiled Pauline. Even more outrageous was Belinsky's contention that Makar could have married Varenka, if only because no one other than himself could sacrifice so much on her behalf.

Belinsky had even less use for *The Double*. As with *Poor Folk*, he began with well-meaning if perfunctory praise. Dostoevsky's second work was for him more masterly and bold than the first: a wellspring of intelligence, truth, and art. If *The Double* was not a triumph with the public, though, he knew the reasons why. As with other reviewers of *The Double*, Belinsky charged that what were flaws and failings in Dostoevsky's first novel were now monstrous weaknesses in the second. The young writer had not learned his literary lessons. He was still writing in a slapdash and sloppy way, with little concern for measure, tact, and restraint. Proving his point, Belinsky even added a vicious parody of Golyadkin's utterances in the work.

He was only getting started. If Dostoevsky would have done well to shorten *Poor Folk* by 10 percent, Belinsky complained, he would have done even better to cut *The Double* by a third. The strengths of *The Double*, he continued, only underscored its weaknesses. The piece reached literary heights, but in such a rich and unrelenting way that it left the few readers who finished the piece not only with an aching head and stomach but also with a marked preference for the works of Alexandre Dumas père and Eugène Sue. In a word, *The Double* was a disaster in both content and form.

Belinsky also slammed *The Double* by seeing the hero as a construct that was social, not psychological. In his view, Golyadkin was an exemplar of lower-class urban males who, from frustrated ambition, go off the deep end, courtesy of a sickly if not demonic sensibility and suspiciousness of life. Dostoevsky's bold break-up of Golyadkin into a loser-Senior and a winner-Junior was dismissed as the stuff of mentally illness, the prerogative of doctors, not poets.

Dostoevsky's "Mr. Prokharchin" fared even worse. The sporadic flashes of talent in the work, the critic contended, were mired in darkness and pretense. In a parting blow to Dostoevsky's early fiction, Belinsky claims he had to force himself to finish "A Novel in Nine Letters."

With his misgivings about the four works after *Poor Folk*, Belinsky burst the bubble of Dostoevsky's alleged genius and fame. In no uncertain terms, he declined to anoint Dostoevsky the new messiah of Russian literature, the heir-successor to Pushkin, Lermontov, and Gogol. Such accolades, Belinsky declared, were childish and absurd. They led nowhere and explained nothing. Dostoevsky did not stand higher than his predecessors, the critic continued. He did not even stand alongside them as an equal; rather, he had only had the good fortune to come after them.

Not pulling any punches, Belinsky also proclaimed Dostoevsky's dependence on Gogol. Even more brutally, perhaps, he insisted that the author of *Dead Souls* would remain for the young writer a father figure, a Columbus to help him navigate his way through art. How much, Belinsky lamented, did the writer of *Poor Folk* have to learn from the writer of *Dead Souls* in both substance and style. Gogol was a writer for the masses, but Dostoevsky a dallier for dilettantes. Gogol showed no contradictions in his writing, but Dostoevsky, in his works, had muddled content and form. Belinsky make the ranking painfully clear. Expanding the aesthetic distance further, he insisted that readers and reviewers eschew listing Dostoevsky along with Pushkin, Lermontov, and Gogol.

Needless to say, Dostoevsky was stung deeply by the critics' reviews. He was not stupid. He saw that behind the clamor and delight over his writing, there were serious reservations about his talent. Also rankling to Dostoevsky were charges that *Poor Folk* and *The Double* were boring, flaccid, and difficult if not impossible to read. Even more hurtful, if not insulting, was the claim that there was little difference between him and his ill-fated characters—he and Makar Devushkin shared the same mug.

The pièce de résistance was the assertion of ties, even subservience, to Gogol. Here Dostoevsky's anger knew no bounds. In no way would he acknowledge dependence on the great master. He was more profound than Gogol, the young writer ranted. He analyzed people and things in ways that Gogol never could or would, he raved. Far more than the writer of *Dead Souls*, the author of *Poor Folk* and *The Double* was doing something very new and dramatic in Russian literature. Why else, Dostoevsky reasoned, were people reading and rereading him in such a frenzied way? Why else was *The Petersburg Miscellany* (read: *Poor Folk* as the main attraction in the publication) selling like hotcakes in the provinces? Why were fans treating his works as lavish feasts, reading only a chapter a day so as not to exhaust themselves, but to smack their lips with pleasure? Alexander Herzen and Ivan Goncharov might be nipping at his heels, but he need not worry, Dostoevsky told himself and others. He still held first place among contemporary Russian writers. Indeed, he hoped to stay there forever. Dostoevsky may have been bloodied, but he was unbowed. He would show them all.

Or so he thought.

Ironically, in the two years after *Poor Folk*, the more Dostoevsky swelled externally with self-induced accolades and applause, the more he shrank internally with self-inspired doubt and despair. The devolution was sudden and swift, with sins of omission and commission everywhere in view.

If, consciously or unconsciously, in 1846 and 1847 Dostoevsky entered upon what he later recalled as a sad and fateful time, he had only himself to blame. The sudden success of *Poor Folk* had so inflated the writer's being that he lost contact not only with reality but also with everyone and everything that had afforded him harmony, stability, and peace. Dostoevsky did not forget his roots so much as he ripped them out with his hands. The values and verities instilled in him by father Mikhail and mother Maria stabilized him no longer. The parental lessons of faith, hope, and love that he had internalized during the first twenty-four years of his existence he expunged almost entirely in the following two. For one thing, Dostoevsky forgot God. If, before the success of *Poor Folk*, he had filled letters with appeals to the Almighty, or comments on deific mercy, justice, and goodness, he did not do so now. Not once in his missives in 1846 and 1847 was there the slightest mention of a supreme being. (Professed shock at Belinsky's disparagement of Christ at this time Dostoevsky recalled many years later, in 1873 entries of *Diary of a Writer*, after he had got religion.)

For another thing, Dostoevsky abandoned family and friends. Beyond occasional notes to brother Mikhail, he lost contact with brothers and sisters, uncles and aunts. Members of the clan often had no idea where he was or what he was doing. With the prodigal son or nephew, they rejoiced over rare missives or contacts. Friends, too, were cast aside, recipients of letters that were sporadic, fleeting, and scribbled on scraps of paper. Women also continued to be absent from his purview. At gatherings and events, Dostoevsky engaged members of the opposite sex only in occasional dances or in brief and polite conversations. Even more serious, perhaps, Dostoevsky no longer kept mental company with the theologians and philosophers, writers and artists, who had so excited his childhood, adolescence, and youth. Indeed, he stopped reading them altogether.

The ill-treatment shown to family and friends was extended to others. Not content with alienating members of the Belinsky circle, Dostoevsky also estranged other agents of the Russian literary world. He quarreled with booksellers for bleeding him dry and for withholding his works from the public for better prices and profits. He also ran afoul of editors and publishers, setting high-handed terms for unwritten works, failing to keep promises, and insisting that he and his writing were worth more, much more, than he was offered.

More than ever, Dostoevsky wounded himself. Disorder and dissoluteness claimed heavy tolls. Debts, loans, and IOUs mounted precariously. Illnesses—real and imagined; past, present, and future—promised an early grave. Complaints included a body that was fevered and trembling, nerves that were sick and shot, and a heart that palpitated dangerously. Bouts of apathy and boredom gave way to pipe dreams of life in Italy, to spells of sadness, lethargy, and dread, and to preparations for his wake and funeral.

Even more painful, perhaps, Dostoevsky wondered if the critics were correct in their claims. Increasingly, he found writing difficult. *The Double*, the young writer admitted, had given him fits. With "Mr. Prokharchin," "The Landlady," and "A Novel in Nine Letters," he seemed to be declining, even disintegrating, as a writer. In a rare moment of honesty, Dostoevsky also acknowledged that he had failed expectations, and that exhaustion and haste had ruined *The Double*. It took no arm-twisting on the young writer's part to agree, implicitly, with Belinsky's disavowal of his second work as muddle, foulness, and trash.

More than once in 1846 and 1847, Dostoevsky saw the collapse of projects and plans, leaving him to flop and flounder like the very people he despised. Despite claims to the contrary, he was facing stiff competition from colleagues who had also begun their careers with a bang—admittedly, not with the furor of *Poor Folk*, but with strength and speed in subsequent writing. With or without the author of *Poor Folk*, Russian literature, particularly works of social exposé, was alive and well. In those same two years, Goncharov published *A Common Story*; Grigorovich, *The Village* and *Anton Goremyka*; Alexander Druzhinin, *Polinka Saks*; Ivan Turgenev, "Khor and Kalinych"; and Alexander Herzen, *Who Is to Blame?*, *Mimoezdom*, *Doctor Krupov*, and *The Thieving Magpie*. Dostoevsky ran the danger not just of being outpaced and outclassed but of being forgotten altogether. For the umpteenth time in his now twenty-six years of existence, Dostoevsky questioned if he had what it took to be a writer, if he could endure the difficulties and labor needed to establish himself in the Russian literary world.

In this dark time, though, there were bright spots. If Dostoevsky was anything in 1846 and 1847, he was a survivor who, by sheer will, moved from swamp to sun. He was not entirely downcast. He still had goals. He still needed success. When life was not dreary and cold, it could be warm and rich.

Although the young writer had lost touch with much of his family, he held fast to brother Mikhail—and, by extension, to his sister-in-law Emiliya and their two children. Here Dostoevsky was his old self, with demands for solace and support that were swift and sure, overbearing and outrageous. Would Mikhail be kind enough, Dostoevsky asked boldly, to manage his affairs, support his dreams, and fund his projects? Even more extreme, could his brother kindly take a leave of absence several months before his formal retirement from state service to join Dostoevsky in St. Petersburg earlier than planned? As before, Dostoevsky struck pay dirt. Ever the loyal brother, Mikhail agreed to everything.

Dostoevsky also became friends with Stepan Yanovsky, a physician and himself a character in the cast of the young writer's life. In the first two years after *Poor Folk*, he was a kindred spirit, a guardian angel, a psycho-spiritual brother, and, even more than Mikhail, Dostoevsky's closest friend and contact with reality.

Dostoevsky and Yanovsky had much in common. They were "doubles" in a positive sense. The two were relatively close in age: When they met in late 1846, Yanovsky was thirty-one. Dostoevsky twenty-five. Both came from serf-owning families of petty gentry. Both had spent their early years in provincial Russia. Dostoevsky summered near Tula, some one hundred miles south of Moscow. Yanovsky hailed from Kursk, approximately two hundred miles southwest of Tula, near the border with Ukraine. Both men had studied science. Dostoevsky had taken up engineering at the Main Engineering Academy in St. Petersburg; Yanovsky had turned to medicine at the Surgical-Medical Academy in Moscow, after which he was a teacher of natural history and a doctor for the members of the Forestry Institute and of the Preobrazhensky Regiment in St. Petersburg. In spring 1846, when Yanovsky met Dostoevsky, he had just transferred to the Department of Public Medical Training in the Ministry of the Interior. He had also begun a private practice.

Dostoevsky and Yanovsky loved fiction and had similar aesthetic tastes and worldviews. (While studying medicine, Yanovksy also audited lectures in literature by Stepan Shevyryov.) Both thought empirically. Both shunned cards as well as wine, women, and song. To the mix, Yanovsky added fervent beliefs in God and country, tenets, it will be recalled, set aside by Dostoevsky.

Yanovsky found Dostoevsky in rough shape. Beyond the writer's already noted complaints, Yanovsky diagnosed additional problems. Some were physical; most were mental. Scurvy and anemia wracked the writer's body. Hallucinations, panics, and fears of paralysis and strokes warped his soul. In his newfound friend, Yanovsky encountered an even more disturbing complication. To him Dostoevsky confided that death was no stranger, having come for him more than once. In fact, the young writer often feared that he would die in his sleep.

Treatment by Yanovsky was part conventional science, part common sense. Two or three comforting words were often all that was needed to set the young writer at ease and to convince him that most of his illnesses were in his head. In Yanovsky, too, Dostoevsky found what he cherished most: conversations, intimate and intense, which allowed him to hold forth on literature and life.

Doctor also gained from patient. Dostoevsky was for Yanovsky a mesmerizing teacher, virtuoso, and guide who imparted lifelong values and ideals. Not for nothing did Yanovsky compare Dostoevsky to Socrates.

Several claims Yanovsky made about Dostoevsky during the first two years after *Poor Folk*, though, require clarification. The first was Yanovsky's avowal that in 1846 and 1847 the young writer experienced occasional bouts of "falling sickness" or *"epilepsia"*—several times to a life-threatening degree. The observation must be taken *cum grano salis*, for several reasons. First,

Yanovsky made the remark only as a passing comment in a letter to a Russian newspaper in 1881, almost forty years after they were supposed to have occurred (and two weeks after the writer's death). Absent from the good doctor's allegations were precise details about these afflictions. The two cited instances were maddeningly vague. It was also only in the second one that the young writer was said to have had convulsions. Further undercutting Yanovsky's claim as to Dostoevsky's epilepsy was his admission not only that his patient was a notorious hypochondriac but also that he sensed the onset of "falling sickness" at specific times and places—trips to Haymarket Square, a key setting in his major novels, were a common trigger—a foreboding that Yanovsky himself dismissed as neurosis, not neurology.[1]

Three things complicate matters further. First, Apollon Maykov, an alleged witness to one of Dostoevsky's bouts, never noted such an event in writing. Three others individuals—Alexander Poretsky, Pyotr Tseidler, and Ivan Lkhovsky—who, along with Maykov, were named by Yanovsky as having been informed of Dostoevsky's attack three days later, were also silent about the episode.

Second, independent of the doctor's account was the testimony of Mikhail Yazykov, who, in an article written two weeks after Yanovsky's, claimed that Dostoevsky suffered an epileptic attack at a gathering in his home in the summer of 1847.

Weaknesses in Yazykov's account of Dostoevsky's alleged epilepsy mirrored those of Yanovsky. Yazykov stated that Dostoevsky showed initial symptoms of the attack—a facial expression that was agitated, eyes that were frightened, a voice that was anxious and hollow, together with sudden confusion over his surroundings and mad dashes for air—all in the presence of Panaev, Pavel Annenkov, Turgenev, and possibly Nekrasov. Although these individuals would have delighted in having new ammunition to use against the writer, again, none of them noted such an occurrence in writing then or later. Even more revealing, perhaps, all four men were conveniently gone or exiting the scene (it is not clear which) when the real fun began: Dostoevsky, allegedly doused with cold water, fled the premises and ran down Liteinyi Prospket in central Petersburg before being stopped by Yazykov in a carriage, who now, *mirabile dictu*, found the young writer conscious, calm, and heading for home.[2] Third, and even more serious, perhaps, is the fact that Dostoevsky himself admitted in 1849 that he suffered not from "falling sickness" but from hypochondria three years in a row. Also, looking back on physical failings in this period almost a decade later, Dostoevsky reiterated that he had been seized not with epilepsy but with great spiritual illness and hypochondria, often to a powerful degree.

To return to Yanovsky, it is also conceivable that he held Dostoevsky in such awe that for him the young writer, via "fainting sickness," perceived, if not inhabited, unearthly realms. Just as students at the Main Engineering Academy saw Dostoevsky as a mystic, divorced from everyday persuasions and preoccupations, so could Yanovsky have come to see Dostoevsky-cum-*epilepsia* as a prophet or "holy fool" who embraced more, much more, than others could.

Still another observation by Yanovsky in this period requires discussion. Most certainly, Dostoevsky in 1846 and 1847 was not, as the doctor claimed him to be, a patriot, a believer in Christ, or an advocate for the poor. As has already been noted, in the first two years after *Poor Folk*, God and country were the last things on Dostoevsky's mind. Earlier concerns for the insulted and injured had also fallen by the wayside. If unfortunates did figure in the writer's thoughts and travels at this time, it was only marginally or, as with Ivan Karamazov in Dostoevsky's final work, as constructs that tormented mind, not heart. It should also be recalled that the heroes of his first five works were not from the lower reaches of society. They had jobs, salaries, and skills—even humane superiors. For the young writer, social or economic injustice was not an issue. No liberal or radical was he.

The discrepancy between Dostoevsky during the first two years after *Poor Folk* and Yanovsky's account of him can be explained simply. The Dostoevsky recalled in 1881 was not the young writer thrashing about in literature and life; rather, he was a much older, established, and successful individual who, after years of searing trial and error, believed that only God and Russia promised happiness and salvation. In no way was the Dostoevsky of 1846 and 1847 the Dostoevsky of 1881.

In 1846 and 1847, Dostoevsky did not always have to be the star of the show. He could take comfort in things outside of himself. Music, particularly Italian opera and Russian singers, captured his fancy. So did interests in medicine, crania, nervous systems, spiritual disorders, and illnesses of the brain.

Dostoevsky also enjoyed the company of select families such as the Vielgorskys, the Beketovs, and the Maykovs. Even more revealing, he loved to arrange gatherings with close colleagues and friends. Dinners at restaurants and hotels were modest and cheap—no more than two rubles per person—but embraced merriment and inspired memories long afterward.

At these gatherings, Dostoevsky was the consummate host. True to form, he drank little—a thimble of vodka, a quarter glass of wine—but he was the life of the party. He loved to toast guests, to engage them in an open and sincere way, and to give them hearty send-offs and encouraging words before they reentered the cold, cruel world. In contrast to the get-togethers with the Vielgorskys, Beketovs, and Maykovs, the dinners at restaurants and hotels had an unwashed, bohemian flair. In the writer's idea, all present were self-styled proletarians who eschewed the daily grind and regular paychecks to pursue dreams as writers and students of literature, philosophy, and art. Amidst such company, Dostoevsky held court and continued unimpeded as teacher-mentor to novice writers with ambitions similar to his own.

Equally important, Dostoevsky still had his fans. Alexei Pleshcheev saw the writer as a bright new star. Valerian Maykov deemed Dostoevsky highly original, hardly Gogol's sidekick. Indeed, Maykov hit the nail on the head when he said that Gogol was a social writer, but Dostoevsky was a psychological one. Gogol, Maykov continued, traveled the length and breadth of Russia, whereas Dostoevsky inhabited the even vaster, if more challenging, expanses of the mind. Maykov agreed that Dostoevsky was not an easy read, but that the results were worth the time and effort. It was, he said, only after readers and reviewers explored *Poor Folk* and subsequent stories a second or third time that they could grasp the profundity, perception, and psychology in Dostoevsky's writing. Remarkable also was Maykov's prescience, that is, his striking ability to light upon virtues in Dostoevsky's early works that would be the seedbeds of his later ones. When Maykov called the final encounter between Makar and Varvara tortured, oppressive, and despotic, he unknowingly pointed to the torturous ties between men and women in Dostoevsky's major novels, for example, how Nastasya Filippovna abused Rogozhin and Myshkin in *The Idiot*; or how Katerina Ivanovna and Grushenka assaulted Dmitri in *The Brothers Karamazov*.

Maykov also had high if singular praise for *The Double*. In his second work, he asserted, Dostoevsky was a scientist of the body, a psychologist of the mind, and a seer of the soul. Just as Maykov foreshadowed the battles of the sexes in *The Idiot* and *The Brothers Karamazov* with comments on Makar and Varvara in *Poor Folk*, so now did he foresee the birth of the hero in *Notes of the Underground* and of Raskolnikov in *Crime and Punishment* with claims that Golyadkin was a slave but bent on personhood in life. Given such insights into Dostoevsky's early work, it is a pity that Maykov did not have Belinsky's authority. It is an even greater tragedy that Maykov left life so early—he died of a stroke at age twenty-four while swimming, just before, according to Turgenev, he would have been named Belinsky's successor as a critic[3]—since he might have steered readers and reviewers to see *Poor Folk*, *The Double*, and other early works in a more positive and accurate light and thus save Dostoevsky from the disastrous mistake, his involvement in the Petrashevsky affair, which almost ended his life, let alone his literary career.

In the first two years after *Poor Folk*, Dostoevsky held fast to his dream as writer. He would not accept failure or a humdrum existence. Thrown from his metaphorical horse, the young writer got back up on his feet, dusted himself off, and started again. He also had scores to settle. Pen in hand, Dostoevsky again waged war on all. Indeed, he seemed almost glad for his quarrels with Nekrasov, Belinsky, and others so that he could burn, if not blow up, bridges behind him and work unimpeded, and independently, for his idea of art.

In his mind at least, Dostoevsky had ample albeit inflated proof for his revolt. He could still tell a good story, spellbinding listeners with tales of drunkards and other "poor folk" that, taken from real life, were merciless, comical, and humane. Ideas and images that he deemed more original, lively, and bright begged for paper. His pen moved to inspiration from his soul. He was swamped with work, writing day and night, and seeing better days ahead. "The Landlady" was as crisp and successful as *Poor Folk*. The beginnings of a novel that would be *Netochka Nezvanova* was giving him no peace. Plans to publish the story, along with *Poor Folk* and a revision of *The Double* as separate and illustrated works, appeared with schemes for a series of translations, courtesy of brother Mikhail. Within two years, Dostoevsky mused, he would have a complete edition of his writings in print. Previous readers, reviewers, and booksellers be damned! Other people would take their place and applaud, defend, and publish him.

Beyond fictional works, Dostoevsky was also trying his hand at feuilleton-style journalism: a series of 1847 articles, titled "The Petersburg Chronicle," in which, via the breezy, gossipy style that would become a hallmark of many speakers in his mature works, Dostoevsky made clear his likes and dislikes in literature and life. It can be argued that more than any other work to date, "The Petersburg Chronicle" was his most significant step as a thinker and an artist. That is, whereas in *Poor Folk*, "The Double," "Mr. Prokharchin," "The Landlady," and "A Novel in Nine Letters," Dostoevsky painted muddy canvases of individuals disaffected with life, he, in "The Petersburg Chronicle," conceptualized, logically and simply, many of the images and ideas that he would sanction or censure in his later fiction.

In "The Petersburg Chronicle," Dostoevsky defended Russian history and nationality against what he saw as the attacks of stupid Frenchmen, armchair intellectuals, and the public at large. Vengeful ridicule of circles and salons merged with insightful musings about beings who shifted, at will, between sinners and saints, oppressors and oppressed.

Equally revealing, in these articles Dostoevsky praised outlooks and views that, later in life, he would condemn with a vengeance. Peter the Great, his city, and his idea for Russia drew only praise and applause from the twenty-six-year-old writer. Indeed, Dostoevsky sounded very much like Belinsky and the other Westernizers of the time when he rejected the worldview of the Slavophiles as dreamy and dead. In its place, the young writer put forth St. Petersburg as model and exemplar for native minds, hearts, and souls. For such a reality, though, Dostoevsky foresaw a rough and rocky road. The Russian window on the West, he said again à la Belinsky, was clouded with garbage and dust; but such disorder was necessary for national renewal and rebirth.

Changing metaphors, Dostoevsky saw St. Petersburg as a sturdy sapling that had been planted in a swamp but spread its roots throughout Russia, to industry, trade, science, education—and, of course, literature. In no way, Dostoevsky continued, were denizens of the northern Venice perishing under European influence. They were not soulless Germans: walking dead. Rather, citizens of St. Petersburg and elsewhere in Russia were experiencing a union of East and West: positive and principled, healthy and whole.

He had ample evidence for such a view. *Peterburzhtsy*, Dostoevsky insisted, were stoic fatalists no longer. Rather, they were curious, analytical, and discerning. Even more revealing and salutary, they were open, even confessional about their failings and faults. It came as small wonder, Dostoevsky went on to say, that Russian readers and reviewers wanted the same in their literature. Equally unsurprising, he added, was the public impatience and ire with contemporary writers. The demand was for literati to pick up pen and paper with no holds barred. Everyone and everything were subjects for them to disclose what people thought, said, and did.

In "The Petersburg Chronicle," though, Dostoevsky was under no illusions as to what he saw as shortcomings in the national character. Particularly annoying to him was the penchant of Russians to become excited by causes and ideas but never to follow through. Rather than pursue meaningful goals, they wasted time and lives in drink, duels, and cards. Presaging the moral monsters of Dostoevsky's mature fiction, they gave in to specious ideas and goals which, after painful, near-fatal trial and error, they later despised as sentimental and silly.

The most important aspect of "The Petersburg Chronicle," however, was Dostoevsky's fascination with dreamers. As he saw it, dreamers were men and women, as well as children, adolescents, and youths, who yearned for action and life but who experienced catastrophe and upheaval.

So intrigued was Dostoevsky with dreamers, though, that in the style of the "physiological" writing of the time, he not only embarked on engaging sketches of such types but also, unwittingly, set in motion characterizations of the wishful thinkers of his later writing. Externally, Dostoevsky saw dreamers as dark and dismal, terse and tense, weary and wan. He deemed such individuals overheated ideologues, burdened by skull-cracking thoughts and impressions, the content of which he, sadly, did not care to define. Additionally, Dostoevsky assessed dreamers as unbalanced dualities who are both happy and sad: egoists and boors.

Dreamers, Dostoevsky went on to say, were also failures and freaks at odds with the world. They withdrew into themselves. They hid from people and life, in corners that were inaccessible, disordered, and dirty. Dreamers also relished idleness and ease. Any effort—physical, mental, and spiritual—was for them anathema.

In Dostoevsky's view, dreamers dwelled between a rock and a hard place. On the one hand, they so feared life that they were submissive and inert. On the other hand, they struck back at their lot by seeing reality not as it was but as it should be—or, more accurately, as they wanted it to be. Such individuals, Dostoevsky insisted, did not plumb existence for ideas; rather, they imposed ideas on existence, to trap the world in structures and systems that were self-fashioned, self-serving, and self-preserving.

With idle minds as devil's workshops, Dostoevsky asserted that dreamers sought life in sensations, impressions, and moods. Sometimes these arose from a book, music, or memory, other times from daily trivia and trifles. More seriously, they often assumed a cerebral form. Indeed, dreamers for Dostoevsky could be so seduced by images and ideas that they lost all sense of reality and self. The thrills and spills that such yearning souls missed outside their bodies they more than relished inside them. They stepped forth as heroes and heroines of stories, novels, and tales. Religious myths competed with romantic intrigues; swashbuckling adventures vied with bloody melodramas; epic struggles contended with charming fairy tales. There were joys and sorrows, heavens and hells. There were captivating women and damsels in distress. There were heroic gestures, activities, and struggles. There were horrors and crimes. There was even an eternal if not apocalyptic flair. Space disappeared. Hours became minutes; eternities turned into moments.

It was also sensations, impressions, and moods that made Dostoevsky's dreamers feel alive, if not resurrected from the dead. With God and Christ not moving them to spiritual joy, and women not bringing them to physical bliss, Dostoevsky's wishful thinkers had only themselves with whom to experience delight. They also encountered alone their version of utopia and Eden. Indeed, for Dostoevsky, dreamers were so aroused by sensations, impressions, and moods that they entered into paradises that were splendid, grand, and filled with peace and love. Once there, they encountered physical and spiritual ecstasy. Their pulse quickened, their eyes filled with tears, and their cheeks became fevered and moist.

Such joy did not last, though. When it was over, it left dreamers hurt and hung over, even more dissatisfied, unfulfilled, and apathetic than previously. They also took away nothing from the experience. They recalled little of what had allegedly transpired, other than the beating hearts that returned them to earthbound and expanded hells.

Tragically, dreamers were for Dostoevsky a stiff-necked lot. Having refused to learn from their mistakes, they—willingly, perversely—committed them anew. It was a measure of their pathos that, in Dostoevsky's idea, not only did wishful thinkers celebrate the anniversaries of their fantasies and adventures but also, after denying efficacy, responsibility, and will for their actions, they marked their calendars for times when they deemed themselves happy and could dream anew. They appealed to existence not for life lessons or truths but for stimuli to reignite minds, hearts, and souls. Chance was a key and crucial factor. A book that fell into their hands, or a woman they saw on the street, was all they needed to fly through the air with the greatest of ease, and to re-create an impotent if self-destructive bliss.

Having lived vicariously as heroes, even as man-gods, Dostoevsky's dreamers refused to accept what the writer saw as a key truth, namely, that life is an endless contemplation of nature and daily being, Such a concept was for Dostoevsky's fantasists too quiet and mundane, too genuine and prosaic, and too dangerous and demeaning to be of value. Reflection on nature and being threatened ego and self. Even worse, it destroyed their view of the world. In no way could or would Dostoevsky's dreamers accept that running the show was God and life, not they. Equally abhorrent to them was the idea that they were specks in the universe, not its core or center. For Dostoevsky, such resistance got dreamers into trouble. It forced them to forsake ethics and morality. Twenty years before the fact, Dostoevsky laid the foundation for "all is permitted."

If Dostoevsky wrote insightfully about dreamers, it was because he—and everyone else—created life in their own image and likeness. Tired of the daily grind and fearful that he would destroy his talent and youth, Dostoevsky also went out on mental limbs, taking as truth self-styled, convoluted, and contradictory versions of people, places, and events. However paradoxically, Dostoevsky believed that the decline in his fame brought him closer to success. Even with a string of failures to his name, Dostoevsky held fast to the view that he held the public's love, fascination, and hope.

He clung fast to a grand view of self. Editors and publishers were inundating him with offers; they were throwing money at his feet. No doubt about it, Dostoevsky told himself (and anybody else in proximity), he would regain fame, even primacy as a writer.

It would not be Dostoevsky if he did not assert internal change as well. Things, distasteful and unpleasant, were giving way to changes that were useful and good. In a move that would make the villains of his later fiction blush, Dostoevsky professed that he was being reborn, physically and spiritually. Never before, he continued, had he experienced such abundance and clarity, equilibrium and health. *Mirabile dictu*, Dostoevsky even claimed to be debt-free!

For all the hoopla and good cheer, Dostoevsky failed to move forward. "The Landlady" was a failure. "The Petersburg Chronicle" ended as quickly as it had begun. Refusing to publish unfinished pieces, Dostoevsky had nothing to give to editors and publishers, from whom he often hid rather than approach them with empty hands. It would not be until 1849 that Dostoevsky published the first three parts of *Netochka Nezvanova*.

The young writer was also hardly secure financially. Even as funds came in from the publication of *Poor Folk*, he simply could not manage money. He owed everyone in town. He succumbed to fanciful schemes. He helped (or was exploited by) one and all. As Dostoevsky was the first to admit, if it were not for the kindness of others—the Maykovs, for one—he would have perished.

Stresses from without triggered strains from within. Despite Yanovsky's counsel and care, Dostoevsky went about in hazes and dazes. He suffered rushes of blood to the head. Existence, he told brother Mikhail, was becoming dual. External realities were overwhelming and fearsome. Internal ones ascended dangerously. Floods of fantasy inundated his being; surges of nerves plunged it into bottomless voids.

With an eye to readers and reviewers, particularly the members of the Belinsky circle, Dostoevsky charged that society championed false prophets and Pharisees, shamans and sages who, useless, repulsive, and vile, upheld the status quo. As with biblical demons, their name was legion. As with folk woodcuts, their message was cheap and mass-produced.

Striking out blindly, Dostoevsky chased away the people he loved—and who loved him—the most. Brother Mikhail was (again) first in line. In the first two years after *Poor Folk*, Mikhail moved from being Dostoevsky's sounding board for his hopes and dreams to a whipping boy for his frustrations and fears. Insult followed injury. In sporadic and scribbled notes, Dostoevsky engaged Mikhail in classic self-projection, chiding his brother for failings and wrongs of which he himself was guilty. Dostoevsky berated

Mikhail for withdrawing in silence and neglect, for eschewing a healthy lifestyle, for failing to be vibrant and bold, and for disparaging the thought of better times ahead. Even worse were moments when Dostoevsky, not unlike Varvara with Makar in *Poor Folk*, tormented Mikhail with elaborate, outrageous, and costly errands and requests. With Mikhail's wife and children, Dostoevsky could even be cruel. On a visit to his brother and his family in Revel (now Tallinn) in Estonia, Dostoevsky noted that he had been awkward and difficult. To Mikhail's wife, Emiliya, he was rude; to Mikhail's five-year old son, Fedya, spiteful.

Mikhail protested the injustice, but such complaints fell on deaf ears. At times, the young writer challenged Mikhail's objections as unjust. At other times, he engaged in self-recrimination and rebuke. For his misconduct toward Mikhail, Dostoevsky blamed illness and nerves. More revealingly, perhaps, he indicted himself for being repulsive and heartless: a mass of contradictions beyond comprehension and control. Only when external circumstances or incidents wrenched Dostoevsky violently from himself could he show heart and love. At still other times, Dostoevsky sought to mend fences with Mikhail by proclaiming himself to be the lesser of the two and by professing ultimate affection and sacrifice, saying that he was ready to die for his brother and his family.

Dostoevsky, though, had no intention of changing his ways. Akin to the characters in both his early and mature fiction, he regaled Mikhail with confessions that were false. The lists of failings and flaws were too swift and schematic; they lacked moves toward reconciliation, restitution, and true remorse. Indeed, one wonders if with Mikhail—not unlike the villains in, say, *Devils* and *The Brothers Karamazov*—Dostoevsky was boasting of his sins rather than disclosing them. Even more outrageous, perhaps, the young writer demanded that Mikhail—and by implication others—accept him, warts and all. After all, Dostoevsky complained self-pityingly if defensively, if only Mikhail, and the world at large, knew how he had suffered constantly and unjustly. Whatever Dostoevsky thought he was doing—or not doing— in his rapprochements with Mikhail, his breast-beating ended as quickly as it had begun. Other cares and concerns—his despair over *The Double* and his excitement over "The Landlady" and *Netochka Nezvanova* were key examples—diverted his attention. His own Underground Man, Dostoevsky spent days and nights alone. Even more like his infamous hero, he wondered how Mikhail, and anyone else for that matter, could love him. In truth, in 1846 and 1847, few could or would.

It comes as little surprise that when Dostoevsky reflected on his youth in the twilight of his existence, he saw the first two years after *Poor Folk* as a time when he both cursed and embraced the darkness. It is also safe to say that later in life, Dostoevsky came to understand the years 1846 and 1847 as an initial foray into a self-styled, self-imposed, and self-directed Golgotha, during which twelve years of crucifixion were followed by twenty years of gradual resurrection. Whether Dostoevsky attained the latter is a matter of debate; whether he achieved the former, especially in the first two years after *Poor Folk*, is beyond a doubt.

PART ONE

Pride before the Fall

Belinsky and the Aftermath of Poor Folk

When Vissarion Belinsky first met Dostoevsky in May 1845, he was thirty-six years old. He would die of tuberculosis exactly three years later, concluding a decade-long search for truth and meaning in life. Initially, Belinsky had espoused the German romantic idealism of Friedrich Schiller, Friedrich Schelling, and Georg Hegel and their universalist notions about poets, nations, and societies.

Then, in a famed "reconciliation with reality," he had looked to such French socialists as Pierre-Joseph Proudhon, Henri de Saint-Simon, Robert Lamennais, Charles Fourier, Étienne Cabet, Louis Blanc, and Pierre Leroux, who advocated secular worldwide brotherhoods as well as scientific restructurings of reality. More recently, Belinsky had become enamored with such left Hegelians as David Strauss and Ludwig Feuerbach, particularly their ideas on mechanistic and moral determinism, as well as their demands that communist worlds replace Christian ones. In the last two or three years of Belinsky's life, Annenkov wrote, the great critic was "concerned with the emerging definitions of the rights and obligations of man, with the new truths proclaimed by economic doctrines that were liquidating all notions of the old, displaced ideas about the moral, good, and the noble on earth, and, in their place, was putting formulas and theses of a purely rational character."[1]

At the core of Belinsky's quest were two additional, stirring beliefs. The first was his absolute faith in the sanctity and greatness of humankind. The second was his equally unshakeable confidence in the Westernizing path that Peter the Great had chosen for his homeland. Peter was for the eminent critic his "philosophy, [his] religion, [his] revelation to all that concerns Russia."[2]

In his final years, though, Belinsky was in even worse straits than the young Dostoevsky. For one thing, he was trapped in an unhappy marriage. Just a month before his nuptials to Maria Orlova, he confessed to his fiancée on October 13, 1843, that there was "nothing fiery, nothing ardent" in their relationship. Three years later, Belinsky chastised the woman on July 30, 1846, writing, "Nothing, neither living together nor separating [from each other], will teach you to understand my character."[3]

For another thing, Belinsky knew that his days were numbered. "I began to realize with horror and fear that I do not have long to go," he wrote to Vasily Botkin on February 6, 1843. Three years later, he confessed to Herzen his fear not only of death but also of familial ruin. "It is a terrible thing," he wrote, "to leave wife and daughter without a crust of bread."[4]

Even more serious, perhaps, Belinsky was tired of the literary grind. Successful as the great critic was, he struggled to make a living materially and mentally. "The walls of my quarters are hateful to me," he wrote to Botkin on December 9–10, 1842. "Like a prisoner returning to jail, I return to them with despair and repugnance in my soul." On February 6, 1843, he continued, telling Botkin, "Work on *The Fatherland Notes* has come to disgust me to the point of morbidity." Three years later, Belinsky had had his fill of the publication and its editor, Andrei Kraevsky. "Working against a deadline for a journal sucks the living strength out of me," he complained to Herzen on January 2, 1846, "like a vampire . . . ever ready to suck the blood and soul of a person and then to throw him out the window like a squeezed lemon."[5]

His new position at *The Contemporary* only exacerbated his angst. If Dostoevsky had had difficulties with Nekrasov and Panaev, so did Belinsky. He wrote to Turgenev on March 1, 1847, "Nekrasov was one of the worst; perhaps only Panaev is worse." On February 6, 1847, he complained to Botkin: "My repugnance for literature and journalism *as a trade* grows from day to day, and I do not know what will become of it. It is more difficult to fight repugnance than need; it is a disease."[6]

Needless to say, Belinsky felt alone, socially and spiritually; but again, as with the young Dostoevsky, his isolation was self-imposed. The more extreme his convictions, the less he shared them with the few friends he had. The more radical his thinking, the greater his fear and frustration for his country and its citizens. Belinsky was experiencing a Dostoevskian duality all his own. If he was split in mind and soul, it was because of his insistence that art maintain absolute integrity, but also that it serve sociopolitical ends.

Dostoevsky was conflicted deeply over Belinsky, particularly during the eighteen or so months of their close relationship. On the one hand, he saw Belinsky as a personal and professional success. The great critic was a gentleman and a scholar who cared for his family as much as he did for Russia. He was also a being who understood national life better than anyone else. Equally unusual for the young Dostoevsky, Belinsky was a man of thought and action: an individual who not only crashed through walls—political, social, and aesthetic—but also pondered how they stymied Russia and Russians. For Dostoevsky, Belinsky was not "superfluous." He did not yield to apathy; he did not brood about life and fate. Energized by ideas and warmed by progress, he was the happiest man in his homeland. Animated and intense, Belinsky brimmed with confidence and aplomb. Pragmatic and philosophical, he championed men and women, railroads and art. His only sadness was that growth came slowly. "Why not today, why not tomorrow?" was his mantra-like lament.

With hindsight, Dostoevsky saw Belinsky as a mentor and guide, even as a parental figure who extended the life lessons of father Michael and mother Maria in his childhood, adolescence, and youth.

On the other hand, Dostoevsky became increasingly hostile to Belinsky, for straightforward reasons. He chafed against the great critic's attempt to bend him to his aesthetic will and to make him a critic of political and social ills. More to the point, Dostoevsky never forgave Belinsky for the fact that he had applauded *Poor Folk* but castigated *The Double*, "Mr. Prokharchin," "The Landlady," and "A Novel in Nine Letters."

More important, perhaps, with the hindsight of some thirty years after events—a period during which Dostoevsky became increasingly conservative politically and socially, and was also writing his political novel *Devils*—his anger with Belinsky assumed a darker and deeper cast.

Belinsky, he charged, had been the catalyst for personal and national catastrophe. Having appealed to Western liberals, socialists, and communists for deliverance and salvation, Belinsky had led both Dostoevsky and Russia astray. He had moved from God-man to man-gods, from solid and sacred values of the past to seductive and shimmering fantasies of the future. Belinsky, Dostoevsky claimed, deified reason, science, and economics; he had debunked Christ and religion; he had renounced private ownership, traditional values, and individual responsibility. Even as Belinsky foresaw the mess, even monstrosity, he was creating—the dream-turned-nightmare of the sociopolitical ant heap—he carried on with this personal and political madness. Belinsky, Dostoevsky continued, was hardly the solution to Russia's ills. He was part of the problem, shameful and stinking.

The rancor was unending. Belinsky, Dostoevsky declared, was stubborn and spiteful, pushy and proud. He was also petty and powerless, but with a dangerous and destructive streak. On good days, Belinsky was an ideologue, a retrograde, and a traitor. On bad days, he was a louse and a "shitty insect." The man was a host of contradictions: a fanatic who swung wildly between extremist rights and lefts, as well as a nihilist who covered the world with spittle and shame. No one escaped Belinsky's venom and wrath. Westernizers suffered the same reprimands and rebukes as Slavophiles. Russians were chronic basket cases, beyond resurrection and renewal. Indeed, Belinsky believed that if Russia traveled a special path, it was not to a third Rome but over a cliff into an abyss. Even as an émigré, Dostoevsky added, Belinsky would have been Turgenev's Rudin come to life: an empty talker of spurious causes and campaigns.

Given such personal and professional shortcomings, Dostoevsky concluded, it was not surprising that as a critic, Belinsky was so wrong about so many things. His views on Pushkin's *Eugene Onegin* and Gogol's *Dead Souls* topped the list. How could it be otherwise, Dostoevsky noted, when aesthetics concerned Belinsky but little. Literature that indicted and propagandized, that chose fact over fiction, that stressed sensation and scandal, and that grabbed readers by their necks and throttled them was for the critic the stuff of the national literary expression. Anything else was muddle and mess.

Good or bad, Belinsky loomed large in Dostoevsky's life. He was for the writer the father who had given him professional life, but with sins that were visited on his most famous son.

1846 and after
Fyodor Dostoevsky, from *A Writer's Diary*

> My entrance onto the literary scene—God knows how many years ago—was for me a sad and fateful time.

1846 and after
Fyodor Dostoevsky, from dictated notes

> He first retired [from service] and then wrote his rather large story, *Poor Folk*. . . . Its success was rare in the full sense of the word. But then in the next few years, his lack of health harmed his literary activities.

1846 and after
Fyodor Dostoevsky, from an 1858 letter to Mikhail Katkov

> Work for money and work for art are for me two incompatible things. Because of such a thing, I suffered the entire three years of my literary activity in Petersburg. I did not wish to profane my best ideas, my best plans for stories and novels. I worked hurriedly for deadlines. I so loved [these ideas and plans] that I wanted to create in an unhurried way, with love, so much so that, it seemed, I would rather die than to engage my best ideas in a dishonest way. Always being in constant debt to A. A. Kraevsky (who, by the way, never extorted work from me, but always gave me time [to write]), I was tied hand and foot.

1846 and after
Fyodor Dostoevsky, from his testimony to the Investigatory Commission for the Petrashevsky affair

> I have been sick constantly, suffering from attacks of hypochondria for three years running.

1846 and after
Stepan Yanovsky, from his memoirs

> During the entire time of my acquaintance with Dostoevsky, I never once heard that he was in love or that he loved any woman with passion. Before his exile to Siberia, I never saw him even hint at such things, that is, to study and analyze the character of the women or girls we both knew.

1846 and after
Nikolai Grech, from his memoirs

> A certain freedom in print proved very useful to the government, informing the powers that be who were their friends and enemies. In such a way, the vile *Fatherland Notes* before 1848 could serve as the best telegraph to show what kind of people Belinsky, Dostoevsky, and Herzen (Iskander) were.

1846
Pavel Annenkov, from an article

> The year 1846 was a remarkable one. By strange coincidence there appeared remarkable monuments of Russian literature . . . I. A. Goncharov's *A Common Story*, F. M. Dostoevsky's *Poor Folk*, and D. V. Grigorovich's *Anton Goremyka*.

1846
Anna Dostoevskaya, from her notebook

> From Balzac, Dostoevsky liked *Cousin Pons* and *Cousin Bette*.[7]

January–March 1846
Vera Dostoevskaya-Ivanova, from a letter to Fyodor Dostoevsky

> How guilty I am before you, dear brother, that I did not answer your letter right away, but it was not from laziness. Not knowing where to send my reply, I decided to wait to write a letter to [brother] Andryusha and to include one to you.
>
> I do not know how to thank you, dear brother, for your letter.... You have brought me to tears of happiness.

January 1, 1846
Vissarion Belinsky, from a review

> This coming year ... will awaken powerfully the attention of the public to a name that, it seems, is fated to play in our literature a role given to extremely few individuals. Who is this name, and why is he noteworthy—this we will keep silent for a while, all the more so since readers will find out about him in the next few days or so.[8]

January 2, 1846
Vissarion Belinsky, from a letter to Alexander Herzen

> By Easter I am coming out with *Leviathan*, a huge thick almanac.... Dostoevsky is giving me a story.[9]

Before January 24, 1846
Dmitri Grigorovich, from his memoirs

> During the publication of *Poor Folk* ... Dostoevsky was in a state of extreme nervous excitement.

After January 24, 1846
Ivan Panaev, from his memoirs

> The appearance of any new remarkable talent in Russian literature was always a holiday for Sollogub. He did not have the slightest trace of that literary envy or unpleasantness over another's success which, unfortunately, one often meets with among very talented writers and artists.... Enthusiastic over Dostoevsky's *Poor Folk*, he kept asking us: "But who is this Dostoevsky? For God's sake, show him to me, introduce me to him!"

After January 24, 1846
Vladimir Sollogub, from his memoirs

> *Poor Folk* featured such talent, such simplicity and force, that it led me to ecstasy. Having read the work, I immediately set out to see the editor of the journal—it seemed it was Andrei Alexandrovich Kraevsky—to find out about the author.[10] He told me it was Dostoevsky and gave me his address. I went there right away and came across a small apartment on one of the far-flung streets of Petersburg. . . .
>
> [There I met] a pale and sickly-looking young man. He wore a rather worn house frock coat with unusually short if seemingly unattached sleeves. When I introduced myself and told him in glowing terms the profound and surprising impression that *Poor Folk* had made on me, that it was unlike anything that had been written at that time, Dostoevsky became embarrassed and confused. He offered me an old-fashioned chair, the only one in the room. I sat down and we talked. To tell the truth, I talked more, a sin that I am always guilty of. Dostoevsky answered all my questions in a modest and even evasive way. Immediately I saw that this was an individual who was shy, proud, and reserved, but to a high degree also talented and pleasant. After twenty or so minutes, I stood up and invited him to my place in an informal way.
>
> Dostoevsky took on a frightened look.
>
> "No, Count, forgive me," he muttered bewilderingly, rubbing his hands one against the other, "but to tell you the truth, I have never been in high society and in no way can I bring myself to. . . ."
>
> "But who is talking about high society, dear Fyodor Mikhailovich? True, my wife and I belong to such circles . . . but we will not let them into our home!"
>
> Dostoevsky burst out laughing, but he remained adamant. It was only two months later that he first visited my home.

January 26, 1846
Vissarion Belinsky, from a letter to Alexander Herzen

> [*The Petersburg Miscellany*] is going great guns; more than 200 copies have been sold from January 21st to January 25th.

January 26, 1846
Apollon Grigoriev, from a review

> Devushkin and Varvara are a strange pair. They could see each other on a daily basis . . . but they talk in letters . . . so that neighbors will not see them together. . . .

Varvara sees Devushkin not as a mailman but as a mail horse. First she burdens him with orders for her wedding; then she leaves him for her new husband.

January 26, 1846
Nikolai Kukolnik, from a review

> *Poor Folk* has no form. It is founded entirely on details that are tiresome and monotonous, and that induce such boredom the likes of which you have never experienced. . . . It is like a dinner in which sugar is served instead of soup, and sauce instead of beef.

January 30, 1846
Pyotr Pletnyov, from a letter to Yakov Grot

> I did not care for *Poor Folk*, the much-vaunted novel by Dostoevsky. . . . The entire thing sounds like Gogol and Kvitka. . . . One should buy it only for a university library.

January 30, 1846
Leopold Brandt, from a review

> Mr. Dostoevsky's *Poor Folk* is made up of letters—a narrative that demands unusual talent, great experience, masterly exposition . . . and profound emotion so as to remedy the shortcomings . . . of writing of this type. . . .
>
> Mr. Dostoevsky . . . has taken into his head to write a *poema*, a drama. But despite all his pretenses to create something that is profound, highly poetic . . . and artistically simple, he has come up with *nothing*.
>
> Makar Devushkin, an elderly chancellery clerk who, for some thirty years, has been copying papers in some department, and Varvara Dobroselova, a woman of fallen virtue and guilty innocence, are the main and almost only characters of the work. Although the two live in the same building, they daily, sometimes twice a day, write to each other extremely long letters in which they complain bitterly about their poverty and fate. . . . The tie is generous and touching, but where precisely is the drama, the novel? How does one fill up 166 pages on such trifles? Involuntarily, one runs into . . . repetitions, into endless expositions of one and the same thing.
>
> In the personage of an uneducated, simple . . . and stupid old man, the author wishes to give to the world a type of simple-hearted goodness, unconscious nobility, disinterested honesty, and noble "humanity,"

even if this [model of] elevated humanity cannot withstand the blows of fate and sometimes gets drunk, causing the "virtuous" Varvara Alexeevna to issue forth extremely.

Now it is the fashion to seek out by force, to squeeze, so to speak, from the most usual, simple situations, something that is legendary, highly significant, and meaningful; "precisely" (a very sickly precisely) to analyze the "inner world" of the heart and soul; and despite reality and truth, to advance the most ordinary characters to some unattainable ideal—in other words, to make a mountain out of a molehill.

"Here is mystery, here are the heights, here is the triumph of art!" exclaim eccentric critics.[11] Like Varvara Alexeevna, inexperienced youth is deluded by such wise theories. . . .

How does this "naively . . . and profoundly simple" story of *Poor Folk* end? Oh, the surprising conclusion, the "artistic denouement"!

Varvara Alexeevna Dobroselova, crushed by grief, need, and the sufferings of the "noble, but incomprehensible world" of her soul, resolves to marry her vile (but, as you see, still rather honest) seducer. An ill-starred sacrifice! But this "sad, forced" union does not prevent her from thinking about the attire for her wedding (another precise reproach to feminine nature!), and from turning her priceless friend, Makar Alexeevich, into a sacrificial agent who upon her instructions . . . and edifying "notations" . . . runs about like a madman, to jewelers and fashionable stores. . . . Furthermore, this virtuous Varvara Alexeevna, "God knows how seductive" in her youth, gets carried away by games, by extremely feigned roles of oppressed sacrifice and innocence! . . .

Do not the following lines arouse the deepest empathy:

"Tell Madam Chiron that without fail, she [must] change the blond lace to conform to yesterday's patterns. Also tell her that I have changed my mind about the satin, and that it should be embroidered with crochet. Also, the letters for the monograms on the dresses should be done in tambour. Are you listening? In tambour, not smooth work. Make sure that it be done in tambour. One more thing, before I forget. Tell her, for God's sake, that the lapels for the fur coat must be raised and that the collar be done with lace. Please, Makar Alexeevich, tell her these things!"

Unhappy sacrifice! Does such a request not tear at your heart? Are these touching words about lace and trimmings the voice of the most cruel feminine suffering?. . . .

And poor Makar Alexeevich! What has happened to him, this truly virtuous old man, as his name "Devushkin" makes clear?[12] He is in despair that his beloved "little mother" (so he usually calls Varvara) is getting married and leaving him in such sadness that one fears he will not be able to carry on. So the novel ends.

The reader, moved to the depths of his soul, and shedding tears over the fate of these mournful "sacrifices to fate," lets the book fall from his hands . . . but, perhaps, for another reason. . . . It weighs on his arms with its heaviness . . . and a great, great deal of "pathos."

We, of course, would not have gone on at length about this first unsuccessful attempt of a young writer if it were not for the fact that . . . several weeks before the appearance [of *Poor Folk*] . . . people claimed that it was the work of a new and unusual talent, a piece that was great, even greater than the writings of Gogol and Lermontov. Immediately, a hundred rumors carried the pleasant news throughout the "length and breadth of Petrograd." Curiosity, expectation, and impatience were everywhere.

Rejoicing spiritually over a new talent amidst our insipid contemporary Russian literature, we set about [reading] Mr. Dostoevsky's novel greedily; but together with our readers, we were disappointed cruelly. "You will see a model of genuine, noble beauty and a peaceful, profound drama, written in a masterly style!" So we were told on the day it appeared. But alas, after reading the novel with the most complete and sincere goodwill, we, in our obtuseness and lack of taste, saw no such thing.

Would you like to see an example of the false simplicity in Devushkin's letters? Here are several lines: "As soon as it gets dark, my Varenka, I will *run* to you for a tiny hour. Now it is getting dark early, so I *will come running*. I, little mother, will today, without fail, *run* for a teeny-weeny hour. . . . You will now wait for Bykov (the seducer), but as soon as he leaves, I *will come running* to you. But just wait, little mother, I *will come running*."

What is this? Simplicity or humor or comedy? In truth, we do not know. We could put forth twenty examples of similar simplicity, but the size of our newspaper will not admit such long lists. We also note that Devushkin, in a large part of his letters, talks about the poor condition of his shoes and boots. This is his *idée fixe*. . . . He so fusses and fumes over such things that the entire novel, one can say, is written *à propos de bottes*.[13]

In each literary work, we try diligently to find a good side; so we will not say that this new author is not completely without talent, but he gets carried away by the empty theories of "principled" critics who, in our country, are confusing the younger generation [with their ideas].[14] The work has several tolerable places, but they do not make up for the rest. . . .

In future attempts, let Mr. Dostoevsky move away from the temptation of external imitation, from the absurd theories of the magicians of art, and perhaps he will be more successful. But this time, pardon us, the first pancake has turned out lumpy,[15] the mountain has given birth to a mouse, the "rumors" about Mr. Dostoevsky have been false and have even hurt him greatly, since they have led the public to expect something unusual.

Late January 1846
Varvara Dostoevskaya-Karepina, from a letter to Mikhail and Emiliya Dostoevsky

In my letter, dear brother, I saw to my surprise that you still did not know about the marriage of our sister Verochka. . . . The engagement was on December 2, 1845, and the wedding on January 7, 1846. Her husband, Alexander Pavlovich Ivanov, is a very kind and intelligent individual, about thirty-two years old. He so loves and worships sister that it is fun to see the two of them together. He has a mother who also cannot get enough of Verochka. In a word, she is so happy that it seems she cannot want for anything else. Do you know, dear brother, anything about brother Fedinka? We have not seen hide nor hair of him as to whether he is well or not. Write, please, and let us know if he wants to reenter service [to the state].

Circa February 1846 and after
Fyodor Dostoevsky, from an 1867 letter to Apollon Maykov

I have finished with that damned article "My Acquaintance with Belinsky." There was no way I could delay it or set it aside. In truth, I worked on it in the summer, but I found it so torturous to write . . . that I dragged it out to this very moment and, gritting my teeth, finished it. . . . Like a fool, I took on such a piece. As soon as I began the thing, I realized right away that with the *censorship*, there was no possible way I could do it justice (since I wanted to write the entire story). A hundred and fifty pages of a novel would have been easier than those thirty-two pages! The result was that . . . I rewrote the accursed article at least *five times*, then crossed it all out and put it all back together again. Somehow I have come up with an article—but it is such a rotten piece that it makes me sick to my stomach. How much valuable material was

I forced to throw out! As I might have expected, what was left was the most worthless "golden mean." *Garbage!*[16]

Circa February 1846 and after
Anna Dostoevskaya, from her memoirs

When [in 1867] it was proposed to Fyodor Mikhailovich that he write an article, titled "About Belinsky," he set about this interesting theme with pleasure. He planned to write . . . a serious article on the man, to offer a most elementary and sincere opinion of this individual who in the beginning was dear to him, but who in the end treated him with such hostility.

It became evident, though, that Fyodor Mikhailovich was not yet settled in his thinking [about Belinsky]; that many things needed to be thought through and resolved; and that many doubts remained. The article had to be written at least five times, and in the end Fyodor Mikhailovich was dissatisfied with the piece.

Circa February 1846 and after
Fyodor Dostoevsky, from *A Writer's Diary*

Belinsky was the most intense person I have ever met.

Circa February 1846 and after
Vsevelod Solovyov, from his memoirs

[Dostoevsky said:] "Belinsky was not like the others. If he said something, he would also do it. His was a nature that was simple, whole, and for whom word and deed were one. Others got lost in thought a hundred times over before they decided to do something, if they ever decided at all. But Belinsky was not like that."

Circa February 1846 and after
Fyodor Dostoevsky, from a *Writer's Diary*

Belinsky . . . compared an excessive "concern" [for an audience] to a "depraved talent" and scorned it openly, implying, of course, its antithesis: even in the most ardent poetic mood, [the writer must] keep this concern [for his audience] in check.

Circa February 1846 and after
Fyodor Dostoevsky, from his "Notes" on *Devils*

One time Dostoevsky met Belinsky at a railroad station under construction. "I cannot wait patiently [for its completion]." he said. "I choose to stroll here every day so I can look at the work that is going on."

Oh, the poor man, if only he knew how many others looked at the railroad with the same glance, how dear the construction was also to them....

Dostoevsky also talked to him . . . about future railroads, about heated coach cars, and about heating [homes] in Moscow, where wood was becoming more and more expensive. [He also talked] about the future, about the crisscrossing of railroads in Moscow, and how much more costly still wood would become. Perhaps, Dostoevsky said, wood would be brought in on railways from countries with forests.

Belinsky laughed long and hard at [what he saw as] such a poor knowledge of life. "Now he wants to bring wood on railways!" he said. Such a thing seemed to him to be monstrous. Imagine that Belinsky thought that only passengers traveled on trains, and that the only goods that moved on rails were the most delicate and costly articles from Paris. That was Belinsky's knowledge of life. But he understood it better than anyone.

Circa February 1846 and after
Fyodor Dostoevsky, from *A Writer's Diary*

This most blessed among men, who possessed a remarkably tranquil conscience, had his occasional sad moments. But his sadness was of a special kind. It came not from doubts or disillusionment—oh, no—but from the questions "Why not today, why not tomorrow?"

In all of Russia there was no one in a bigger hurry [than Belinsky]. Once when I met him near the Znamensky Church[17] . . . he told me:

"I often drop by here to look at how the construction is progressing." (The station for the Nikolaevsky railway was still being built).[18] "It makes my heart rest a bit easier to stand and watch the work: at long last we will have at least one railway. You will never believe how at times such a thing comforts my heart."

This Belinsky said well and with passion: He never put on airs. We set off together. I recall he said, "When they lay me in my grave" (he knew that he had consumption), "only then will they realize whom they have lost."

Circa February 1846 and after
Fyodor Dostoevsky, from *A Writer's Diary*

Belinsky was as good a husband and father as Herzen.[19]

Circa February 1846 and after
Fyodor Dostoevsky, from *A Writer's Diary*

> Were there many genuine liberals [in the 1840s in Russia]? Were there many truly suffering, pure, and sincere people such as Belinsky?

Circa February 1846 and after
Fyodor Dostoevsky, from his 1876–77 *Notebook*

> Belinsky's very errors, if he had any, are higher than any truth, if not everything, that you have created and written.

Circa February 1846 and after
Fyodor Dostoevsky, from *A Writer's Diary*

> Belinsky . . . was no *gentilhomme* at all—oh no. (God knows what his origins were. I think that his father was an army doctor.)

Circa February 1846 and after
Fyodor Dostoevsky, from *A Writer's Diary*

> Given such a warm faith in his ideas, Belinsky was, of course, the happiest of men. People were wrong in writing later that if he had lived longer, he would have joined the Slavophiles. Belinsky would never have ended up a Slavophile. He might have ended by emigrating [from Russia]. . . .
>
> As a small and rapturous man whose former warm faith never permitted him the slightest doubt, Belinsky would have made the rounds of various congresses in Germany and Switzerland; or . . . run errands on behalf of the women's movement.

Circa February 1846 and after
Fyodor Dostoevsky, from an 1868 letter to Apollon Maykov

> I will never believe Apollon Grigoriev's statement that Belinsky would have ended up with Slavophilism.[20] Belinsky could not end up like that. He was just a little louse and nothing more. He was a great poet in his time, but he could not have developed any further. He would have ended up at the beck and call of some local Mme. Goegg[21] as an adjutant for the woman question at meetings and would have forgotten how to speak Russian without having learned German.

Circa February 1846 and after
Fyodor Dostoevsky, from an 1870 letter to Apollon Maykov

> At the time [in exile] I was still under the sway of a mangy, yeast-like Russian liberalism, propagandized . . . [by people] like the shitty insect Belinsky and others.

Circa February 1846 and after
Fyodor Dostoevsky, from an 1871 letter to Nikolai Strakhov

> That stinking insect Belinsky . . . a precisely small, feeble, and powerless individual . . . who cursed Russia and consciously brought to it much harm.

Circa February 1846 and after
Fyodor Dostoevsky, from an 1868 letter to Apollon Maykov

> Recall the best liberals—recall Belinsky: Surely was he not a conscious enemy of the fatherland, a retrograde?

Circa February 1846 and after
Fyodor Dostoevsky, from *A Writer's Diary*

> Belinsky, an individual who, by nature, was passionately carried away [by everything,] . . . was almost the first of the Russians who attached themselves directly to European socialists, who had already rejected the entire order of European civilization, even as at home, in Russian literature, he waged a war to the end against the Slavophiles, apparently for completely the opposite cause.

Circa February 1846 and after
Fyodor Dostoevsky, from *A Writer's Diary*

> For some the Slavophile doctrine even now means only kvass and radishes as it did in the old days of Belinsky. . . . Belinsky *really* went no further than that in his understanding of Slavophilism.

Circa February 1846 and after
Fyodor Dostoevsky, from his 1876–77 *Notebook*

> Truly, Belinsky understood Russia little, or, better to say, he understood it in a prejudicial way and knew it extremely little. He knew Russia factually, although he grasped it terribly via instinct, premonition.

The entire European order Belinsky applied directly to Russia, without pondering the differences [between the two], and it was in such things that he differed from the Slavophiles.

Circa February 1846 and after
Fyodor Dostoevsky, from his 1876–77 *Notebook*

Belinsky saw only order. He loved the people, but he differed from the Slavophiles in that he had no hopes for their transformation and did not believe in and studied little . . . the paths that they had proposed for the rebirth of Russia in the spirit of the folk. Apparently, also, Belinsky read little of the Slavophiles' works. As if in despair, he began to await universal renewal in the nascent social movements in Europe and was carried away by them passionately.

Nonetheless, Belinsky also expressed a serious negation of civilization in rejecting Europe, falling in with the Slavophiles but in a different spirit. In order to explain this curious phenomenon of Russian life, I add that Belinsky was incomparably a more conservative Russian than the Gagarins.[22] But, having adhered to the *extreme left*, he spoke unconsciously as an extreme Russian and thus became close to the Slavophiles, in contrast to Westernizers at the time who worshiped the West over Russia and moved to Catholicism (in its right wing). . . .

I repeat, those who adhered to the left, extreme left, of Europe changed their minds completely and declared themselves to be the most Russian, negating European culture with native revulsion. Belinsky, for example.

Circa February 1846 and after
Fyodor Dostoevsky, from his 1880–81 *Notebook*

Belinsky. An unusual striving for the acceptance of new ideas [along] with an unusual desire . . . to trample on everything that was old with hatred, spittle, and shame. As if thirsting to revenge the old, I burned everything that I had worshiped.

Circa February 1846 and after
Fyodor Dostoevsky, from *A Writer's Diary*

Even well before the Paris revolution of 1848, we were caught up by the fascinating power of . . . ideas. Even in 1846 Belinsky had initiated me into the entire *truth* of this coming "regenerated world," into the entire *sanctity* of the future communistic society.

Circa February 1846 and after
Fyodor Dostoevsky, from *A Writer's Diary*

> I found Belinsky to be a passionate socialist, and with me, he began directly with atheism. That was for me very significant—precisely his amazing feeling and his unusual capacity to penetrate an idea in the most profound way, to become totally inspired by an idea. . . .
>
> Cherishing above all reason, science, and realism, Belinsky understood, more profoundly than anyone, that reason, science, and realism alone could create only an ant heap and not the social "harmony" in which humankind could get on with life. He knew that moral beginnings are the basis of everything. He believed in the new moral foundations of socialism (which, to date, have shown nothing but vile distortions of nature and common sense). He believed [such things] to the point of madness, without any reflection at all.

Circa February 1846 and after
Fyodor Dostoevsky, from *A Writer's Diary*

> As a socialist, Belinsky first had to dethrone Christianity. He knew that necessarily, the revolution must begin with atheism. He had to dethrone that religion from which came the moral foundations of the society he was rejecting. Radically, Belinsky rejected the family, private property, and the moral responsibility of the individual.

Circa February 1846 and after
Fyodor Dostoevsky, from *A Writer's Diary*

> As a socialist, Belinsky was absolutely bound to destroy Christ's teachings and to label them as a false and ignorant philanthropy that was condemned by contemporary science and by economic principles. Still, there remained the most radiant image of the God-man, its moral unattainability, its marvelous and miraculous beauty. But Belinsky, in his endless and unending enthusiasm, did not pause even before this insurmountable obstacle, as did Renan, who proclaimed in his *Life of Jesus*, a book filled with unbelief,[23] that Christ is still the ideal of human beauty, an unattainable type, never to be repeated in the future.

Circa February 1846 and after
Fyodor Dostoevsky, from an 1871 letter to Nikolai Strakhov

> You never knew Belinsky, but I did and understood him fully.
>
> This individual (Belinsky) . . . could not note how much he and others harbored petty ambition, spite, impatience, irritation, and the

main thing, pride. Cursing Christ, Belinsky never said to himself that when we put ourselves in His place, we are so vile. No, he never pondered the fact that he himself was vile. He was extremely satisfied with himself . . . personal, foul-smelling, ignominious, and obtuse.[24]

Circa February 1846 and after
Fyodor Dostoevsky, from his "Notes" on *Devils*

> The deceased Belinsky cursed Christ in an abusive way, but he himself would not harm a chicken.
>
> As to reality and his understanding of real-life things, Belinsky was very weak. Turgenev was right when he said that Belinsky knew very little, even in a scientific way,[25] but he understood things better than anyone else. You laugh because you feel like saying, "But he understood things nonetheless." But, my friend, I do not pretend to understand the pieces of genuine life. . . .
>
> I recall the writer Dostoevsky[26] who was still a youth at that time. Belinsky attempted to turn him toward atheism, but to the objections of Dostoevsky, who defended Christ, he cursed [the Savior] in an abusive way. "When I swore, Belinsky always made such a sad and crushed face . . . [before] he pointed to Dostoevsky with well-meaning and innocent laughter."

Circa February 1846 and after
Fyodor Dostoevsky, from *The Brothers Karamazov*

> [Kolya Krasotkin:] "If you wish, I am not against Christ. He was a completely humane personality. If he had lived in our time, he would have joined the revolutionaries, and perhaps would have played a visible role. . . . Even with failure."
>
> "And where did you pick that up from?" Alyosha exclaimed. "What fool have you been hanging out with?"
>
> "Have mercy. You can't hide the truth. . . . Even old man Belinsky, people say, said such a thing."

Circa February 1846 and after
Fyodor Dostoevsky, from *A Writer's Diary*

> "But do you know," Belinsky screamed one evening (sometimes if he was very excited, he would scream) as he turned to me. "Do you know that one cannot count a man's sins, nor burden him with obligations and turnings of the other cheek when society is set up so basely that a

man cannot help but do wrong, when he is driven economically to do so; and that it is absurd and cruel to demand from a man something which, by the laws of nature, he cannot fulfill, even if he wanted to. . . ."

We were not alone that evening. One of Belinsky's friends, an individual whom he respected highly and listened to often, was present, along with a certain young beginning writer who won fame in literature later.[27]

"It's touching just to look at him," Belinsky said, breaking off his furious exclamations suddenly and turning to his friend as he pointed to me. "Every time I mention Christ, his whole face changes, as if he wanted to burst out crying. . . . But believe me, you naive fellow," he said, attacking me again. "Believe me that your Christ, if he were born in our time, would be the most unremarkable and ordinary of men; he would have faded away among today's science and movers of humanity."

"But no-o-o-o-o!" Belinsky's friend chimed in. (I recall that we were sitting, while Belinsky was pacing back and forth around the room.) "But no. If Christ appeared now, he would have joined the movement and become its head. . . ."

"Yes, yes," Belinsky agreed suddenly, with surprising haste. "He certainly would have joined the socialists and followed them."

Circa February 1846 and after
Anna Dostoevskaya, from her memoirs

Despite Fyodor Mikhailovich's high opinion of Belinsky's critical acumen, and sincere gratitude for the man's encouragement of his literary gifts, he could not forgive Belinsky's mocking and almost blasphemous attitude toward his religious views and beliefs.

Circa February 1846 and after
Fyodor Dostoevsky, from *A Writer's Diary*

The forces that advanced humanity, which [Belinsky believed] Christ was destined to join were all Frenchmen: George Sand,[28] the now totally forgotten Cabet,[29] Pierre Leroux,[30] and Proudhon, who was then only beginning his work.[31]

As far as I can recall, Belinsky held these four in the greatest respect. . . . He would discuss these men for entire evenings at a time. There was also one German to whom Belinsky paid great tribute and that was Feuerbach.[32] (Belinsky, who, throughout his entire life, could not master a single foreign language, pronounced it "Fierbach.") Strauss was also spoken of very reverently.³³

Circa February 1846 and after
Fyodor Dostoevsky, from an 1871 letter to Nikolai Strakhov

> If Belinsky, Granovsky, and that entire bunch of riffraff could take a look [at life] now, they would say: "No, we did not dream about that; [what is happening now] is a deviation; we will wait further and light will appear, progress will rule, and humanity will be rebuilt and will be happy!"
>
> In no way would they have agreed that once you have set out on this road, you end up only at the Commune and Felix Pyat.³⁴ They were so obtuse that even *now*, after the event . . . they would continue to dream.
>
> I cursed Belinsky more as a phenomenon of Russian life than as a person: a most stinking, obtuse, shameful, and inevitable phenomenon of Russian life. . . . I assure you that Belinsky would now reconcile himself with the following thought: "Truly, the Commune was a failure above all because it was French, that is, it preserved in itself the infection of nationality. What is needed are people in whom there is not a drop of nationality and who are slapping their mother's (Russia's) face in the way I do."
>
> Foaming at the mouth, Belinsky would again have rushed to write his vile articles, defaming Russia, denying her great phenomenon (Pushkin)³⁵ so as once and for all to make Russia an *impassive* nation capable of leading a *universal cause*.

Circa February 1846 and after
Fyodor Dostoevsky from an 1873 letter to Alexander III

> Our Belinskys and Granovskys would not believe it if they were told that they were Nechaev's direct fathers.

Circa February 1846 and after
Fyodor Dostoevsky, from an 1871 letter to Nikolai Strakhov

> You say that Belinsky was a talented individual. Not at all. . . . I recall my youthful surprise when I listened to several of his purely artistic judgments (for example, on *Dead Souls*).³⁶ He was outrageously superficial and careless in the way he related to Gogol's type.³⁷ He was happy only that Gogol *indicted*. During these four years, I have reread his criticism. He abused Pushkin whenever the writer sounded a false note. . . . With amazement, he proclaimed the nothingness of the Belkin tales.³⁸

In Gogol's story "The Carriage," he found nothing artistic in the entire composition of the work, but saw it only a comic story.[39] He rejected the ending of *Eugene Onegin*.[40] He was the first to put forth Pushkin as a Gentleman of the Emperor's Bedchamber.[41] . . . He said that Turgenev would not be an artist, and did so during a reading of his extremely remarkable story "Three Portraits."[42] I could put before you many such examples as proof of the falseness of his critical sense and his "impressionable trembling." . . . We still judge Belinsky and many phenomena of our life through a multitude of extreme prejudices.

Circa February 1846 and after
Fyodor Dostoevsky, from an 1870 letter to Apollon Maykov

Do they still give to graduates from high schools books like the complete collection of Belinsky's works in which he cries over why Tatyana remains faithful to her husband?[43] No, long have such things not been eradicated.

Circa February 1846 and after
Fyodor Dostoevsky, from testimony to the Investigatory Commission for the Petrashevsky affair

I often reproached Belinsky for the fact that he tried to give to literature a personal and unworthy significance, and that he lowered it to description . . . only to newspaper facts or scandalous events. Namely, I objected to the fact that bile attracted no one, that it tired everyone in a mortal way, and that it grabbed passers-by the buttons of their frock coats and taught and propagandized by force.

Circa February 1846 and after
Fyodor Dostoevsky, from his novel *The Insulted and Injured*

[Ikhmenev:] "Is B. still writing?"
  "Yes, he is writing," I answered.
  "Ekh, Vanya, Vanya," he concluded, waving his hand, "but what kind of criticism is it?!"

Circa February 1846 and after
Ivan Turgenev, from his memoirs

Occasionally Belinsky treated beginners with great tenderness, getting carried away most charmingly, almost amusingly.
  When he got hold of Mr. Dostoevsky's *Poor Folk*, he was positively delighted. "Yes," he used to say proudly, as though he himself had been

responsible for some terrific achievement, "yes, my dear fellows, let me tell you, he may be a tiny bird," and he would his hand about a foot from the floor to show how tiny he was, "but he's got sharp claws!" . . .

In his paternal tenderness toward a newly discovered talent, Belinsky treated Dostoevsky like a son, just as if he were his own "little boy."

Circa February 1846 and after
Avdotya Panaeva, from her memoirs

> Belinsky avoided all serious discussions with Dostoevsky so as not to upset him. Such a response Dostoevsky took for coldness. . . .
> When people told Belinsky that Dostoevsky saw himself as a genius, he shrugged his shoulders sadly and said:
> "What a misfortune! Dostoevsky has indubitable talent, but if instead of developing it, he imagines himself already to be a genius. His giftedness will not move forward. Without fail, he must receive medical treatment . . . for his terribly unstrung nerves. It must be that life has worn him out, poor soul! These are difficult times, one needs nerves of steel to withstand all the conditions of contemporary life."

Circa February 1846 and after
Stepan Yanovsky, from his memoirs

> I know that Fyodor Mikhailovich, by virtue of his mind and the power of his convictions, did not love to submit to any authority. . . . He often told me how he talked to Belinsky: "That's all right, Vissarion Grigorievich, you just keep quiet; there will come a time when you will start talking your head off." (So Fyodor Mikhailovich would say apropos of the fact that Belinsky had praised *Poor Folk* to the skies, but that he had seemingly ignored his other works, and [that] the silence about his [later] writing was more bitter than abuse.)

Circa February 1846 and after
Pavel Annenkov, from his memoirs

> Belinsky wanted to do for Dostoevsky what he had done for other writers, for example, Koltsov and Nekrasov, that is, to free his talent from moralizing tendencies and to invest it with strong nerves and muscles so that he could possess his subject immediately, directly, without strain.
> But [from Dostoevsky] Belinsky met with a decisive rebuff. . . .
> At Belinsky's, the new author read his second story, *The Double*, a sensational depiction of a person who moves between two worlds—real

and fantastic—without allowing him the possibility of settling in either one of them.

Belinsky liked the story by virtue of its power and skillful handling of an original and strange theme. It seemed to me, though—(I was present at the meeting)—that the critic also had an ulterior motive which he did not think necessary to articulate immediately at that time.

Belinsky constantly drew Dostoevsky's attention to the necessity of *hitting the nail on the head,* as they say in the literary world, to free oneself from the difficulties of literary exposition, to acquire the ability to render one's thoughts in a free and easy way.

Belinsky apparently could not accustom himself to Dostoevsky's then still diffuse manner of narration with its constant returns to the same old phrases, and its ad infinitum repetitions and rephrasings. Belinsky ascribed this manner to the young writer's inexperience, his failure as yet to surmount the stumbling blocks of language and form. . . .

Dostoevsky heard the critic's recommendations in a mood of affable indifference. The sudden success of his novel had sprouted seeds and germs of high self-regard and self-esteem already in this soul. It more than liberated [him] from the doubts and hesitations that normally accompany the first steps of a writer. It took him to a prophetic dream auguring laurel wreath and chaplets.

With Belinsky, Dostoevsky soon parted company. . . . Life took them in different directions, although for a long time their views and thinking were the same.

Circa February 1846 and after
Fyodor Dostoevsky, from a draft of *A Writer's Diary*

> Mr. Annenkov . . . could not have been a witness to [his claim] of arguments between me and Belinsky as we never did such things.

Circa February 1846 and after
Avdotya Panaeva, from her memoirs

> Dostoevsky was annoyed at Belinsky for playing preference[44] and for not speaking to him about his *Poor Folk.*
>
> "How can such an intelligent individual spend even ten minutes over such an idiotic activity as cards," Dostoevsky said with some bitterness. "Belinsky does so for two or three hours at a time. Truly, one cannot tell the different between bureaucrats and writers: they both spend time in the same dull way."[45]

Circa February 1846 and after
Fyodor Dostoevsky, from *A Writer's Diary*

> Having scrutinized Nekrasov's character . . . [I found him to be] reserved, almost fleeting, cautious, and almost non-communicative.

Circa February 1846 and after
Anna Dostoevskaya, from her memoirs

> [Dostoevsky] considered Nekrasov the friend of his youth and esteemed his poetic gifts.

Circa Feburary 1846 and after
Anna Dostoevskaya, from her memoirs

> Nekrasov figured in memories of [my husband's] youth and of the beginning of his literary career. After all, Nekrasov was one of the first who recognized the talent of Fyodor Mikhailovich and facilitated his success in the intellectual world of that time.

Circa February 1846 and after
Lyubov Dostoevskaya, from her memoirs

> Nekrasov published *Poor Folk* in his journal[46] and it was a great success. Suddenly, my father became famous. Everyone wanted to meet him. "Who is this Dostoevsky?" was heard on all sides. For a long time Father had visited literary salons, but no one had paid any attention to him.[47] This shy individual always took refuge in a corner, on a window seat, or behind a screen.
>
> But now he was no longer allowed to hide. People surrounded him and flattered him; they forced him to speak and found him enchanting. . . . They invited him to their homes and accepted him wholeheartedly.

Circa February 1846 and after
Stepan Yanovsky, from his memoirs

> Fyodor Mikhailovich loved to listen to music, as a result of which, with any opportunity, he attended Italian operas. . . .
>
> He especially loved *William Tell*. . . . With delight he listened to Mozart's *Don Giovanni*, especially the role of Zerlina, and he went into raves over *Norma*. . . . He also went wild over the debut of Meyerbeer's opera *Huguenots* in Petersburg. . . .[48]
>
> About ballet, Fyodor Mikhailovich knew only from hearsay; he never attended performances.

Circa February 1846 and after
Anna Dostoevskaya, from her memoirs

> It is possible that many of the unhappy impressions that Fyodor Mikhailovich retained from his tie with Belinsky were the result of gossip and innuendoes, of "friends" who, at first, acknowledged Dostoevsky's talent and spread it hither and yon, but who later, for reasons inexplicable to me, began to persecute the shy author of *Poor Folk*, to write lies about him, to compose epigrams, and to try his patience in every possible way.

Circa February 1846 and after
Lyubov Dostoevskaya, from her memoirs

> Dostoevsky's friends, young writers who were setting out on their own path in literature, could not bear his sudden success. They began to envy my father, driving themselves to distraction with the thought that this shy and modest individual had been accepted in the salons of famous personalities to whom they had no access. They could not value *Poor Folk* for its worth. The work seemed to them to be silly. They parodied it in their poetry and prose, and poked fun at the writer in a merciless way. To harm him in society, they spread humorous anecdotes about him.
>
> Dostoevsky's friends insisted that success had gone to his head, and that he demanded that every page of his second novel, which was to appear in Nekrasov's journal, should be surrounded by a border so as to distinguish it from other works in the issue. This was apparently a lie. The novel *The Double* appeared without any borders.[49]

Circa February 1846 and after
Dmitri Grigorovich, from his memoirs

> The sudden change from people worshiping and raising the author of *Poor Folk* almost to the level of genius to their cruel rejection of him crushed such an impressionable and proud individual as Dostoevsky.
>
> He began to avoid the people of the Belinsky circle. He became withdrawn completely, and irritable to the highest degree. Unfortunately, whenever Dostoevsky met Turgenev ... he gave full vent to the indignation that had been welling up inside him, saying that he was not afraid of anyone and that just give him time and he would drown all of them in mud. I do not recall what caused such an outburst ... but the conversation was seemingly about Gogol.

It was Dostoevsky who was at fault. Turgenev lacked all passion and fervor. He could even be reproached for his gentleness and pliancy.

Circa February 1846 and after
Avdotya Panaeva, from her memoirs

> Dostoevsky often visited us in the evenings. His shyness had passed. He even showed a certain passion [for things]. He got into arguments with everyone. Apparently from stubbornness, he contradicted others. From youth and nerves, he could not control himself. In an extremely manifest way, he gave witness to his authorial pride and high opinion of his writing talent.
>
> Stunned by his unexpectedly brilliant entry into the fictional enterprise, and showered with praise from competent people in literature, he, as an impressionable individual, could not hide his pride before other young writers who had set forth modestly into fiction.
>
> As if on purpose, Dostoevsky tore at his colleagues with his irritability and condescending tone, saying that he was an incomparably better writer than they. They responded by making him the object of gossip, by pricking his pride with jibes in conversations.

Circa February 1846 and after
Avdotya Panaeva, from her memoirs

> Dostoevsky became terribly suspicious after a friend told him everything that people were saying about him and his *Poor Folk*. . . .[50] Dostoevsky suspected jealousy . . . and believed that everyone wished to ridicule him and belittle his work.
>
> He visited us seething with anger . . . as if to pour on envious peers all the bile that was suffocating him. But our jests, rather than soothing a sick and nervous individual, irritated him more forcefully.

Circa February 1846 and after
Ivan Panaev, from his memoirs

> Belinsky said that *Poor Folk* revealed a great and immense talent, and that the author would surpass Gogol. . . .[51] *Poor Folk*, of course, is a remarkable work and fully deserving of the success it enjoyed, but Belinsky's enthusiasm for the novel was extreme.

Circa February 1846 and after
Ivan Turgenev, from his memoirs

> The exaggerated praise that he gave to *Poor Folk* was among Belinsky's initial blunders and demonstrated clearly his declining powers.[52]

Circa February 1846 and after
Ivan Panaev, from an 1855 article

Any new appearance in literature, any new talent made for me an indescribably joyful impression. I rejoiced over any literary success; never did the slightest feeling of jealousy possess me. Just the opposite, I needed authorities in literature with all my being . . . and in the absence of genuine heroes, I worshiped little idols who were erected by people close to me, and whom I respected and believed in.

We put little idols on pedestals and worshiped them with genuine enthusiasm. . . . With incense and bowing, we almost lost our minds. One of these little idols made us happier than others. We carried him in our arms around the city gates; we showed him to the public, crying: "Here is a recently born small genius who in time will kill all our present and past literature. Bow to him! Bow to him!" . . .

We heralded him everywhere, in salons, on the streets. One lady, blond and shapely, with airy curls and a brilliant name, read his work. Having heard so much about him, she wanted to meet him. A certain individual . . . brought the man to her, saying with ecstasy: "Here he is! Look! Here he is!"

Gracefully, the lady with the airy curls, moved her lips, licking them with her small tongue. To our idol, she wanted to drop a most charming compliment: one of those accolades which one of my acquaintances, a seminarian, having studied in a noble home, calls a "fragrant, enlightened trifle," and which, always off the mark, he also tells his wife is a *"dear absurdity."*

As soon as the lady with the airy curls gifted our little genius with this fragrant, enlightened trifle, he turned pale suddenly and started to sway. He was carried off to the back room and sprayed with eau de cologne. He regained consciousness but would not return to where the woman with the airy curls was sitting, illumined brightly by oil lamps and candles. . . .

From that time on, our little genius became unbearable. In no way did he want to feel the earth under his feet. . . . Invariably, he demanded that we lift him as high as possible so that everyone could see him. Constantly he raged at us and cried out: "Higher! Higher!" Our arms grew numb as we raised him . . . but still he raged and cried out, "Higher!"

When we tried to cut our little genius down to size, he began to reproach us for being jealous of him, for hating him, for lacking the strength to lift him higher. In a fury, he jumped from our hands, dashed about, raised his head back completely, and in an unusually majestic way, marched through the crowd, surprised that people did not notice him and fall at his feet when they saw him. . . .

Offended by the crowd, he rushed to his small attic, where before him appeared the aristocratic lady with the airy curls who kept telling him: "You are a genius! You are mine! I love you! . . . Together we will go to the cathedral of glory, to our bright and brilliant salons where you will never hear a Russian word. You must meet *our kind of people*, because only our kind will preach genuine glory. . . . The world is divided into two types of people . . . *connus* and *inconnus,* and you will never become famous until you know the first group. . . ."

She wound her downy hand around his and touched his face with her airy curls.

At first, he did not to believe in such a division of people. Involuntarily, his entire nature rose up against such a strange separation. But when her hand touched his, a most shallow and pitiable pride rose up in him and possessed his being. . . .

He imagined himself in gold in a hall, glittering and magnificently lit, in the very center of those people whom the lady with the airy curls had called the *connus*. Although such individuals were coming to shake his hand, she was beckoning him elsewhere . . . to lavish and mysterious boudoirs with diffuse light and elegant couches as in ancient Russian stories . . . [bidding] that he keep following her there, there!

But then the vision disappeared suddenly . . . and again he saw himself in his poor attic, on the coarse Turkish couch which he had bought at a flea market. Having wiped his eyes and glanced around, he sobbed, and in horror covered his face with his hands. . . .

Once, after such a vision, he walked about his room in an agitated way. Suddenly, he ran to the editor of a journal to whom, several days previously, he had given a small article. At that moment he was for the editor the same as he was for everyone else: a little idol.

Our idol demanded that without fail, the piece be published at the beginning or end of the book, and that it make a striking visual impression, being set off from the others with a golden border or edge. The editor agreed to everything, and having patted the man on the shoulder, began to sing:

> "I will make a fuss over you
> I will set forth, a scoundrel on the mend
> I will surround you with a border
> And put you at the end."[53]

From that moment on, our little idol began to rant and rave. Soon he was hurled down from his pedestal and forgotten completely. The poor soul! We ruined him! We made him laughable! He could not keep to the heights to which we had raised him. We ourselves were carried away in a way that was sincere, disinterested, and well meaning. But were we guilty? . . . Can one indict people for their youth, enthusiasm, passions, and delusions?

Circa February 1846 and after
Nikolai Nekrasov, from *The Stone Heart*[54]

On that day at eleven a.m. Trostnikov, gasping for breath, ran with *The Stone Heart* to his friend Mertsalov. With enthusiasm, he said to him:

"Grigory Alexandrovich! Read this, for God's sake, read this manuscript as soon as possible! If I am not mistaken, fate is sending our literature a new brilliant figure! In my opinion, it is a most splendid thing!"

Mertsalov was an individual of precise literary taste. Deservedly did he have the distinction of being an excellent critic. He was a key contributor to a journal that, at the time, enjoyed a widespread and honored reputation, and, one can say without exaggeration, Mertsalov was the reason. A sharp, irritable tone; an impartiality that bowed neither to ties nor to advantage; and an irony, if not always exacting, always wicked and precise—[such things] made the man many enemies who spread God knows what rumors about him. Mertsalov was for them a scourge of everything that was gifted and splendid; a literary bandit who, if only to indulge his youthful boldness, was merciless with anybody and everybody.

In truth, though, there was never a more kind, noble, and delicate individual [than Mertsalov]; and if he sometimes attacked unworthy literary phenomena with greater fervor and indignation than they deserved, it was because of his ardent and passionate love for literature. Like a tender father toward a favorite child, Mertsalov wished to see only virtue in literature. Any untalented, unscrupulous, appalling, or scandalous phenomenon brought him to despair. It aroused in him all manner of bile, which he often expressed in reviews of such works.

As a result, no one greeted new signs of talent with such love, with such warmth and encouragement. Indeed, his enthusiasm for such giftedness was that for one good feature of a piece, he overlooked ten poor ones, In so doing, Mertsalov gave his enemies cause to accuse him not only of exaggerated censure but also of overblown praise, which they called idol worship. Generally speaking, such extremes were for him key in both literature and life. There was no middle. An individual or book that was dear to him today risked arousing his repugnance tomorrow. Such shifts always took place suddenly and sharply, preceded by an inner and painfully burdensome process of thinking which led him to conscious mistakes.

Both orally and in writing, Mertsalov did not hesitate to admit his errors. If he was not always consistent in his views (something that some see as a necessary hallmark of a great mind) . . . his opinions flowed from profound convictions. It should also be noted that in him fate did not observe a particular disposition. He was very unhappy in life, a condition that, naturally, intensified his irritability.

Mertsalov heard Trostnikov's enthusiastic praise of *The Stone Heart* with the mild smile of disbelief with which, typically, experienced critics receive people who take it upon themselves to pronounce positive verdicts on matters belonging exclusively to them. Personal enthusiasms, followed by bitter disenchantments that wounded one's pride, had also taught Mertsalov to be more careful. If he could not change his nature, then at the very least, he tried to greet every new occurrence [in literature] in a calmer and more sober way, and that taught by time and experience, he would not surrender to passion.

Mertsalov was just under forty years old, but—to tell the truth—thanks to rich and perceptive personality, he was younger than any twenty-year-old.

"Oh, you youth, youth!" he said with a grin. "You barely finish reading something, you like it, it begins to stir your heart, and right away, a superb, truly, even a brilliant work."

"First of all, read it—and tell me what you yourself think."

"Read it? Now look here: Is it worth reading? I am very busy now."

"It's worth it, I assure you, it's worth it!" Trostnikov answered enthusiastically. "Only begin to read it—you will not be able to tear yourself away from it!"

"Really? You judge for yourself! But enough! I am not a kid like you. Right now there is not a book that exists which I could not tear away from whenever I please—even for an empty conversation."

"I will stop by," Trostnikov said.

"This evening? Fine, do so."

"And you will give me your opinion."

"Right away? You think that I will drop everything and start reading?"

"But it is an excellent thing. Read it today. . . ."

"I cannot today. I have just begun a splendid book. I have to finish it."

"But when will you read it?"

"Well . . . I will read it sometime," Mertsalov answered lazily.

Trostnikov left. In truth, Mertsalov had no intention of continuing what he had been reading. No sooner had Trostnikov left than, in a lively way, he seized the manuscript of *The Stone Heart*. He read the title, ran past the epigraph, which contained several lines from one of his own critical articles, and began to read. After several lines, his face became inflamed. He put down the manuscript and with quick steps walked around the room. Then he summoned his servant, ordered that he not be disturbed, and began to read again.

Around eight in the evening, Trostnikov, burning with impatience, ran to Mertsalov's home.

When the bell sounded, Mertsalov was lying on the couch. His facial expression was greatly excited. In his hands was the manuscript of *The Stone Heart*. Having heard the bell, he jumped off the couch and met Trostnikov with words that expressed both annoyance and impatience:

"Where have you been?"

"Me? I had supper. . . . I dined with Glazhievsky at the Hôtel de Paris."

"I was waiting for you. I waited and waited. I was even thinking of sending my servant for you. . . . So tell me, is he a young person?"

Seeing the familiar manuscript in Mertsalov's hands, Trostnikov guessed whom he was referring to.

"He is young," he answered.

"How young?"

"I think he is about twenty-four or twenty-five."

"Thank God!" Mertsalov exclaimed with delight and exhaled as if a stone had been lifted from his chest. "Such a question was very much on my mind. I am simply exhausted, waiting for you. So you say that he is only twenty four?"

"In no way is he more than twenty-five!" Trostnikov responded.

"But he is such a genius!" Mertsalov pronounced with emphasis.

"I told you so," a delighted Trostnikov noted.

"You said so? You told me? But could you really tell me? Can one really talk about such a thing? You came, turned around, left a manuscript, and disappeared!. . . . It is a splendid thing, but it is not enough that it is splendid. Such a description could also be attached to a trifling vaudeville, a business file. But this is a brilliant artistic work!" Mertsalov continued, inspired.

"I will tell you, Trostnikov," he went on, his face so inflamed that it turned red, and making a sharp gesture with his hand, he added: "I would not exchange *The Stone Heart* for all of Russian literature!"

He then talked about the merits of *The Stone Heart*, its artistic significance, the profound principles at its base, the unusual composition of its parts, and the complete nature of the whole (such words were in great use in the literary language of the time).

Mertsalov also talked (extremely intelligently, and with great animation) about each character in the novel. In a decisive way, he could not praise the art of the author enough.

"The main thing," Mertsalov said in passing, "is the [author's] remarkable ability to put forth, before the eyes of the reader, a character as if alive, defining him with only two or three words, but in such a way that if another writer had covered ten pages with writing, his character would not step forward in such sharp relief. And what profound and warm sympathy toward poverty, toward suffering! Tell me, he must be a poor individual. Has he suffered much in life?"

Trostnikov told Mertsalov everything that he had managed to learn about Glazhievsky's character and existence. Mertsalov was interested to know even the man's mannerisms and his physiognomy. From everything that Trostnikov told him, he made more or less accurate references to *The Stone Heart*, explaining, as they loved to say at the time, that the author is his work, and the work is its author. If, from a lack of facts, these considerations were remiss in truth, they also showed wit and intelligent subtleties . . . [of which] Mertsalov was a great master and enthusiast. It was enough for him to have the most insignificant fact [about an individual] for his imagination to conjure up the entire personality; or, if the matter concerned an event, it afforded the missing piece. In a masterly and completely logical way, Mertsalov explained the causes of the departure [of someone] from the straight path and its likely outcome. One only had to listen how, on his lips, a scrap of fact, an event or an item in a newspaper . . . took on form and soul, something orderly and whole, like a seed that had been tossed on the ground but that gradually became a tall and splendid tree with a powerful trunk and wide, beautifully spreading leaves. It was amusing to see (and also annoying because Mertsalov developed his points in such a witty way that the listener was always carried away and believed them) how completely he demolished the first half of an idea with the second, destroying the entire edifice he had built in such a painstaking and logical way—an edifice he had come to see as fact, not fiction.

Mertsalov was a great master . . . of developing a thought in a logical way, with the most far-reaching consequences, but he did not always pursue the direction of his thought . . . and sometimes came up with extremely strange conclusions. The faithfulness with which he pursued truth, together with the endless generation of friends who listened to him like an oracle, did not restrain the innate liveliness of his imagination.

Mertsalov told Trostnikov that, while waiting for him in tormented agony (he loved to express himself forcefully), he was on the verge of conjuring up . . . an external portrait of the author of *The Stone Heart*, but that his picture did not accord entirely with the original.

"Most of all, I rejoice," he said, "that he is only twenty-four-years old. If he had been middle-aged, then most likely nothing would have come of him. One would have seen *The Stone Heart* as the result of the entire and best half of the life of an intelligent and observing individual who had experienced and felt a great deal in life. But to write such a thing at age twenty-five, that only a genius could do, someone who, by force of his understanding, has seized upon things in a way that would demand of the average person many years of experience!"

Mertsalov also talked about the shortcomings of *The Stone Heart* (as a precise critic, he could not but notice them; after all, it was his very calling to be enjoined to find them), but such shortcomings—its prolixity, long-windedness, inappropriate repetition of one and the same words, and certain exposing affectations—he attributed to the youth and inexperience of the author, which of course indicted neither him nor his work.

Circa February 1846 and after
Nikolai Nekrasov, from *The Stone Heart*

Deep into the night the friends chattered about *The Stone Heart* and its author. Trostnikov left, promising on the following day to bring the new man of genius. But despite its being so late, Trostnikov ran straight to Glazhievsky's place and openly, with youthful enthusiasm, told him Mertsalov's opinion of *The Stone Heart*.

During his brief acquaintance with Glazhievsky, Trostnikov had many occasions to see joy on the face of the new writer, [an emotion] which stood out even more sharply since Glazhievsky's countenance usually resembled a hazy, grayish autumnal cloud which, at any minute, could end up in rain, sleet, and snow. But never had Trostnikov seen such happiness on Glazhievsky's face as when he told him about

Mertsalov's praise [for *The Stone Heart*]. It was something akin to the fainting spells that greeted Glazhievsky at night.

Several times in the same week, in a nervous and trembling voice, Glazhievsky asked Trostnikov precisely what Mertsalov had said, repeating the critic's observations as if entering into them and weighing the significance of each word. Every minute he broke into a tinkling nervous laugh, struggling in vain to keep a stolid and calm face.

Not without foundation, Trostnikov thought that if there had been witnesses, the man of genius most likely would have danced about happily, as would any mortal in moments of extreme joy. But Trostnikov also noted that his own praise of *The Stone Heart* was no longer received by Glazhievsky in such a happy way. It now seemed so insignificant to him.

Glazhievsky asked offhandedly:

"Is that really what Grigory Alexandrovich [Mertsalov] said?" When Trostnikov added that Mertsalov agreed with what he himself had thought [of *The Stone Heart*], something akin to suspicion appeared on Glazhievsky's face, or so it seemed to Trostnikov.

"But there is also Razbegaev," Glazhievsky noted in passing. "After all, he is a decent fellow with taste and tact. . . . A good soul, an exceedingly good soul, and not the least bit envious! I smiled when he called my *Stone Heart* a work of genius, and now Grigory Alexandrovich says the same thing! And you seem to think so too?"

In this remark, Trostnikov thought he heard a reproach, since, in his first meeting with Glazhievsky, he had never called *The Stone Heart* a work of genius, but he did not deem it important to comment on Razbegaev's praise because to do so would be empty and shameful.

Such a thing surprised him somewhat.

Circa February 1846 and after
Nikolai Nekrasov, from *The Stone Heart*

On the following day, Trostnikov waited for Glazhievsky to take him to Mertsalov's home. The appointed time passed, but he had not appeared. Knowing Mertsavlov's impatient attitude, Trostnikov rushed to Glazhievsky's place.

The man of genius was not dressed. His features bore traces of long indecision, of a struggle of weakness with himself.

"What's the matter with you?" Trostnikov asked reproachfully.

"I'm not going to Mertsalov's," Glazhievsky answered.

"What? Why not? What's going on?"

"Well, just . . . truly. . . . Would it not be better if I didn't go?" He spoke less decisively, having lowered his eyes to the floor.

"But why?"

"I have thought about this. . . . I have thought about it the entire night. . . . After all, you said that he asked about me, even about my face . . . I'm afraid . . . if—"

Here he stopped suddenly, as if he had said something he shouldn't have. Then he added more decisively:

"No . . . I'd better not go . . ."

"What childishness!" Trostnikov exclaimed heatedly. "Are you really afraid that when Mertsalov sees you, the impact of your work will be destroyed?"

"Where did you get that from? How do you know what I am thinking?" the man of genius objected sharply, offended that Trostnikov had guessed the reason for his thoughts. . . .

"I simply will not go because I have decided that I have no reason to be there. What am I to him? What role will I play with him? What do we have in common? He is a learned man, a well-known man of letters, a famous critic, but I . . . who am I?"

"Osip Mikhailovich! Osip Mikhailovich!" Trostnikov noted in sharp rebuke. What humility! And before whom? Have I not read *The Stone Heart*? Has not Mertsalov also read it?"

"So you think there is something in there?" Glazhievsky pronounced quietly and ingratiatingly, restraining a smile of satisfaction.

"As if you did not know, as if you have not been told that even if Mertsalov does not know your personal qualities, there is still your work. . . ."

The face of the man of genius took on a happy look. Every freckle became filled with joy. But seeking to hide such a thing, Glazhievsky interrupted Trostnikov with feigned annoyance and humility:

"Enough! Enough! Perhaps you think so. But does he? Yesterday he praised it . . . but now, perhaps, he has grown cold to it and already thinks something entirely different. . . ."

Once again the shadow of genuine doubt and fear showed on his face which, we have noted, had the habit of changing a thousand times a minute, first suggesting a threatening cloud ready to pour down rain and sleet, but then suddenly shining forth with a bright, playful light like the sun lighting up frost.

"Mertsalov is not that kind of individual, and *The Stone Heart* is not that kind of work [for one] to become disenchanted quickly,"

Trostnikov replied (during which time the face of the genius again changed to frost). "He is accustomed to pronounce judgment in a careful and thought-out way."

"Splendid, splendid!" Glazhievsky countered. "So what else does he need? He has read the novel; he has come to a conclusion about it. So let him write something, even if it be an entire book. As you told me yesterday, he will write something. . . ."

"So you will not go?"

"No . . . perhaps another time when . . . after . . . there will still be time. . . ."

"Well, as you wish!" Trostnikov answered with annoyance, tired of begging him. He also had no desire to come up for a second time with proof why Mertsalov was interested in seeing him [Glazhievsky] or why Glazhievsky should call on him, having added:

"What would he find interesting in a person, who . . . who . . . ?"

"Good-bye!" Trostnikov said in place of an answer and left.

Hardly had Trostnikov take ten steps onto the sidewalk, though, when he heard a cry behind him:

"Tikhon Vasilich! Tikhon Vasilich!"

Trostnikov turned around and saw [the servant] Terentiy, running after him without a hat.

"What is it?"

"The master is calling for you. He has ordered me to tell you that he will go, that he will get dressed right away."

Trostnikov returned.

"I thought," Glazhievsky told him, "what would be the harm in going? Perhaps he is waiting for me. . . . It is all the same; there would be no great harm if I were to make a quick visit there, right?" he asked, as if he were still doubting if there would be any harm in doing so.

"How could there be any harm, when Mertsalov himself has asked and is waiting for you? How many times have I told you that?"

Glazhievsky got dressed and the two took off. All along the way, Glazhievsky kept asking about Mertsalov's habits. He also kept saying that he himself was not a refined man, that he did not know how to make an entrance and how to greet or talk to people he did not know. Trostnikov answered that with Mertsalov, one had to behave simply and nothing more!

They arrived at the staircase, and Trostnikov made for the bell.

"Wait!" Glazhievsky pronounced in such a severe and shuddering voice that Trostnikov became frightened and dropped his hand instinctively.

"Now what?"

"No, truly. . . . No. . . . I have decided that I must not go. I will not go! You go by yourself," Glazhievsky said as if Trostnikov were an emissary from hell who had come to drag him into the kingdom of darkness.

He rushed down the stairs.

"As you wish," a furious Trostnikov answered.

"Will he be angry?"

Trostnikov had not managed to say a final word when Glazhievsky was again standing alongside him, his hand searching for the doorbell. He kept looking for the thing, unaware that the handle was on the other side of the door. Glazhievsky's eyes and, generally speaking, his entire face resembled a stormcloud . . . [with] a strong autumn wind in full force; looking at it, one could hear the shrill and plaintive howling of the gale. . . .

Only then did Trostnikov understand Glazhievsky's prolonged indecisiveness, seeing to what an astounding degree the author of *The Stone Heart* had become timid, imagining himself before the severe eyes of the critic. In moments of extreme shyness, Glazhievsky had the habit of shriveling up, of taking leave of himself to such a degree . . . that it could be characterized by the phrase "to descend into nothingness.". . .[55]

Suddenly, Glazhievsky's entire face became owl-like. His eyes disappeared under his eyelids, his head hung down to his shoulders; his voice, always suffocating, lost all clarity and freedom, as if the man of genius were in an empty barrel without sufficient air. His gestures, words, and glances, as well as his constantly moving lips, expressed suspicion, danger . . . [and] something tragic that precluded all possibility of laughing.

Circa February 1846 and after
Nikolai Nekrasov, from *The Stone Heart*

The simple and tender reception of Mertsalov, especially the accolades he did not hesitate to sprinkle over *The Stone Heart*, returned Glazhievsky to his senses. The young man even went to the opposite extreme, taking it into his head to flaunt an undue familiarity, to purr a line from a song, and to tell an anecdote about his [servant] Terentiy, who, because he could not read or write, once ate some kind of medical plaster which had been prescribed for external use. The anecdote was not funny, but its exposition was marked by affectation and two or three extended sarcasms.

"Well, God be with your Terentiy," Mertsalov said. "But tell me, did it take you a long time to write *The Stone Heart?*"

Glazhievsky became somewhat confused.

"Me? . . . Not long . . ."

"Well, how long?"

After a while, Glazhievsky answered.

"How long? I began it in May . . . and finished, er, put an end to it . . . the same year."

To Trostnikov, such an answer seemed somewhat strange. After all, it was not that long ago that Glazhievsky had told him that he had worked on his novel for four years and that he had rewritten it sixteen times.[56]

"Is he really unashamed to tell Mertsalov the truth?" Trostnikov thought.

"So quickly!" Mertsalov responded. "But in truth, when it comes to creativity, time means nothing. Pushkin wrote several of his pieces in an usually quick way; by contrast, others cost him a great deal of work. I have happened to see several chapters from *Eugene Onegin*: every word was crossed out and scribbled over ten times. But the result is the same: Whether one of Pushkin's works was written quickly or over a long time, with pronounced effort, it reads easily, with identical delight. They were all works of genius! Byron wrote very quickly. He wrote *Manfred* in twenty-two days, and several verses in *Don Juan* in no more than a single night.[57] The story goes that our Gogol found writing to be so difficult . . . that he paused several times over a single word. His manuscripts were a complete mess, but could one know that such even, flowing, and picturesque prose cost its author such effort? I have the autographs and several manuscripts of many famous writers. Would you like to see them?"

Mertsalov spoke in a good-natured way, not thinking of the impression his words were making. But if he had followed what was transpiring on Glazhievsky's face, he would have seen that it was not his words or the autographs of great people that were engaging his listener so much as that the great Russian critic had begun to talk about Pushkin, Byron, and Gogol. All the more eloquently did the face of the author of *The Stone Heart* show the emotions aroused by such flattering associations. And with this face, Trostnikov, already having begun to understand Glazhievsky, guessed immediately what was going on in the young writer's head!

"What an intelligent man!" Glazhievsky said to Trostnikov when Mertsalov left to get the writers' autographs. "And how remarkable that he understands elegance so precisely! Here is a genuine critic!"

Mertsalov was truly an intelligent individual, but his mind, of course, did not make itself manifest in scenes and circumstances like this one. Very quickly did he move from the role he had thought to assume, having resolved firmly to be moderate in his praise. Sufficient was one phrase to which Glazhievsky responded with unusually gentle humility:

"Are you, perhaps, exaggerating the merits of my novel?"

The kindhearted Mertsalov, having flared at such a remark, began to prove why he considered *The Stone Heart* to be an artistic work of great genius.

From time to time Glazhievsky threw in a word (not without design, as it was beginning to seem to Trostnikov), which had the effect of pouring oil on a fire. Mertsalov became more and more impassioned; he lost all restraint in his expressions, repeating anew and solemnly the phrase of the previous day, that [in exchange] for *The Stone Heart*, he would not take all of Russian literature!

"So you will see: I will write. Only then will the great significance of *The Stone Heart* be revealed. About such a novel, one could write an entire book, twice as thick as the original!"

"Enough, Grigory Alexandrovich! Truly, you have been so kind to me—no matter what you write about my work! I confess that if I were in your shoes, I would not know how to fill even a short review. Praise should be short; if it is drawn out, it will be boring . . ."

"That only goes to show," Mertsalov replied, not without some pride, "that you are not a critic and that you do not know how to engage such a work. To analyze such a piece means to show its essence, its meaning, so much so that one can dispense with praise easily. The matter is absolutely clear and speaks loudly for itself. But the essence and significance of such an artistic creation [as yours] is so profound and significant that one cannot merely allude to such qualities in a review."

"Well, that is your affair, your affair entirely," Glazhievsky replied, letting it be known that the critic's arguments had convinced him completely.

The conversation continued like that for an hour and a half more. . . .

Bidding farewell to Glazhievsky, Mertsalov announced that he hoped to see him again at his place.

"In a few days I will be gathering one or two of my friends and we will introduce you into our literary circle. All the people there are very good. I will prepare for them a good time. We will read *The Stone Heart*."

After three days Glazhievsky indeed received a note with this content:

"Dear Osip Mikhailovich! Today at my place there have gathered several good friends. They will be happy to meet the author of *The Stone Heart*, which you will be so kind and read to us, etc.

"Mertsalov."

After he had read the note, Glazhievsky's face extended into a long question: To go or not?

Circa February 1846 and after
Nikolai Nekrasov, from *The Stone Heart*

With unusual speed, news about the new novel of genius, and about the new literary genius himself, spread in the literary circle where Mertsalov was the center and guiding light.

Friends and visitors always saw him with *The Stone Heart* in his hands, from which he began immediately to read excepts, praising them and paying necessary tribute of surprise at the talent of the author.

The literary circle which had gathered about Mertsalov was made up of everyone who, at that time in literature, was young, talented, and noble. Along with writers, though, were several individuals who had never written anything and most likely never would. Nonetheless, they had no circle other than a literary one in which they could spend all their time, free from work or other activities.

Such individuals were tolerated . . . thanks to the patronage of Mertsalov or another writer with authority, their introduction . . . always being justified by virtues with which their patrons and others had discovered in them.

"Although he does not write poetry, he is a poet in his soul," they said about one of them. "Look how he understands the splendid! How he is able to notice each most precise feature in a poetic work!"

Another was called the noble personality, surprising everyone with his far-reaching ability to sympathize with the splendid, his supporters telling one and the same story about him as proof of his remarkable moral force. A third was hailed for his unusual humor.

In this group were also a great many who were able to feel; that is why they were called "literary sympathizers." In truth, they were good souls, most of them being completely indifferent [to things], but able to be indispensable luminaries by virtue of their connections and riches, or simply by a special obsequiousness and ability to flatter.

The Poet in Soul was rich. Once a week the entire circle dined at his place with truffles and champagne. In important cases, he loaned money to writers of whom, with credit that was moral but not real, he did not hesitate to take advantage.

The Noble Personality distinguished himself by his unusual inclination for sleep, apathy, and corpulence, but he had become a necessity thanks to his untiring ability to fulfill orders. If a member of the circle was . . . a person of substance, and if he needed a book, to get a dress on credit, deal with a bookseller, get hold of funds, or have someone host a dinner and invite precisely so-and-so and such-and-such, the noble personality set aside his personal affairs and with passion, rushed to fulfill his wish. If a writer was leaving for somewhere far away and needed help with correspondence: no one could be more faithful than the noble personality. With incomprehensible fervor, the noble personality took it upon himself to inform you about everything that was going in literature in your absence, to manage your peasants if they were in Petersburg, and to send you your favorite cigars. And he did it all with such readiness and civility, so disinterestedly and so meticulously, that the fame of the noble personality grew with unusual speed. Not content with one literary circle, he soon made his way into other groups . . . [so that] a description of his exploits at his home would take up in our notes several chapters, and perhaps even an entire volume.

The Artistic Nature was like the poet in soul, but with this difference: the dinners that, with heavy heart, he sometimes gave to maintain his dignity were unbelievably poor. With great difficulty, he also lent money in small sums, but with sizable collateral and an eye to respectable profits.

The Practical Head, having left the stock company where he worked "because of an unpleasant turn of events" . . . took it upon himself to help writers . . . to acquire funds when there was no other way to obtain some. Being on good terms with booksellers, and knowing the moral credit of each writer, he was a most practical head.

The Element of Good Breeding was kept on for albeit secondhand news and gossip . . . to which, generally speaking, all writers were extremely susceptible.

The Library furnished writers with rare and expensive editions and all kinds of necessary books.

The Newspaper . . . roamed, from morning to night, the various corners of Petersburg, eavesdropping [on conversations], and writing in his little book everything that he happened to hear on the street.

Finally, *The All-Around (and Also Embracing) Nature* gained entrance into the circle because he knew everything, saw everything, sympathized with everything, and, in a profound way, embraced to his bosom every manifestation of life, every work of pen, chisel, and brush, and, like a bee, collected from them the juice of their delights. So people said about him, noting how worthy of envy was his fortunate ability to delight in everything, understand everything, and sympathize with everything, without giving himself over to anything exclusively. In truth, he was a weighty being because in the three years he had been abroad, he had seen all the famous galleries in Paris and London and, with unusual impudence, talked about everything—even if it be Chinese grammar—sharply, decisively, with the scholarly air of a connoisseur.

Circa February 1846 and after
Nikolai Nekrasov, from *The Stone Heart*

The literary sympathizers included two or three scholars . . . who would be at home in any circle. The rest . . . were kept on because of their ample means and also for their unfailing and ample flattery, servitude, and obsequiousness. . . . Many were happy if a writer ordered them to copy one of his compositions, claiming that in so doing, they felt rapturous tremblings and shed tender tears. Others submitted to voluntary humiliation, enduring rather unpleasant scenes, such as when Mertsalov, having becoming irritated rather suddenly, found himself in momentary disarray. In such moments he did not consider it untoward to tell a literary sympathizer who had come at an inopportune moment, "Get out of here!" or to say something like:

"Where the hell have you been? I have been in desperate need of *Conversational Lexicon*. I have asked you to get it three times. You are never here when I need you, and when I have nothing for you, you always show up! So why have you come? I asked for *Lexicon*, not you. Have you brought it?"

"No, I gave it to Lyukoshin."

"You gave it to Lyukoshin! You always do something like this! Who asked you to give it to him?"

The poor sympathizer was silent, daring not to remind [Mertsalov] that he owned the library and was willing to lend out his books.

If the dinner that a sympathizer gave turned out to be a poor one, he was immediately subject to the most severe judgment:

"This is shoe leather, pal, simply shoe leather!" one would cry out, stabbing his cutlet with his fork and sticking it under the nose of his host.

"This is vinegar!" said another, having tried the sauterne.

"A scandal!" said a third, pouring his red wine on the plate.

Sometimes the dinner ended with the host in tears. But soon the passion for the literary circle imbued him with the most patient submission. Within a week he again invited his friends to dinner.

"Look sharp!" the invited guests told the literary sympathizer in one voice.

"Look sharp!" proclaimed Parutin in a bass voice, speaking to everyone without exception in the familiar "you," and threatening his host with his finger in an expressive way. . . .

A limited individual who, rarely and reluctantly, was admitted into the literary circle (in passionate attempts to attain such happiness, he even traveled abroad despite his complete ignorance of French), sought to draw closer to writers by announcing his desire to host a dinner. Shyly, he informed Parutin of his wish.

"Will there be dinner?" Parutin asked sullenly.

"There will be dinner, there will be dinner."

"With champagne?"

"How can there not be champagne?"

"Make sure that there will be enough champagne."

"There will be enough, believe me, there will be enough. Only allow me to ask: My wife also wishes to be with writers. . . . You understand, she finds it all interesting. So can she come too?"

"Your wife?" Parutin exclaimed. "Your wife! Absolutely not! Not even the slightest trace of her!"

"But she will leave right away. She only wants to take a look. . . ."

"No, no, no!" Parutin objected, moving his pipe about threateningly in his mouth. "No wife, and no kids either. . . . Are you listening?"

So the timid sympathizer chased away his wife and children so as to have only gentlemen writers for dinner.

Young sympathizers, still under the care of their mommies and daddies, also sometimes wished to get together with writers. Long did they fight off such a temptation. But in the end, apparently, everything was arranged well. Fortunately their room was on the second floor, with parents not at home. So the sympathizer hastened to take advantage of the favorable situation and to summon the group.

The feast was in full swing. . . . The champagne flowed like a river, and under its lively influence, the conversation became more and more animated. A passionate debate turned into screams and cries.

Suddenly, amidst the merriment, there arrived an old man, stepping softly, in slippers, robe, and nightcap, and with an irritated, flushed face, and a tallow candle end in his hand. Like a bombshell, he fell upon the merry company, and for a moment, everyone grew silent. He fixed a questioning and unpleasant stare upon the sympathizer, trembling and white as a sheet. A deep silence reigned, followed by the threatening, thundering voice of the old man:

"You brat! What's going on here? And you, gentlemen. . . ."

"Papenka! I have the honor of presenting to you my friends: Mr. Glazhievsky, the author of *The Stone Heart*; our famous critic Trostnikov, Mertsalov, also a critic, Lyukoshin—the translator of Calderón. . . and all kinds of other things. . . ."

The poor soul! He thought that the importance of the guests would soften the anger of his irritated parent. But in a threatening way, the parent interrupted him, exclaiming:

"Quiet! Clear out and get to bed, brat! Obey me. Wine! Lamps! Candelabra!"

He went up to the lamp and candelabra and extinguished the candles. The room became semi-dark, now lit dimly only by the candle in the hand of the old man. . . .

The guests seized their hats and, as a group, took their leave, accompanied by the threatening muttering of the old man, who did not observe any proprieties in his expressions for them or his son, whom he threatened to flog.

"I should do the same thing to your friends!" he cried out loudly, within earshot of the departing guests.

Swearing at the young sympathizer, the guests left, laughing as they did.

For a long time the young sympathizer did not show himself in the literary circle until, finally, he, having performed an important service to Mertsalov, or having brought him some important bit of news, had the doors opened to him anew.

But even more powerful than the dinners, the flattery, and the petty services were the tongues of the sympathizers, which, obedient and insatiable . . . made them indispensable. Through them the luminaries of the circle could exert their will in any and all directions, since they were assured firmly that praise, censure, news, and opinions would enter the mainstream with incredible speed and art. One must not think that such things came about as a preliminary strike. God forbid! Among writers and sympathizers there reigned a spirit of truth, perhaps because the luminary of a circle was distinguished by genuine integrity or, to speak literarily, conscientiousness. Evil acts were subject to the most severe judgment; regularly it was decided not to shake hands with someone who . . . had treated his wife badly. . . .

The newest sympathizer abhorred being the weapon of whoever came by. Everyone wanted his own opinion and, more than anything, to assert his independence. The worship of luminaries was so absolute, though, that it took only one of them to let loose any kind of absurdity that within the hour all the dilettantes would repeat it among themselves and to their acquaintances who came their way on Nevsky Prospekt. Their fervor for the glory of their patrons was so great that when a writer did not agree with the consensus and reviewed an extolled work in a sharp way, he caused sympathizers sometimes to become so impertinent that they attacked the individual and accused him of bias and envy.

Such escapades, infrequent as they were, usually ended up in shame for diligent sympathizers. The writer was driven so insane by their insolence that finally, in a serious way, he took up proving his opinion about the shortcomings of the disputed work. He was joined by other writers and even often by the author of the work himself. Here one had to see the confusion and embarrassment of the poor sympathizers, which, incidentally, did not last for long. Suddenly, they made an about-face, avowing the opposite opinion as seeming to come into view. . . .

Circa February 1846 and after
Nikolai Nekrasov, from *The Stone Heart*

Now for the writers. . . . Let not the reader think that I am going to put forth before his eyes a series of bright, impeccable portraits, edifying examples for non-writing humanity. As one thinking reviewer said profoundly, a man is always a man and will always be a man. . . . Trivial weaknesses, petty motives, and base emotions are part and parcel of the people who write good books, as well as the people who read them. As the most simple mortals, they

> gossip and slander
> boast and envy.

Their gossip is all the more unforgivable since they know splendidly and understand soundly to what extent such deeds are degrading.

What is even more horrible, under the guise of concern for you, in the name of justice, and/or in the name of new and enlightened ideas, they consider it their duty to interfere in your affairs, to analyze your domestic life. Without permit or permission, they also give advice, at first indirect, but if you are slow-witted, also direct, striking and overwhelming you with coarse and unforgivable frankness and with unceremonious attachment as to such aspects of your life, even those of your heart, on which, even with the most delicate hand, you could not be touched without pain and indignation.

And good God! What these characters who succumb to their influence will not do! . . . Terrible is their lot: They are called dim-witted, backward, almost schismatic. . . . About them writers invent fantastic facts, predict their ruin, count every copeck in their pockets, write caustic remarks and even reprimands without reprieve, and, finally, find fault with their small foreheads unable to accommodate vast minds. . . .

Nowhere is it possible for these poor sacrifices to show themselves. . . .

Ladies with sadness, almost with tears, look into their eyes and then lower their heads slowly.

Sympathizers also droop their heads, sigh, shrug their shoulders sadly, and converse with them more pliantly.

As soon as these poor souls leave, there immediately rises a general cry of sympathy which is so genuine, so warm, that a bystander visitor would inevitably burst into tears. . . .

"Poor, poor Vetugin, or Balakleev, or Trostnikov! What a terrible thing: Such a splendid, intelligent, and educated man B., his wife beats him!"

"She does, she does! I myself saw such a thing! . . . I went to his place, and he came out with red eyes."

"Perhaps he was asleep?"

"No, no! What sleep! One of his cheeks was somewhat swollen."

"I went to his place, no one was in the dining room. . . . I went further—into the dining room, the nursery. Finally, I entered the bedroom, and a terrible picture unfolded before my eyes. He was sitting on the floor, leaning his head against the bed, and Natalya Karpova was beating him around the legs terribly and crying: 'So you don't want this? So you don't want this?' What was wanted, I do not know, but her hair was tousled and her face was aflame, shrew-like."

"Oh, the unhappy man!"

In truth, the situation of the unhappy, sacrificial sympathizer became worse with each passing day. He was the topic of conversation with the Element of Enlightenment, the All-Embracing Nature, the Sympathetic Nature, and the Poet in the Soul. Even the Brat cried out about him, saying how he himself had seen how, in his presence, Lyukoshin had gotten into a fight with his wife and would not show himself in public because he had a black eye. The Noble Personality, setting his friend aside, whispered sadly, shaking his head in a mysterious way:

"My wife and I were not able to fall sleep for the entire night."

"Why?"

"Poor, poor Lyukoshin! . . . and so forth."

The Sympathetic Nature, having feared a rumbling in his stomach and refusing to drink champagne, said:

"I cannot talk about it, my friend, I cannot! Lyukoshin's situation torments me."

"Lyukoshin's situation, Lyukoshin's situation!"—there began anxiety solely about Lyukoshin's situation.

"I wonder what's going on?" remarked the gentleman who loved to give everything a great and mysterious color. "Why is Lyukoshin so silent? Why does he not want to unburden his soul, having revealed the secret to his friends? I hope that he knows that we are his friends, that we wish him well, and that we are ready to do anything we can [for him]. To give advice, even to take action. I will go, I will pay him a visit: let him have his say; what are we and his friends for?"

The gentleman went to see Lyukoshin, and after a brief interlude, said to him:

"Listen here, Lyukoshin: you know how I love you. . . ."

The face of the sympathizer was covered in deathly paleness. He struggled to remain silent, but the inquisitive and obsessive friend had achieved his goal. Certain that he had become an interesting person, he did not waste any time but marched bravely to the wise men of the first order, as well as to each and every one of the sympathizers, to retell Lyukoshin's secret, beginning:

"Well, I was at his place. The scene was a painful one. I cried. Never have I left anywhere with such a burdensome, joyless impression."

Encouraged by his success, others also went to see the unfortunate man. He held out, though, maintaining his silence stubbornly. But the rumors become bolder and more persistent, the sympathy more open, the remarks more straightforward. At the same time, letters flew about to absent wise men and sympathizers with a detailed description of the fight and the disastrous situation of the sympathizer.

After several days, the unfortunate man began to receive letters of an ambiguous and delicate nature in which he was assured that he was loved, that he was respected by everyone, that no one had changed their stance toward him, and that, if he took it into his head to visit, he could expect the most warm welcome. The letters kept ending with all kinds of hints, all straightforward . . . to comfort him and to set his mind at peace!

About such letters people spoke with great importance:

"Trostnikov has written to him. It seems that such a thing has comforted him somewhat. No matter what you say, Trostnikov is a fine fellow!"

The gossip spread to the most incredible degree; people spoke of their sympathy almost in the presence of the victim himself. The poor soul kept seeing that it was already too late to hide, that everything was already known, that friends were attaching themselves to him more and more persistently, and finally, at the conclusion of a lunch or dinner, when the curiosity, warmed by champagne, had become more and more insistent, there occurred the final shameful act of sympathy.

The unhappy man, besieged on all sides, confessed his disgrace to all. Such a stance would have been burdensome even if it were not for the fortunate fact that the unhappy man, noticing that effect he was making and becoming the subject of overall attention, began to tell things about which he should have kept silent. . . .

But then there began another period—a period of overt sympathy, advice, and cavalier interference. But perhaps we would do better if we lowered the curtain which we have scarcely raised.

Circa February 1846 and after
Nikolai Nekrasov, from *The Stone Heart*

Every morning people began to run in droves to Mertsalov, agitated about the rumor of an unusual literary talent. Willingly to each, he told details about the author himself, as well as about his work, enhancing the information with excerpts from *The Stone Heart*, which, as he himself said, had become his bible. In truth he had not let the manuscript drop from his hands, and in conversations, he constantly cited expressions of the new writer, which, incidentally, he did every time he read the remarkable work: such was the impression that it had made on his mind.

In support of his claims, before sympathizers, he read and reread parts of *The Stone Heart*, and in the end, the frequently repeated readings of the work so blunted his taste that he began to find splendid even things that he saw initially as shortcomings of the work.

"In this remarkable composition," he said, "there are no shortcomings. Everything in it is thought out, imagined, and fulfilled in such an artistic way that initially, the work seems somewhat forced, that it does not get to the matter at hand. But look at it more attentively and you will see that such a flaw comes not from the immature talent of the author but from your own inability and limitation to embrace an artistic piece in all its fullness and breadth. Such is the profundity [of *The Stone Heart*] that only via an attentive reading does it reveal itself in all the depth and height of its broad content. . . . Here you will see not just one novel but five, ten, twenty novels; turn to any page and there will pour forth such a splendid thing as to bring fame to an ordinary writer!"

Such opinions were in such great supply as to excite not only sympathizers but also writers for whom Mertsalov's opinion could not but help the new author.

"Have you heard, have you heard?" Balakleev told anybody and everybody who came his way, running with his usual haste along Nevsky Prospekt. "In our literature there has appeared a new genius. Trostnikov and I were the first to discover him, but I have known him even in childhood. We are friends with him. A wonderful thing! Mertsalov said that he has never read a better thing in his life!"

"Have you been to Mertsalov's?" the so-called Noble Personality asked mysteriously, meeting another sympathizer or writer.

"I have."

"Have you heard?"

"I have heard, how can one not hear, it is interesting to read . . ."

"A new epoch in literature: there has never been such a thing like it! Mertsalov says that [in exchange] for it he would not take all of Russian literature. . . . Truly it is an unusual phenomenon. Do you know him?"

"No. Why?"

"My wife is very interested in seeing him. We did not sleep all night."

"How come? Was someone sick at your house?"

"No, thank God, we are well. All night long we talked about *The Stone Heart*. Mertsalov read one scene to me. I told my wife. She has such an impressionable, sensitive nature. She could not fall asleep."

Having bent his ear in a mysterious way toward the sympathizer, the Noble Personality, under strictest confidence, passed on everything that was already known to the literary circle.

"Ach, you will not believe, Lyukoshin, what I will tell you!" the Element of Enlightenment exclaimed in a sweetish, long-drawn-out voice.

"What?"

"Mertsalov has discovered a genius . . ."

And so forth.

When they met among themselves, the sympathizers and writers talked about nothing but *The Stone Heart*. "Will you be at Mertsalov's on Friday?"

"I will. And you?"

"How can I not be there! I should say so!"—and so forth.

Finally, Friday came.

Circa February 1846 and after
Nikolai Nekrasov, from *The Stone Heart*

Literary readings are out of fashion in Petersburg. Now it is *du jour* to be indifferent to literature and to run from such gatherings where whispers fly that one or another gentleman will read his story. Indeed, the best way to chase away guests is to let loose with such rumors. Journalists avoid readings, claiming a lack of time. Writers go their separate ways and come together rarely. It was not like earlier, when several homes supposedly flourished solely to serve as a haven for writers, as so-called literary hotels. A writer could go there whenever he felt like it, to do whatever he wanted. If he wanted to eat, even it if be midnight, people began to cook and fry. If he wanted to sleep, people put a soft pillow under his head and walked around on tiptoe and spoke only in whispers. If he wanted to speak, people listened to him with servility and smiled at his every word. The entire family was rushed off its legs, one racing to offer jam; another, favorite small pretzels with tea; still another, cigarettes. If, without rhyme or reason, a writer took it into his heard to sing Italian arias, the family listened to him with rapture, swearing that they would not [have to] go to the opera, and telling acquaintances later that they had had an opera singer in their home.

Literary sympathizers have also become rare and show to writers an indifference to literature. Only in small literary circles do readings still flourish. Literary dilettantes are still great fans of them, but, incidentally, not for completely unselfish reasons. Enticing writers with the news that a remarkable work will be read at their place, they at first yield the floor to the author who is of interest to the writers, but then once this person finishes his piece (sometimes such a thing goes on until midnight), these dilettantes announce modestly that they also have a new small thing which they would like to read so as to hear the advice of such choice and experienced judges. And under the guise of [receiving] such advice, which they do not follow, they begin to torture writers with their own personal works sometimes until three or five in the morning.

But at the time of our story, literary readings were in full swing. The reason for this was in part because Mertsalov, having directed the tastes of the circle, truly loved his job. The appearance of each new talent was for him a holiday. He treated the individual like his own small child—and not only because the talent was ten times ready to listen to him but also in part because most of the circle was made up of young people.

On Friday around seven o'clock everyone who belonged to the circle and who had the right to be there came running to Mertsalov's home. There even appeared several individuals whom Mertsalov was completely displeased with.

At eight o'clock there also arrived Reshetilov with a small, plausible gentleman around twenty years old . . . a gentle, quiet, reliable young man.

This young man was neither a writer not an artist. He was a special type of literary sympathizer.

He accompanied literary and other celebrities . . . and was called Sputnik. God knows how, but no sooner was there a rumor about a new celebrity than Sputnik was already constantly at his side. Even on close terms, the relationship had a strange, somewhat suspicious character. The two were neither friendly nor amiable; rather, the tie recalled the supple pairing of a modest, efficient, and sharp subordinate with his superior. . . .

The genius, in the heat of triumph, glory, and worship, could not but be flattered by the unknown small man. Sputnik, from the very first meeting, became for him a necessary and many-faceted service.

Every morning Sputnik appeared at the genius's home, passing on to him (seemingly not without exaggeration) everything that he had heard yesterday, flattering items about him and unflattering about his rivals, and also relaying gossip and the behind-the-scenes secrets of the literary circle.

He arrived with every journal and newspaper that talked about the genius.

Quickly, Sputnik also memorized and rendered as general property the witticisms and noteworthy sayings which the genius had uttered in a circle of two or three friends.

Sputnik mediated between the genius and those who wished to meet him. He gave dinners precisely for those whom he wanted to engage. . . .

If the genius wished to set in motion an opinion about his work which he felt it awkward to say himself, he told it to Sputnik. The quick-witted man understood what he had to do.

During solemn readings, Sputnik filled in for the genius's weak chest, lending his trembling voice in pathetic places in the work (being read for the twentieth time) as a sign of staggering emotion.

If a new work was being read, he exclaimed in well-known places: "Shh, shh! A splendid scene is about to begin! . . ." And the attention of the listeners doubled.

As if in reward for such disinterested and many-faceted service, the indirect rays of glory that illumined the body of the genius also fell on Sputnik, affording him his own kind of advantage.

"Do you know whom I was walking with?" he asked, having met a writer.

"With whom?"

"With Reshetilov!"

"You are acquainted with him!"

"How could I not be, we are friends. Do you want me to take you to him?"

"Do me the favor!"

"Without fail. When?"

"What about tomorrow?"

In such a way Sputnik landed in the home of a writer who had known him for ten years but who had never invited him to visit.

"Vladimir Petrovich! Vladimir Petrovich!" Sputnik cried out to a journalist who, having spotted him, rushed headlong the other way. "Vladimir Petrovich!"

"What is it?" the journalist asked angrily, turning around without stopping.

"Yesterday I was at Reshetilov's. He is writing a new story."

The journalist stopped.

"I tried to persuade him to give it to your journal."

The journalist approached Sputnik quickly and offered him his hand in a kind way, saying:

"Hello! Where is he now?"

"But I still do not know. If you want, I will tell . . ."

"Be so kind."

"With pleasure! Without fail! I will tell him simply: 'If you do not wish to give your story to Tomashevsky, I will no longer be your friend!'"

"I will be greatly indebted to you. When can I expect an answer?"

"Whenever it is convenient for you. Perhaps tomorrow. Only where will we meet?"

It ended with the severe and haughty journalist inviting Sputnik to dinner.

Having met a famous actor—unknown actors, writers, journalists Sputnik had no need of and responded to with a bitter grimace, in a contemptuous way—he asked:

"Is your performance soon?"

"I still don't know!" the actor answered carelessly, hardly gracing him with a bow.

"Why do you ask?"

"Well, you know, Reshetilov . . ." So began the same story. He promised the actor that he would advise Reshetilov to give him a drama.

In a word, Sputnik took advantage of the fame of his friend in such a masterly way that he came to regret his own lack of personal glory—as sometimes happens when one pities a hungry poor man who discusses in an artificial way the distribution and use of the capital of others. The phrases "Reshetilov and I," "I was working when Reshetilov walked in," "News, important news: Reshetilov is writing a new novel; I have already heard two chapters; it is splendid!" "Do you know what Reshetilov said about your story?" "What a strange character is this Reshetilov"—these and similar phrases slipped from his tongue, affording him a smile, attention, and acceptance from people whose society he was trying to enter. To dine at the home of a journalist or a well-known writer, to stroll with them along Nevsky Prospekt, or to ride around with them in a carriage, such events were bright spots in Sputnik's life since he understood in a prudent way that he did not have what it took to shine with his own light. . . .

Among the unpleasant and prolonged epochs of a great man's life are when he takes to drink or dies . . . or when he descends into the ranks of ordinary mortals.

Thus did Sputnik disappear instantly, leaving the literary circle with one memory, so very vague, just like his personality.

Circa February 1846
Avdotya Panaeva, from her memoirs

One time Dostoevsky wished to speak to Nekrasov. He was in a very aroused state. I left Nekrasov's study and listened from the dining room. Both men became angry. Suddenly Dostoevsky ran out of the study and into the foyer. White as a sheet, he . . . grabbed his coat from the servant's hands and rushed down the stairs. . . .

"Dostoevsky has simply lost his mind!" Nekrasov said in a trembling and agitated voice. "He threatened that I dare not publish my review of his work.[58] Someone has been telling him stories that I am reading a poetic lampoon that I wrote about him. He was beside himself with anger."

Circa February 1846
Nikolai Nekrasov, Ivan Turgenev, and Ivan Panaev, from a poem

    A Greeting from Belinsky to Dostoevsky.

    A knight of mournful cast,
    Dostoevsky, dear, grand, and tall
    Like a new pimple on literature's nose
    Redly do you glow to all.
    Although a new writer
    Joyfully you dethrone one and all
    The Emperor praises you
    Even Lichtenberg is enthralled.

    To you the Turkish sultan
    Will send his wisest men
    But the grand reception before princes
    No one knows where and when.
    Now a myth and a puzzle
    You have fallen like a Finnish star
    And sneezed your pug-like nose
    At a red-haired beauty from afar.
    How tragically inert
    You looked at the object of your light
    And so close to death.
    Did not perish at your artful height.

    From the envious cliffs
    Bend your ear to my request
    Cast your ashen glance
    Hurl it at me, your guest.
    For the sake of future praise
    (Such extremes, you see, are quirks)
    But separate *The Double*
    From your unpublished works.

> I will fuss over you
> I will set forth, a scoundrel on the mend
> I will surround you with a border
> And put you at the end.

Circa February 1846
Dmitri Grigorovich, from his memoirs

> "A Greeting from Belinsky to Dostoevsky" was written in 1846, when Turgenev and Nekrasov were friends, and was dedicated to Belinsky, who at that time was raving about Dostoevsky. Dostoevsky demanded constantly that *The Double* be included in Belinsky's *Anthology*, and that the work be surrounded by a border to distinguish it from the other selections in the work.

Circa February 1846
Dmitri Grigorovich, from his memoirs

> Turgenev was the master of the epigram. . . . For a good shot, he sometimes would not even spare a friend.

Circa February 1846
Alexei Surovin, from an 1880 article

> F. M. Dostoevsky, now residing in Staraya Russa,[59] where he is taking a cure, has asked me to assert in his name . . . that he "never received verses allegedly composed by Nekrasov and Panaev."[60]

Circa February 1846
Pavel Annenkov, from an 1880 letter to Mikhail Stasyulevich

> Tell Turgenev to remember to write about Nekrasov's epigram on that wild dog howling in the wind.

Circa February 1846
Nikolai Nekrasov, from an 1856 poem

> His voice like a child's, his legs like spokes
> His hands, soft and red,
> A strand of hair like fluffy down
> Marks his beard and head.

Circa February 1846
Stepan Yanovsky, from an 1884 letter to Anna Dostoevskaya

> Fyodor Mikhailovich, describing a visit to the salon of Count Vielgorsky, where he had been together with Belinsky, told me, "We were

invited there as an exhibit, for show." . . . When Belinsky dropped a glass and a tray . . . Fyodor Mikhailovich told me that he heard . . . how Vielgorsky's daughter said to Count Sollogub, "They are not only barbaric and inept but also dumb."

Circa February 1846
Dmitri Grigorovich, from his memoirs

When, at the Vielgorskys' home, Dostoevsky was introduced to the beauty Mrs. Senyavina, he fainted from excitement.

Circa February 1846
Lyubov Dostoevskaya, from her memoirs

Dostoevsky's friends laughed at his shyness with women and spread the story that allegedly, from agitation, he fainted when he saw the legs of a young woman to whom he had been introduced.

PART TWO

Havens from the Storms

The Vielgorskys, Beketovs, and Maykovs

Disillusioned, if not angry, with the members of the Belinsky circle, Dostoevsky looked elsewhere for solace and support. In 1846 and 1847 he was fortunate to find three Russian families who, for the moment at least, provided the young writer with a haven from personal and professional storms.

The first clan were the Vielgorskys, whom Dostoevsky visited in early 1846. Mikhail Vielgorsky was a wealthy count, composer, and writer of romances. He was also a patron of the arts with ties and connections throughout Russia. Equally important, Mikhail was a *barin* of the old school: kind, moral, educated, easygoing, and notoriously absent-minded, but with a precise feeling for art and the finer things in life. As his son-in-law, the writer Vladimir Sollogub, noted, Mikhail "loved and took advantage not only of all that was good but also of all that was sinful." Food was a particular passion. Friends recalled inviting Mikhail to their homes to sample a wine, a dish, or the fare of a new cook and waiting, often with bated breath, to hear "judgments that were authoritative, always sincere, and often even harsh." Nonetheless, Mikhail enjoyed love and respect from all. As Sollogub remarked, "Rarely have I loved an individual as much as Count Vielgorsky."[1]

Mikhail's wife, Luiza, was even more interesting, if only because she served as a type for the "infernal women" of Dostoevsky's mature fiction. As recalled by Sollogub, Luiza—known to all as *matushka* or "little mother"—had two radically different personalities. One moment the woman showed "unapproachable pride . . . [and] the most extraordinary arrogance"; the next she displayed the "most sincere Christian abasement . . . [with] the most touching goodness and kindness."[2]

Whatever their strengths and weaknesses, Mikhail and Luiza were consummate hosts. Receptions featured legendary dinners, as well as concerts not only with the best musicians in St. Petersburg but also—if Dostoevsky's daughter Lyubov is to believed—poor artists whom Mikhail discovered in the darkest reaches of the city. Luiza's parties welcomed prominent members of society. Mikhail's gatherings took place two or three times a week and embraced novice as well as established writers, journalists, and artists; Gogol, for example, was a frequent guest. It is no surprise that Dostoevsky loved the time he spent with the couple. "Father felt especially comfortable at the Vielgorskys'," Lyubov Dostoevskaya recalled. "There one could hear excellent music. He loved music passionately."[3] (Sadly, Dostoevsky never met Gogol in their home.) Again, according to Lyubov, the musicians whom Mikhail found in the attics and cellars of St. Petersburg served as prototypes for Yegor Yefimov, the mad artist in the first part of *Netochka Nezvanova*. Mikhail himself would appear as Prince X in the second part of the work.

A second group came into Dostoevsky's life in the first two years after the publication of *Poor Folk* in early 1846—the Maykovs. Like the Vielgorskys, the Maykovs were a colorful clan. Nikolai, the head of the household, was a handsome retired officer who painted neoclassical portraits of women, as well as icons for St. Isaac's Cathedral and other churches in the northern capital.[4] His wife, Yevgenya, was an equally attractive, if temperamental, dark-haired poetess and prose writer with an aristocratic figure and face. One son, Apollon, was on his way to becoming an accomplished poet who felt most at home in the ancient and medieval worlds. (He had been introduced to Dostoevsky by Belinsky.) A second son, Valerian, the organizer if not the "soul" of the group,[5] was making a name for himself, and not only as a sociopolitical journalist[6] and an advocate of Feuerbach and the utopian socialists. He was also an early member of the circle that gathered around Mikhail Petrashevsky, and an editor of the first volume of the infamous *Dictionary of Foreign Words*[7] who contributed articles on the social significance of art. A third son, Leonid, was a historian, ethnographer, and academician. A sister-in-law, Natalya, was the daughter of the poet Alexander Izmailov as well as an inspector for the Catherine Institute and a friend of the empress, Alexandra Fyodorovna.[8]

The Maykovs mirrored the Vielgorskys physically and socially. They too loved the good life led in spacious and elegant surroundings. They too were connoisseurs of material pleasures but also caretakers of the soul. Good food and drink took their place alongside contemplation and prayer.

The Maykovs had their faults. At any moment they could be proud and aloof or sentimental and silly. Most often they were kind, progressive, and humane—welcome alternatives to the sham glitterati of St. Petersburg. They were also warm and welcoming. Every Sunday, beginning at seven in the evening, they opened their home to an extended family of young writers, critics, journalists, scholars, musicians, and artists who sought collectively to solve the problems of Russia and the world.

Unlike the members of the Belinsky circle, the visitors to the Maykovs' home were not prima donnas seeking praise and perks. Guests read their articles, proposed projects and plans, and debated science, politics, literature, and art in an atmosphere of trust, equality, and bonhomie. Reluctantly, participants departed from the Maykovs' in the wee hours of the morning, if not later.

At the Maykovs' gatherings, writers also read their works. Indeed, fiction was the primary interest of the group. It was here that Goncharov exposed to public scrutiny his first novel, *A Common Story*. It was also at the Maykovs' that Dostoevsky presented not only his writings—"Mr. Prokharchin" was one—but also "atomic analyses" of Gogol, Turgenev, and others.

A final group to provide solace and support for Dostoevsky were the Beketovs. Even more than the Maykovs, the Beketovs enjoyed personal and professional success. Alexei Beketov, it will be recalled, had been a close friend of Dostoevsky's at the Main Engineering Academy in St. Petersburg. He was a universal favorite: virtuous, intelligent, and energetic. He was also outraged by all kinds of injustice. Alexei had two equally gifted brothers, both university students. Nikolai would become an outstanding chemist, physicist, and member of the Russian Academy of Sciences. Andrei would emerge as a leading botanist, a rector of St. Petersburg University, and the grandfather of Alexander Blok. The Beketovs also kept good company. Along with Grigorovich and the Maykov brothers, frequent if not daily visitors included Nikolai Khanykov, a budding orientalist, and the poet Alexei Pleshcheev.

Gatherings at the Beketovs' were more unstructured and spirited than those at the Maykovs'. Rarely did the conversation focus on a single subject. As soon as someone raised an issue or question—Fourier and utopian socialism were frequent topics—everyone expounded on everything before breaking into smaller groups to continue the chaos. With as many as fifteen high-powered types under one roof, egos collided and clashed. Arguments and debates became heated and sharp; cries and outbursts filled the air. Momentary war gave way to enduring peace under the watchful mediation of elders, or with all-night excursions to forests and lakes where participants made merry with story and song.

Dostoevsky found the Beketovs to be practical and intelligent, noble and kind. He also asserted that the members of the family were his salvation, so much so that in October or November 1846, he lived with all three Beketov brothers, as well as with Pleshcheev, Grigorovich, and Apollon Maykov in an apartment "association," until Andrei and Nikolai left for Kazan in February 1847.

In a sense, the Vielgorskys, Maykovs, and Beketovs were the young writer's link to his early years with his family. All three groups provided oases of security, warmth, and love in which Dostoevsky could pursue interests and ideas among like-minded aficionados of culture and art. They were also among the precious few who supported Dostoevsky as a writer during the first two years after *Poor Folk*. Valerian Maykov was the only critic of the period to applaud *The Double* and to see Dostoevsky as a psychologist who would leave Gogol in his dust. If anything, the Vielgorskys, Maykovs, and Beketovs kept the young Dostoevsky out of social and spiritual trouble. Even as the young writer was beset by what he saw as the failures of the four stories after *Poor Folk*, as well as by the betrayals by Belinsky's circle, he could still take heart in the peace and goodness in the world, in a life worth living.

February 1846
Nikolai Melgunov, from a letter to Mikhail Pogodin

> [Nikolai] Pavlov is in ecstasy over Dostoevsky's *Poor Folk*. He cannot praise it enough. Ask him to write a review about the work. I do not think that he will refuse. . . . After all, it would be a shame if it were overlooked.[9]

February 1846
Lyubov Dostoevskaya, from her memoirs

> Without a doubt, *Poor Folk* was written very well, but it was not an original work. It appeared to be an imitation of a Gogolian novel, which, in turn, imitated the French literature of the time.

February 1, 1846
Fyodor Dostoevsky, from a letter to Mikhail Dostoevsky

> First of all, do not be angry at me that I have not written to you for such a long time. Honest to God, there has been no time, and I will prove that to you right now. The main thing that has been holding me

up was that until very recently, that is, until the 28th of last month, *I was finishing up my scoundrel Golyadkin.*[10] It was terrible! So much for human calculations! I would have liked to finish it before August but dragged it out until February! I am sending you the almanac now.[11] *Poor Folk* came out on the fifteenth. Well, brother! What cruel abuse it has met everywhere! In *Illustration,* read swearing, not criticism.[12] In *The Northern Bee,* there was only the devil knows what.[13] But I remember how Gogol was received, and we all know the reception that Pushkin got for his works. Even the public is in an uproar: three quarters of the readers abuse it, but one quarter (not even that much, really) praise it extravagantly. The debates about it are terrible. People rant and rave, but they still read it. (The almanac is selling in an unnatural, terrible way.) In two weeks, let us hope, not a single copy will remain. That is how it was with Gogol. They kept ranting and raving about him, but nonetheless they read him; now they have made their peace and have even begun to praise him. To all I have thrown a dog bone! Let them gnaw on it—the fools are building my fame. To degrade oneself that way the *Northern Bee* does with its criticism is the height of disgrace. How frantically stupid! But on the other hand, brother, what praises do I also hear! Just imagine, all our people and even Belinsky have found that I have even departed far from Gogol. In *The Library for Reading,*[14] where Nikitenko writes criticism, there will be a huge analysis of *Poor Folk,* in my favor. Belinsky will be ringing the bells about it in March. Odoevsky is writing a separate article about *Poor Folk.* My friend Sollogub is too.[15] I have entered high society, brother, and in about three months, I will tell you about all my adventures in person.

Our public has instinct, but like any crowd, it is uneducated. They do not understand how one can write in such a way. In everything, they have grown accustomed to seeing the author's mug; but I did not show mine. It is beyond them to see that it is Devushkin, not I, who is speaking; and that Devushkin cannot talk in any other way. They also find the novel drawn out, but there is not a superfluous word in it. They (Belinsky and others) find in me a new, original style, that I operate by Analysis, not Synthesis,[16] that is, I go into the depths, but by taking things apart atom by atom, whereas Gogol takes the whole directly, and for that reason is not as profound as I am. You will read and see for yourself. I have a brilliant future, brother!

Golyadkin is coming out today. *Four days ago,* I was still writing him. He will take up eleven signature pages in *The Fatherland Notes.* Golyadkin is ten times better than *Poor Folk.* Our people say that not since

Dead Souls has there been anything like it in Russia, and that it is a work of genius. What do they not say about it! With what hopes do they all view me! Truly, I was unbelievably successful with Golyadkin! You will like it like I don't know what! You will like it even better than *Dead Souls*. That I know. Are people getting *The Fatherland Notes*?[17] I do not know if Kraevsky will give me a copy.

Well, brother, I have not written to you in such a long while that I do not remember where I left off. So much water has flowed under the bridge. We will see each other soon. In the summer, I will definitely come to see you, my friend, and I will be terribly busy writing all summer. I have ideas. I am also writing now. For Golyadkin I got exactly 600 silver rubles.[18] In addition, I have also been receiving a ton of money, so much so that I have spent 3,000 rubles since parting with you. I am living in a very chaotic way—there's no joking about that! I've moved from my apartment and I am now renting two marvelously furnished rooms from tenants. I am enjoying life very much. . . .

For heaven's sake, please write. Write whether you like *Poor Folk*. Give my regards to Emiliya Fyodorovna and kiss all the children. I was really in love with Panaeva, but that is passing now, and I still do not know. My health is in terrible shape. My nerves are sick and I am afraid of a nervous fever or an inflammation. I cannot live in an orderly way. I am so dissolute. If I do not get to swim in the sea this summer, it will simply be a disaster. Good-bye, and for God's sake, write. Forgive me for having written this letter in a vile way. I am in a hurry, I kiss you. Good-bye.

P.S. Well, brother, for God's sake, forgive me for not having sent anything to you. I will bring everything this summer. Well, for the third time, good-bye.

I will bring gifts to all of you.

In the summer, my friend, you and I will pass the time in a merrier way than right now. I will not be rich, but I hope to have 800 or 1,000 rubles. That will be enough for the summer.

Verochka is getting married.[19] Did you know that?

February 1, 1846
Fyodor Dostoevsky, from *A Writer's Diary*

[*The Double*] did not turn well at all, but its idea was rather clear. Never in my writing did I express anything more serious. But I did not succeed at all with the form of the tale. Subsequently, some fifteen years later, when I revised it thoroughly for a *Complete Edition* of my works,

I again was convinced that the thing was a total failure, and if I now were able to take up the idea and expound upon it anew, I would opt for an entirely different form. But in 1846, I had not found this form and could not come to grips with this tale.

February 1, 1846
Vissarion Belinsky, from a review

In [Nekrasov's] *The Petersburg Miscellany* is *Poor Folk* by Mr. Dostoevsky— a name that is completely unknown and new but, so it seems, is destined to play a significant role in our literature.

In this issue of *The Fatherland Notes*, the public will read still another novel by Dostoevsky, *The Double*—and will be more than convinced that with *such works*, ordinary talents do not begin their career.

February 1, 1846
Vissarion Belinsky, from an article

What is new in our literature? The latest news is the appearance of a new and unusual talent. We are speaking of Mr. Dostoevsky, whom we recommend to the public with *Poor Folk* and *The Double*—works that would end one's career in a brilliant and glorious way, but with which to begin *so* . . . is something extremely unusual! The public now talks only of Mr. Dostoevsky, the author of *Poor Folk*.

Fame, though, is not without thorns. People also say that mediocrity and a lack of talent eat away at Mr. Dostoevsky's wooden swords and spears. . . . All the better since such thorns do not prick but set a talent in motion. . . . After all, a talent is not a talent if he has no enemies and envious people.

February 1, 1846
Pyotr Pletnyov, from a review

In [*Poor Folk*] there are two poetic elements: serious and comic. The first is far greater than the second in that it bears the tone of *artistic truth*. . . . The comic, though, is somehow artificial and, in a significant way, imitates the tone and even the colors of Gogol and Kvitka.

February 1, 1846
Faddei Bulgarin, from an article

All about town people are talking about a new genius named Mr. Dostoevsky—we do not know if this is a pseudonym (most likely) or his real name—and are praising his novel, *Poor Folk*, to the skies. So we too have read this work and all we can say is: our poor Russian writers! Mr. Dostoevsky is not without talent, but if he wishes to pursue a true path in literature, he should write something decent. Let him not listen to the accolades of the *natural* party and believe that he is being praised at the expense of others.[20] To praise in excess is to obstruct the road to further success.

February 1, 1846
Apollon Grigoriev, from his memoirs

[At that time] two pieces [of *The Petersburg Miscellany*] made an overall powerful impression: [Dostoevsky's] *Poor Folk* and Nekrasov's poem "On the Road."[21]

February 5, 1846
Pyotr Pletnyov, from a letter to Vasily Zhukovsky

Sollogub will send you *The Petersburg Miscellany*. In it is Dostoevsky's novel *Poor Folk*. All the Nekrasovites (people who publish in the almanac of a certain Nekrasov) have lost their mind over it. They are also saying that he spells death to Gogol and everyone else. For the time being I do not think this will happen.

February 6, 1846
Vissarion Belinsky, from a letter to Alexander Herzen

[One of your stories] would make a first-rate article for my almanac and share the ecstasy of the public over Dostoevsky's "Shaved Sideburns."[22]

February 6, 1846
Pyotr Pletnyov, from a letter to Yakov Grot

Yesterday . . . we read a thing or two from *The Petersburg Miscellany*. Not everything in it is to our liking. Even Maykov and Turgenev have turned into *Nekrasovites*.[23] . . . Pyotr Ivanovich was indignant over the boredom of Dostoevsky's story *Poor Folk*. So was I.

February 9, 1846
Pyotr Pletnyov, from a letter to Yakov Grot

I forgot to tell you that yesterday at a gathering . . . we read Dostoevsky's new novel in the second issue of *The Fatherland Notes*. I did not like it, although one could see talent. He is chasing after Gogol. Wishing to obliterate Gogol's *Diary of a Madman*, Dostoevsky puts forth [his own type] of lunatic.[24]

February 9, 1846
Apollon Grigoriev, from a review

> [With *Poor Folk*], Dostoevsky has made a forceful literary debut . . . with a work that will be read by not only educated but also everyday readers . . . with several pages that, we are not ashamed to say, moved us to tears.
>
> *Poor Folk* is so simple, so very simple, that only with very great effort can one regard it as a serious undertaking, to extract from its very poor content an entire internal drama.
>
> A poor, somewhat old and laughable clerk—Makar Alexeevich Devushkin—suffers all possible deprivations and needs . . . for Varvara Alexeevna Dobroselova, one of those unhappy beings who are well known in Petersburg, someone who is unhappy, but profoundly worthy of sympathy . . . a very simple, noble, and poetic girl . . . who chooses poverty and suffering over debauchery and vice.
>
> Here are two people who, to the highest degree, are interesting and enlightened. One is given to human love and suffering; the other . . . to Christian humility. . . . Despite their monotonous sensations, as well as their manifestly petty joys and sorrows, they cannot but arouse our sympathy. . . .
>
> One sees flashes of Gogol . . . but the author analyzes. . . and digs deeper . . . than the writer of *Dead Souls* and "Nevsky Prospekt." . . .[25]
>
> If one judges by his great talent, Dostoevsky seems fated to be without limits . . . [and] to be a reconciling link between Gogol and Lermontov.

February 10, 1846
An anonymous reviewer, from an article

> In a terrible, heartbreaking picture, Dostoevsky presents the extreme unhappiness suffered by the poor in our society. The hero of his novel is a wretched elderly clerk, Makar Alexeevich, who conducts a correspondence with a poor girl, Varvara Alexeevna Dobroselova, for whom he nourishes tender fatherly feelings. Nothing that makes our earthly life luxurious and bright—riches, honors, respect, love, and earthly delights—exists for these two unhappy people. They live and are happy only for their mutual friendship. They share with each other their meager funds. With motherly tenderness they warm each other with news about their poor circumstances and the secrets of their lacerated hearts; but they also hide anything that could destroy their mutual

peace. Everything around them is gloomy and sad, like an autumn evening in Petersburg with its drizzle and slush. You will read these half-amusing, half-sad pages. Sometimes a smile will appear on your lips; but more often your heart will ache and moan, and your eyes will fill up with tears. You will finish the novel, but in your soul there will remain a heavy, ineffably mournful feeling—one that will recall the death knell song of Desdemona.

February 12, 1846
An anonymous reviewer, from an article

> For Mr. Dostoevsky to have complete success [as a writer], he must create his own public. . . . He has hardly entered literature, but already he has met enthusiastic fans on one side, and on the other, quick-tempered detractors. Such an outcome is the best proof of his talent. Does one not recall that Pushkin, Gogol, and Lermontov also began in the same way?

February 15, 1846
Nikolai Melgunov, from a letter to Mikhail Pogodin

> Have you read *Poor Folk*? If Shevyryov slams it, I request a spot [in *The Muscovite*] to defend the work . . . and to expound upon its artistic and social significance.[26]

February 16, 1846
Mikhail Pogodin, from his diary

> I am reading *The Petersburg Miscellany*. Dostoevsky is not without merit or hope. But in his work are so many repulsive things.

February 18, 1846
Nikolai Yazykov, from a letter to Nikolai Gogol

> According to *The Fatherland Notes*, Petersburg has a new genius: one Dostoevsky. You will find his story in Nekrasov's almanac. Read it and tell me your opinion. I myself have not yet found time to do so, but local benefactors are now praising it!

February 19, 1846
Vissarion Belinsky, from a letter to Alexander Herzen

> In no way is Nekrasov's poem "On the Road" responsible for the success of the almanac. *Poor Folk* is a different thing and thus the object of earlier rumors.

February 28, 1846
Leopold Brandt, from a review

> This confusion of words, all this senselessness and absurdity are being passed off to us as a great talent, as the work of a genius!
>
> Along with us, what will you say to this, reader? Do you know what kind of genius this Mr. Dostoevsky is, and from what corner he has been crowned with *glory*?

February 28, 1846
Leopold Brandt, from a review

> One cannot imagine anything more colorless, monotonous, endlessly drawn out, and deathly tiring as the unimpressive "adventures of Mr. Golyadkin," who, from the beginning of the story to its end, appears insane, and who makes constant stupidities and blunders which are neither touching nor humorous, despite the efforts of the author to show them as such, with pretenses to some "profound," unsatisfactory humor. There is no end to the verbiage—tiresome, annoying, and nerve-wracking—as well as to the repetitions and paraphrases of one and the same thought, of one and the same words so beloved by the writer. . . .
>
> The hero, Mr. Golyadkin Senior, ends his adventures in a madhouse. Indeed, it would have been easier for the hero, writer, and readers to have begun there.
>
> We regret sincerely a talented young man who understands art so falsely, and who has been so led astray by the views of the literary "coterie" who talk of his remarkable genius.[27]

February 28, 1846
An anonymous reviewer, from an article

> As often happens, Mr. Dostoevsky already has avid detractors and adherents who are ready to fight it out to the end. Happy is the author if he sees the praises of his friends as less significant than the disclaimers of his enemies . . . since, to such an individual, the latter is more valuable than the former. . . . Indeed, the fans of a new writer can be a stumbling block, even a millstone. . . .

March 1, 1846
Vissarion Belinsky, from a review

> In [Nekrasov's] almanac, *Poor Folk*, a novel by Mr. Dostoevsky, is the first piece by both place and worth. . . .

In the reading and writing world, the appearance of any unusual talent gives rise to contradictions and discrepancies. If such a talent appears in the early phase of a still unestablished literature, he meets with, on the one hand, enthusiastic cries and unrestrained praise; but, on the other, absolute condemnation, absolute negation. So it was with Pushkin. . . .

Nonetheless, the success of *Poor Folk* is complete. . . .

Upon first glance one can see that the talent of Mr. Dostoevsky is neither satirical nor descriptive but to a great degree creative, and that the predominant characteristic of his talent is humor. Such humor he does not express from a knowledge of life or from a human heart given to observation and experience. No, he knows such things profoundly; but also a priori, in a purely poetic and creative way. His knowledge is his talent and inspiration.

We do not wish to compare Mr. Dostoevsky with anyone because, generally speaking, such comparisons are childish, lead nowhere, and explain nothing. We will only say that this is a talent who is unusual and original; who immediately, from his first work, distinguishes himself sharply from the entire crowd of our writers; and who is more or less indebted to Gogol in character and direction. Hence the success of his talent. . . .

In many parts of both novels of Mr. Dostoevsky (*Poor Folk* and *The Double*), one sees the powerful influence of Gogol, even in his turns of phrase. But in Mr. Dostoevsky there is so much independence that the obvious influence of Gogol will probably not continue and will disappear with other personally characteristic shortcomings. Nonetheless, Gogol will remain with Mr. Dostoevsky forever as, so to speak, a father figure in creativity . . . the Columbus of that immense and inexhaustible realm of creativity which Mr. Dostoevsky must [also] pursue.

Although it is still early to determine decisively what distinguishing features Mr. Dostoevsky will have, so to speak, the individuality and personality of his talent, such things he has, of this we have no doubt.

March 1, 1846
Vissarion Belinsky, from a review

Judging from *Poor Folk*, we are about to conclude that a profoundly human and emotional element, together with a humorous one, makes up a key feature in the character of Mr. Dostoevsky's talent. But having read *The Double*, we have seen that a similar conclusion would be extremely hasty. Truly, in *The Double*, only the morally deaf and blind can fail to see and hear its deeply emotional call, the deeply tragic color and tone. But, as in Gogol's *Diary of a Madman*, humor masks and hides both. . . .

Generally speaking, for all its grandness, Mr. Dostoevsky's talents is still too young to be put forth in a definite way. This is natural: for a writer who introduces everything in his first work, one cannot expect a great deal. . . .

We have said that in both novels of Mr. Dostoevsky, one notices the strong influence of Gogol, but such a claim refers only to parts, to turns of phrase, and nowhere to the conception of the entire piece or the character of the protagonists. In these respects, the talent of Mr. Dostoevsky shines forth with bright independence. If one should think that Mr. Dostoevsky's Makar Alexeevich Devushkin, old man Pokrovsky, and Mr. Golyadkin Senior have something in common with Gogol's Poprishchin and Akaky Akakievich Bashmachkin,[28] then one cannot help but see that the characters in the novels of Mr. Dostoevsky and the stories of Gogol are as different as Poprishchin and Bashmachkin, even though both were created by the same author.

March 1, 1846
Vissarion Belinsky, from a review

One cannot but agree that for a first work, *Poor Folk* and, immediately thereafter, *The Double* are pieces of unusual depth, works with which no [other] Russian writer has begun his literary career. Of course, in no way does this show that as regards talent, Dostoevsky stands higher than his predecessors (we are far from expressing a similar absurd idea), but only that he had the fortune to come after them. With all this, though, such a debut points clearly to the place that, with time, Mr. Dostoevsky will occupy in Russian literature, and that even if he does not stand alongside his predecessors as an equal among equals, we will still have to wait for a long time for a talent that could come close to him. Look how simple is the beginning of *Poor Folk*: after all, there is no story to tell! But necessarily, there is also much to tell if one decides to do so!

A poor elderly clerk of minimal intelligence and without any education, but with an endlessly kind soul and warm heart, relying on an . . . ill-planned or implausible pretext or tie, wishes to tear from the hands of a vile businessman a poor girl of feminine virtue and maidenly beauty. The author does not tell us if love for this girl has forced his clerk to feel compassion, or if compassion has given birth to love. We know only that his feeling for her is not simply paternal or elderly, the feeling of a lonely man who needs to love someone so as not to hate life or . . . to have a being who owes or is obligated to him—an individual to whom he has grown accustomed and who has become accustomed to him. No, the feeling that Makar Alexeevich has for his "little mother, little angel, and little cherub Varenka" is something akin to the emotion of a lover—a feeling which he strives manfully not to recognize in himself, but which against his will, and in time, bursts through the surface, and which he would not begin to hide if he had noticed that *she* regards him as completely inappropriate for her.

The poor soul, though, does not see such a thing, and with heroic self-sacrifice remains in the role of a relative and patron. Sometimes he becomes lazy and spoiled, especially in the first letter, when the talk is about the raised corner of the window curtain, the good spring weather, the birds in the heavens, and that "everything is coming up roses." Having received in answer an innuendo about his age, the poor soul falls into despair, believing that he is being seen as a prankster, and annoyed, asserting that he is not at all an old man. These attitudes, this feeling, this elderly passion merging, in such a wondrous way, with sincere kindness, love, and habit—all this the author develops with remarkable art and inimitable mastery.

Devushkin, helping Varenka Dobroselova, takes advances on his salary, enters into debt, suffers terrible need, and, in intense moments of despair, like any Russian, seeks oblivion in drink. But how delicate is his instinct! Acting as a benefactor, he deprives himself of everything. He robs and pillages his very self—to the last extreme. He deceives his Varenka with his imaginary capital in a pawnshop, and if he lets slip about the truth of his situation, he does so in elderly chatter and in such a simple-minded way! It never occurs to him that with his sacrifices, he has acquired the right to demand the reward of love for love, since, given his limited and narrow understanding, he could foist himself as a husband on Varenka on the natural and extremely just conviction that no one other than himself could love her and make such sacrifices on her behalf.

From Varenka, though, Devushkin does not demand similar sacrifice. He loves her not for himself but for her very self, and to sacrifice everything for her is his happiness. The more limited his mind, the more constricted and coarse his understanding, so it also seems the more noble and delicate his heart. One can say that all of the intellectual capabilities of his head have moved to his heart. Many can think that in the personage of Devushkin, the author wanted to depict an individual whose mind and capabilities have been weighed down and flattened by life. But to think so would be a huge mistake. The intent of the author is much more profound and humane. In the personage of Makar Alexeevich, he shows us how much [that is] splendid, noble, and saintly lies in the most limited nature. Of course, not all poor people of this time are like Makar Alexeevich in his good qualities, and we also agree that such people are rare. At the same time, however, we also cannot help but agree that such people we pay little attention to, are not interested in, and know little of. If a rich person, eating through a hundred, two hundred or more rubles on a daily basis, throws to a beggar twenty-five rubles, such a thing everyone notices and, hoping to get more from him, is moved in his or her soul by such a magnanimous act. But a poor person who gives the same amount to a beggar like himself, the last twenty-five copper copecks, as Devushkin gives to Gorshkov—such an individual does not move one and all, and in the story, written with such mastery, as well as in life, no one wants to see in his deed anything other than something comic. Glory and honor to the young poet who loves people in attics and cellars and talks about them as if they lived in golden palaces. "After all, these people are also our brothers!"

March 1, 1846
Vissarion Belinsky, from a review

[In *Poor Folk*] pay attention to the old man Pokrovsky—and you will see the humane thought of the author. At first the false husband of a seductive, deceitful woman, then the oppressed mate of a reckless shrew, as well as a drunkard and clown, but he is also a *man*. You may laugh at his love for his would-be son, not unlike the shy love of a dog for its master. But if, laughing at such affections, you are also, at the same time, not touched by it, if the picture of Pokrovsky, with books in his pocket and under his arm, without a hat on his head, running in the rain and the cold, looking like a madman, at the coffin of his son [whom] he loved in such a laughable way, if this does not make a tragic impression on you—do not say anything about this to anyone, so that some Pokrovsky, a clown and a drunkard, will not blush for you as a man. . . .

Generally speaking, a tragic element pervades the entire novel in a profound way. This element is all the more remarkable since it is conveyed to the reader not only in the words but also in the thoughts of

Makar Alexeevich. At the same time [it seeks] to amuse and shake profoundly the soul of the reader, to force him to laugh through tears—what skill, what talent! And without melodramatic springs, without anything resembling theatrical effects! Everything is so simple and ordinary, like the everyday, humdrum life that swarms around each of us, as well as the vulgarity that comes to an end with the sudden death of first one, then the other!

All the characters are drawn so fully, so clearly . . . in a word, every character who appears in passing, or is mentioned in absentia, so stands before the reader as if acquainted with him for a rather short period of time.

One should note, and not without basis, that the personage of Varenka is not completely defined or complete; but such is the lot of Russian women. Russian poetry is not on good terms with them, that is all one can say! We do not know who is guilty, Russian women or Russian poetry. We know that only Pushkin, in the character of Tatyana, managed to seize upon several features of the Russian woman . . . to inform her character with definition and independence.[29] Varenka's journal is splendid, but as to mastery of exposition, it cannot compare to Devushkin's letters. Here the author is not completely at home; but he has dealt with a difficult situation in a brilliant way. The memories of childhood, the arrival in Petersburg, the disorder of affairs with Dobroselov, the education in school, especially life in the home of Anna Fyodorovna, the tie of Varenka with Pokrovsky, their rapprochement, the portrait of father Pokrovsky, the gift to the young Pokrovsky for his name day, the death of young Pokrovsky—all this is told with remarkable mastery. Dobroselova talks neither about a single delicate circumstance, nor about the dishonorable views of Anna Fyodorovna about her, nor about her love for Pokrovsky, nor about her subsequent involuntary fall, but the reader sees everything so clearly that no explanations are needed.

It would be superfluous to tell the plot of this novel or to take copious notes on it. . . . Readers, though, should recall their personal impressions [of the work] and summon them as evidence for the justice and accuracy of our opinion of the high worth of *Poor Folk*. This is why we consider it necessary to cite several passages from the letters of Makar Alexeevich. . . . [In so doing] we will force them to reread the work anew and to see that they have understood it only after a second reading. Works like *Poor Folk* are not understood the first time around; they demand not only reading but also study. . . .

In this picture, painted with such a broad and powerful brush . . . are also the melodramatic effects of modern French feuilleton novelists. But with what terrible simplicity and truth! But who is telling this story? The limited and laughable Makar Alexeevich Devushkin! . . .

We will not point further to the splendid parts of this novel. It is easier to reread the entire piece than to retell everything that is wonderful about it because the entire work is remarkable. We need only to note the last letter of Devushkin to his Varvara: the tears, the sobbing, the wails lacerating the soul. Everything is so truthful, proud, and great, and writing it all is still the limited, laughable Makar Alexeevich Devushkin! And reading him, you yourself will want to sob, and at the same time laugh. . . . How much shattering love, grief, and despair in these simple words of an old man who is losing everything that is dear to him in life. "Do you only know what lies there, where you are going, little mother? You, perhaps, do not know, so ask me! The steppe, my beloved, the steppe, open and bare as the palm of my hand! There goes the unfeeling old woman, the drunken illiterate peasant."

March 1, 1846
Vissarion Belinsky, from a review

By the way, we think that now we should say a few words about [Mr. Dostoevsky's] *The Double*. . . . As an unusual talent, the author in no way repeats himself in his second work. Here he presents a completely new world. The hero of the novel—Mr. Golyadkin—is one of those people, sensitive and crazed from *ambition*, whom one often meets in the lower and middling levels of our society. It always seems to him that people offend him in words, looks, and gestures, and that they are undermining and intriguing against him. Such a stance is all the more laughable, since neither by position, nor rank, nor job, nor intelligence, nor capabilities can he arouse envy in anyone. He is neither smart nor stupid; neither rich nor poor. As a character, he is very kind and soft to the point of weakness. He could get on in the world in an absolutely good way, but the sickly sensibility and suspiciousness of his character is the black demon in his life and is fated to make a hell out of his existence. If you look more attentively around you, you will see so many Mr. Golyadkins, both rich and poor, both stupid and smart!

Mr. Golyadkin is in ecstasy over one virtue . . . the fact that he does not wear a mask, that he is not an intriguer, that he operates openly, and that he goes along a straight path. Even in the beginning of the novel, in his conversation with Doctor Krestyan Ivanovich, it is no wonder that Mr. Golyadin is disturbed mentally. Indeed, the hero of the novel is a madman! The idea is bold and done by the author with remarkable mastery! We consider it superfluous to follow the plot of the work, or to point out particular episodes, or to marvel at the entire creation. For anyone privy to the mysteries of art, one can see right away that in *The Double* there is still more creative talent and depth of thought than in *Poor Folk*. But in the meantime, almost the entire general voice of readers in Petersburg have decided that the novel is unbearably long-winded, and for that reason intolerably boring, and furthermore, that the author has been trumpeted in vain and that in his talent there is nothing unusual! . . .

But is such a conclusion just? Without indicting ourselves, we will say that on the one hand, such an assessment is extremely false, and but on the other, there is also a basis [for such a view] as often happens with the judgment of the mob who does not understand its own self.

Let us begin by saying that *The Double* is in no way long-winded, but one cannot also say that it is not tiring for the average reader who does not understand or value the talent of the author in a profound and truthful way. The fact of the matter is that so-called long-windedness is of two types. One is from a lack of talent—that is true long-windedness. The other is from the riches of a particularly young talent who has still not matured. Such a thing one should call not long-windedness but excessive fecundity.

If the author of *The Double* had put a pen in our hands with the unconditional right to exclude from the manuscript of the work everything that seemed to us long-winded and superfluous, we would not be able to put a hand to a single individual place, because every individual place in this novel is the height of perfection. But the fact of the matter is that there are so extremely many superb places in *The Double* which occur one after another that no matter how awesomely superb they are, they tire and bore [readers]. Demyan is famous for his fish soup, and his neighbor Foka eats it to his heart's content; but in the end, he still flees from his host.[30] It is evident that the author of *The Double* still has not mastered the techniques of measure and harmony. This is why, not completely without foundation, many readers reproach the writer for long-windedness even in *Poor Folk*, although such reprimands are less with this work than in *The Double*. The most extreme fecundity only serves as evidence for the greatness and extent of the writer's talent. What should this young author do now? Should he continue on his own path alone, not listening to anyone—or should he wish to accommodate the mob, to try to acquire a premature, and consequently artificial, maturity . . . and a sham sense of proportion? . . .

In our opinion, both extremes are equally destructive. Talent must travel its own path, and in a natural way, with each passing day, rid itself of its key weaknesses, that is, of youth and immaturity. At the same time, however, it must, it is obliged, to *take into account* what particularly dissatisfies the majority of readers. Even more, it must take care to despise their opinion, but also always to seek to discern the basis of such a view, because such a strategy is almost always sensible and just.

If one can consider *The Double* to be long-winded, it is because of the frequent and often unnecessary repetition of one and the same phrase, as, for example: "*I have been reduced to misfortune! Thus I have been reduced to misfortune!* . . . *Goodness, after all, such misfortune!* . . . *Goodness, after all, such misfortune has conquered!*" . . . Italicized phrases are also completely superfluous, and there exist a sufficient number of them in the work. We understand their source. A young talent, conscious of his power and gifts, is seemingly amused by humor; but his work has so much genuine humor, the humor of thought and deed, that he can boldly dispense with the humor of phrases and words.

March 1, 1846
Vissarion Belinsky, from a review

> Generally speaking, *The Double* bears the imprint of a talent that is great and powerful, but still young and immature. Hence all of its shortcomings, but also all of its strengths. Both are tied together so tightly that if the author would take it into his head to rework his *Double* completely, to keep certain strengths, and to exclude all its weaknesses, we are sure that he would spoil it. The author relates the adventures of his hero from himself, completely in his own language and concepts. On the one hand, this aspect shows a wealth of humor . . . an endlessly powerful ability for the objective contemplation of the appearances of life, the ability, so to speak, of migrating into the skin of another, a being completely different from himself. But, on the other hand, this very same feature also somehow obscures many of the circumstances of the novel. A reader is completely correct not to understand or suspect that the letters of Vakhrameev and of Mr. Golyadkin Junior, Mr. Golyadkin Senior has, in his disordered imagination, written to himself—and even that the surface likeness between Golyadkin Senior

and Golyadkin Junior is really not so great and striking as it seems to him in his disturbed mind. Generally speaking, also, about the very madness of Mr. Golyadkin, not every reader would guess quickly. . . .

We have touched extremely lightly on both works of Mr. Dostoevsky, especially the second one. . . . But such an inexhaustible wealth of fantasy one does not often happen to find in talents of great depth and breadth—and this wealth, apparently, both torments and burdens the author of *Poor Folk* and *The Double*. Hence the imaginary long-windedness which people complain about, individuals who love to read but who, incidentally, do not find *Mysteries of Paris*, *The Eternal Jew*, or *The Count of Monte Cristo* long-winded.[31] And, on the one hand, readers of this type are correct. Not everyone can know the mysteries of art . . . or how to feel and think in a profound way. Thus readers have the full right not to know either the cause or the genuine significance of that which they call "long-windedness." They know only that reading *Poor Folk* tires them somewhat but also that they like the work. *The Double*, though, not many have the strength to read to the end. This is a fact. Let the young author understand such a thing and take it as useful information.

May the god of inspiration save Mr. Dostoevsky from the proud thought of despising the opinions even of the profaners of art . . . just as may this deity save him from the degrading idea of reworking his pieces to flatter the taste of the mob. Both these extremes are the Scylla and Charybdis of talent. Aficionados of art, even if they become somewhat tired from reading *The Double*, nevertheless will not tear themselves away from the novel. . . .

Most readers say that *The Double* is a poor work, and that rumors about the unusual talent of the author are exaggerated. . . . But Mr. Dostoevsky has little cause for concern: his talent belongs to those individuals who are not acknowledged and understood right away. . . . There will be many talents who will stand apart from him, but who will disappear and be forgotten at precisely the same time that he will achieve the heights of his fame. When there appears a new story from him, these very people, with unconscious curiosity and greed, will seize upon it, knowingly, wisely, and decisively.

March 1, 1846
Alexander Nikitenko, from a review

The indisputable talent of the author of *Poor Folk* draws from the fact that he cares little for the shallow desire to render *his own* impressions, *his own* abstract or weighty thoughts on life. Rather, he wishes to understand life from personal lessons . . . to probe its cherished mysteries. . . .

We are tired of the endless abuse [in literature] brought about by invented and unimaginative fantasies, the twists and turns of daydreams and apparitions with claims to reality. [We are bored by] humorous stories, essays that give us a slanted or nearsighted view of things . . . [as well as by] dramas, novels, and the like which violate history, distort our mores, and engage in hypocrisy, lies, and exaggerations of everything including virtue and vice. . . .

Mr. Dostoevsky's novel distinguishes itself . . . as an intelligent . . . analysis of people at all levels of society and in all the phases of life. . . . From all this comes truth. . . .

We understand why one kind and intelligent woman . . . having read to the middle of *Poor Folk* said, "I am crying, I cannot finish the work." Such a simple-hearted emotion is worth more than any critical assessment. . . . Having finished the novel, you feel as though you have been on a pleasant but exhausting stroll.

March 1, 1846
Osip Senkovsky, from a review

[In *The Petersburg Miscellany*] is an article, namely, *Poor Folk*, a *novel* by Fyodor Dostoevsky—that is what this little article is called: novels have now become *tone-poems*, and little articles have now become *novels*. Of all the articles [in the anthology] *Poor Folk* is the longest— much longer than the subject of the story—but it is distinguished by a touching interest. Sometimes tiresome, *Poor Folk* is, for the most part, enjoyable. Seemingly, though, the work has frightened many people. Some have seen it as gifted—as art—the horror!—and decided to praise it right then and there. Others have decided to abuse it so as to wipe out every trace of the work altogether. Some say there is no genius [in our literature] and pronounce the author of the article to be the ranks of such individuals. And what individuals they are—the world has seen nothing like it!—it simply beats everything. Others claim that there is nothing truly extraordinary [in it] and begin to downgrade the writer, so bitter are they over the newborn talent of the writer of *Poor Folk*. . . .

The poor young man! . . . Although I confess that at first I thought that the author of *Poor Folk* was not a young person . . . and even now I am not convinced completely that the writer is not a girl—a claim that I ask you take not as a reproach but as its own kind of praise! . . . The poor young man! Why do you praise [Dostoevsky] so cruelly, why do you abuse him in such a flattering way? . . . What has he done to you? . . . He, a most modest, quiet, dear, and comely individual? He who does not even dare to speak *ore rotundo* but expounds on everything in diminutives? . . . "In the grove are *small birds* running about the *small edge of the wood* . . . so *very dear*, even *most merry*. The *little birch tree* was arrayed in such talkative and trembling little leaves . . . forcing you to jump over *the little pond* and across the grass under you *harmonically*."

The ideas are the most tiny, the details are the most minuscule, the sentences are so pristine, the small pen is so repulsive, the observations are so small, the feelings and emotions are so tender and dainty that unwillingly I cry out: this is a very sweet little talent! . . . No matter how many times I have been deceived, I have a weakness for the future of any beginning talent, and I am convinced that soon . . . Fyodor Dostoevsky will force me, with full voice and deep bass, to proclaim him a most dear writer! But meanwhile, his microscopic little words, objects, characters, and details have so narrowed and compressed my lips that I, like he, must also speak in diminutives.

March 1, 1846
Leopold Brandt, from a review

We would not burden the columns of *The Northern Bee* and the patience of readers with excerpts from assessments from *The Fatherland Notes* if, unfortunately, we were not convinced that this journal, constantly, over the course of several years, has harnessed all its energies toward spreading false and perverse ideas about poetry and art, thereby confusing both the young generation and young writers. An example of the latter we see in Mr. Dostoevsky, a storyteller not without talent but hopelessly carried away by empty and pitiful theories of that group who announces that only the "new school" writes well and that only its works are read by the public.

March 1, 1846
Leopold. Brandt, from a review

In the crowded confectionary store Izler's, on Nevsky Prospekt, there is on public view a magnificently pictorial advertisement for *The Petersburg Miscellany*.[32] At the top of this superbly drawn advertisement are bright flowers . . . and the large figures of Makar Alexeevich Devushkin and Varvara Alexeevna Dobroselova, the hero and heroine of Mr. Dostoevsky's novel *Poor Folk*. Makar is writing on his knees,

Varvara is reading letters, delighting in their torment. As noted by this advertisement, there is no doubt that *The Petersburg Miscellany*, with its themes of *envy* and *injustice*, will be a great success. . . .

March 3, 1846
Stepan Shevyryov, from a review

One cannot but marvel at the activity of our Petersburg writers! One need only to look around! Was it all that long ago that *The Physiology of Petersburg* appeared in two volumes? Now we have this colossal *Petersburg Miscellany*, so heavy for the table. Five hundred and sixty pages of small and close-set print! There is also a huge story: *Poor Folk* by F. Dostoevsky. This alone is an entire book! . . .

This is a new name in literature—Mr. Fyodor Dostoevsky! With great trumpets, journalistic rumor mills have announced his appearance. Errand boys have traveled the length and breadth of Muscovite living rooms . . . [announcing] that a star of the first magnitude has appeared in the sky of our starless literature.

As we see it, though, not only has all this hustle and bustle been in vain, but also it has harmed this new talent. A writer for one Petersburg journal was extremely just when he said that a "new talent, great or ordinary, can now step forth bravely into literature without the protection of journals and other entities. Now a new writer is acknowledged for who and what he is." So why must he be trumpeted in advance? Let him come forth peacefully: readers themselves can assess his worth. Preliminary praises can raise expectations that are not always in sync with newly arrived glory. . . .

Of course, in the almost barren field of our contemporary graceful literature, *Poor Folk* is a remarkable phenomenon. What is the theme of this work?

In our northern capital beneath the majestic world of European splendor, luxury, and comfort lies a world invisible to the eye . . . Here belong the poor clerk-copyists, the hardly noticeable screws in the big and bulky machine that is government. Nonetheless, they are people in their own right. For all of Russia, they supply an endless amount of documents necessary to run the country. They are also, though, the butt of vaudevilles, comedies, stories, satires, and sketches. . . . Hardly does an evening go by in the theaters in Moscow and Petersburg where the public does not laugh at them. . . .

In his first story, Mr. Dostoevsky . . . depicts one of these poor clerks with the most noble sentiments toward all poor people. Makar

Devushkin lives alone, in a quiet, unassuming way. He has a sheeplike heart. He loves dearly to use diminutives in his speech . . . a sign of his meekness and humility. . . . He has only one concern: he is a copyist, but by both the style of his letters, as well as by his many genuine thoughts and observations, he is, unlike Akaky Akakievch, not at all lacking in ability; indeed, he could do something else with his life.

With a most pure and compassionate love, Devushkin is tied to a another poor being, an educated girl, Varvara Dobroselova. . . .

Dostoevsky surrounds his hero with a poverty-stricken world. Everything that is unfortunate and sad touches Devushkin's heart; such things cling to him instinctively. Here also is the Gorshkov family, the organ-grinder, and the lad with a note asking for alms. . . .

Along with such innate love of humankind, though, is Makar Devushkin's ambition. He fears social opinion, he thinks a great deal about what people will say. He drinks tea only for others, for show, for social airs, because it is shameful not to drink tea. For the sake of [other] people, he wears an overcoat; shoes he needs for his honor and name. That is why he becomes so terribly angry at Gogol's [story] "The Overcoat," which stings him to the quick, touching upon his ambition. Literature which he once loved, he now begins to call trash. Seemingly, when Devushkin reads "The Overcoat," he initiates his downfall. The outrage that makes him unworthy to pursue Varvara Dobroselova he carries to the end. For the first time in his life, he gets dead drunk. . . . His fellow clerks, having learned about his friendship with Varvara via a draft of one his letters, misinterpret the tie and call him a Lovelace.[33]

[In *Poor Folk*] Varvara is an insignificant character. She is brought in as a sacrifice to the hero and arouses little human sentiment, especially at the end of the work when, marrying a gentryman by the name of Bykov, [she] informs her friend in an indifferent way and tortures him to the end with her boring instructions for her wedding.

The story is written in manifest philanthropic tones . . . particularly noticeable in the second part of the work. For this reason, we understand this work from two points of view: artistic and philanthropic.

From an artistic standpoint, we note in this narrative observation and feeling. Much about Makar Devushkin is rendered in a very truthful way. All the episodes about the poor people [in the work] are imbued with feeling, especially the story about the student Pokrovsky and his father—probably the best part of the entire story.

Devushkin's letter about the death of the Gorshkov son forces one to become lost in thought.

But does one see this piece as an original work? Initially, such a question is difficult to answer . . . The form of *Poor Folk* still shows such a sharp, irresistible imprint of Gogol that we do not see any escape from it. But one cannot indict the writer [for such a shortcoming]. The influence of Gogol is seen in a large part of our fictional and especially dramatic literature. Indeed, it is difficult for a beginning writer to escape it. The style of Makar Devushkin often recalls the style of characters put forth by Gogol. The humorous escapades [in the piece] are also so redolent of his humor. . . . In a word, the entire coloring of the story shows such a powerful influence of a teacher that we still cannot say a word about the student. What lies ahead [for Mr. Dostoevsky], we do not know.

The philanthropic aspect of *Poor Folk* is more noteworthy than the artistic one.

March 3, 1846
Stepan Shevyryov, from a review

> We do not understand how the author of *Poor Folk*, a work that is so remarkable, could write *The Double*. . . . This work is a sin against artistic consciousness. . . .
>
> [In it] one must appeal constantly to familiar characters from Gogol: Chichikov, the Nose, Petrushka . . . and Selifan.[34] But the work, assuming one gets to the end, is like a most unpleasant and boring nightmare after a rich dinner.
>
> *The Double* is not without thought. In truth, the motif is that of Makar Devushkin, but only half so: the ambition of the Russian clerk, outraged by life. . . . The theme is a rich one. . . . The Russian values what people say about him as long as they esteem his being and personality, as long as others acknowledge them. . . . [Such a thing] Peter the Great understood, and in the Russian he inculcated *ambition* . . . [when] he founded the Table of Ranks, which, although taken from another land, took hold so strongly in our native beginnings.[35]
>
> Golyadkin, a very decent clerk with an eye on marriage in a certain household, has been thrown out bodily from the place. As a result, he goes insane and sees his double everywhere he goes. Again we repeat: the idea demands an observing talent . . . but without such giftedness, it gives rise only to nightmares. . . . Mr. Dostoevsky will understand what we are saying if his talent is genuine.

March 4, 1846
Pyotr Pletnyov, from a letter to Nikolai Gogol

> Here Belinsky and Kraevsky are raving about someone named Dostoevsky. So far I know nothing about him. Can there be something to it?

March 9, 1846
Faddei Bulgarin, from a review

> From where has come this new genius, the cries about whom drown out all previous news? Here has appeared a young writer, Mr. Dostoevsky, who had written two extremely weak stories, *Poor Folk* and *The Double*. They are works that, if they had come out at any other time, would have passed unnoticed in our literature, [like] stories that appear by the hundreds in Germany and France, but without finding readers, if it were not for a party that has seized upon Mr. Dostoevsky and has raised him higher than a standing forest but lower than a passing cloud!
>
> Such a thing is laughable but all the more pitiful. What can one expect from a literature in which the spirit of a party can go to such an extreme, manifestly before the public to proclaim as works of genius trifling stories in which there is neither passionate emotion, nor imaginative force, nor a single idea. There is even no allure in the beginning or charm in the style!
>
> The two stories of Mr. Dostoevsky cannot even compare to a single story by Count Sollogub, I. I. Panaev, Count Odoevsky, or Mr. Pavlov, in a word, with a single work by our new and old writers! About them we will say no more.

March 18–21, 1846
Anna Vielgorskaya, from a letter to Nikolai Gogol

> With this courier we are also sending you Dostoevsky's story *Poor Folk*, which I liked very much. Read it, please, and give me your opinion.

Circa early spring 1846
Dmitri Grigorovich, from his memoirs

> About the Beketovs there gathered, little by little, an entire circle . . . thanks to the oldest brother, Alexei Beketov, a former schoolmate [at the Main Engineering Academy]. . . . At any one time there gathered a great many people, most of them as young as ourselves.

April–May 1846 and later
Fyodor Dostoevsky, from an 1856 letter to Edward Totleben

> For two years in a row I was sick with a strange disease, a moral one. I fell into hypochondria. There was even a time when I lost my reason. I was extremely irritable, impressionable . . . and capable of distorting the most ordinary facts and attach to them different measures and views. But I felt that although this illness had a powerfully negative influence on my fate, it would be a very poor excuse [for my behavior] and even a humiliating one.

April–May 1846 and later
Fyodor Dostoevsky, from an 1858 letter to Mikhail Katkov

> At that time, in addition to everything else, I was sick with hypochondria, often to a most powerful degree. Only youth kept me from wearing myself out, from losing my passion and love for literature.

April–early May 1846 and after
Stepan Yanovsky, from his memoirs

> When I met Dostoevsky . . . I was also treating V. N. Maykov. . . . The name F. M. Dostoevsky was on everyone's lips, the result of the smashing success of his first work, *Poor Folk*. Maykov and I often talked about him, and I always expressed my delight over his work. . . .
>
> Maykov informed me that Fyodor Mikhailovich had asked if he could see me since he, too, was sick. Of course I was overjoyed at the prospect of meeting him. On the following day, Maykov came to my office and introduced me to the person whom I would see every day until his arrest in 1849. . . .
>
> Dostoevsky was small in stature but big-boned, especially in his chest and shoulders. His head was well proportioned to his body. His forehead, though, was extremely pronounced and lined. Dostoevsky's eyes were small, bright gray, and extremely lively. His lips were thin and compressed, but they gave his face an intensely affectionate and kind expression. His hair was not so much light-colored as it was almost whitish and extremely thin and soft. The hair on his hands and legs, though, was considerably thicker.
>
> Dostoevsky was dressed simply but elegantly. He wore a splendid black jacket, a black cashmere vest, a stunningly white Dutch-style shirt, and a fashionable top hat. Two things disturbed the harmony of his appearance: his plain shoes and his awkward demeanor, like seminarians or military students who have finished their course of study.

When I examined Dostoevsky, I found that his lungs were healthy but that his heartbeat was not quite regular. His pulse was also uneven and extremely rapid, as is often the case with women or people of nervous temperament.

On the first meeting and for the next three or four visits, we were doctor and patient. But after that I asked Fyodor Mikhailovich to stop by my office earlier than his scheduled appointment so that I could talk to him at length about topics that had nothing to do with illness. The reason for this was simple. In only a short time, Dostoevsky had fascinated me with his intellect, his unusual humanity, and his extremely precise and profound analysis of people and events.

Fyodor Mikhailovich granted my request. He came by to visit on any and all days not at ten a.m. but at eight thirty; together we drank tea. After several months he started to drop by also at nine in the evening and stayed until eleven. Sometimes he even spent the night at my place. My mornings and evenings with Dostoevsky were for me unforgettable. Never in my life have I ever experienced such joyful and instructive moments.

My treatment of Fyodor Mikhailovich was rather prolonged. When his illness had been cured completely, he continued for three weeks or so to take the home-brewed medicine for the severe scurvy-like anemia that I had observed in him. During the time of his treatment, beginning in late May and continuing to mid-June, Fyodor Mikhailovich visited me on a daily basis, excluding those times when inclement weather kept him at home or when I visited him at his place.

At that time Dostoevsky lived in a very small room with a woman who took in boarders. Every morning, at first around nine a.m. and then exactly at nine thirty, the bell sounded in the foyer. I saw Fyodor Mikhailovich enter the reception room quickly, put his top hat on the first chair that was available to him, and look immediately into the mirror, his hands smoothing down his soft, light-colored hair, cut in the Russian style. Then he turned directly toward me and said:

"Well, it seems that everything is okay. Even today I am doing all right. How are you getting along, old man?" ("Old man" was a favorite and genuinely affectionate expression for Fyodor Mikhailovich, one that he pronounced in an extremely sympathetic way.)

"How does my tongue look?" Dostoevsky continued. "I seem somewhat pale, even nervous. I sleep on and off. I also have been having these hallucinations, old man, and my head hurts."

When Fyodor Mikhailovich told me such things, I examined him in a systematic way. I measured his pulse and listened to his heartbeats. Having found nothing out of place, I sought to set his mind at ease, telling him that everything was fine and that his hallucinations were from nerves. When Fyodor Mikhailovich heard such words, he became happy and content. "Of course, it is nerves," he said. "So there won't be any stroke or paralysis? That's great! After all, if a stroke doesn't strike me dead, I can cope with everything else."

With that, Dostoevsky changed his expression and mood quickly. His intense and frightened look disappeared. His tightly compressed lips relaxed and revealed his strong and healthy teeth. Dostoevsky again went up to the mirror to make sure that he was completely well. He also stuck out his tongue and said: "Yes, of course, it's just nerves. My tongue is white, not yellow! That means I am fine!"

When we sat down for tea, Fyodor Mikhailovich said: "Well, give me just half a cup without sugar. My first cup I will have this way; but my second, I will take it with sugar and a rusk." Every time he said the same thing.

At tea we talked . . . most of all about medicine, social questions, and topics on literature and art. We also spoke a great deal about religion. In such matters, Fyodor Mikhailovich impressed me—and also mutual acquaintances, all of whom were university educated and well read—with his erudition, the singular accuracy of his views, as well as his analysis of people and events in so profound a way that the evidence for his convictions we accepted unconsciously as palpable and concrete.

April–early May 1846 and after
Stepan Yanovsky, from his memoirs

Fyodor Mikhailovich also borrowed books on medicine, especially works that dealt with the nervous system and illnesses of the brain. He was also interested in studies of spiritual disorders and of the development of the cranium à la the fashionable system of Gall.[36] This last item with its drawings so engaged Fyodor Mikhailovich that he often arrived at my place in the evening to talk about the anatomy of the cranium and the brain, the physiological functioning of the brain and nerves, and the meaning of the cranial indentations and elevations to which Gall had attached such significance. Demanding from me an explanation of every nook and cranny of his skull, Fyodor Mikhailovich often extended our conversations deep into the night.

> Fyodor Mikhailovich's skull was truly splendid. His broad forehead ... sharply defined sinuses, equally pronounced edges of his eyelids, and the lack of any elevation in the lower back of his cranium made him look like Socrates. Fyodor Mikhailovich himself was very pleased with such a comparison. . . . He added: "It is a good that there are no elevations on the back of the head. That means that I am not a hat-wearer. I do not like hats at all; but I love bonnets, especially the type that Yevgenya Petrovna wears" (the mother of Apollon and other Maykovs whom we all loved and respected deeply).

April–early May 1846 and after
Stepan Yanovsky, from an 1882 letter to Anna Dostoevskaya

> I have had many good, kind, and honest acquaintances [in my life]. Some I have loved in a powerful way and considered them colleagues, even friends, the latter including Apollon Nikolaevich Maykov . . . [and] Mikhail Mikhailovich Dostoevsky.
>
> But none of them were like Fyodor Mikhailovich . . . whom I followed with my heart and soul . . . nourished by the deep humanity and striving for truth which God had endowed him with so lavishly. . . .
>
> We saw each other almost every day and talked without stopping. . . . Thanks to my friend, I have become sensitive to any lie and falsehood, as well as to a sad and burdensome feeling . . . when I come across some everyday picture . . . of our spiritual life in which truth is distorted . . . in a tendentious Khlestakov-type of way.[37]
>
> Here the image of Fyodor Mikhailovich rises before my eyes. I see his lips compressed from moral unease. I notice the movement of his right hand as he first fixes his hair and then twirls his small mustache. I even hear his voice clearly, saying—"oh, pal, how untrue, how vile"— and I, too, feel burdened and vile.

April 1, 1846
Fyodor Dostoevsky, from a letter to Mikhail Dostoevsky

> I am sending you a helmet with accessories and a pair of epaulets. The covering on the helmet is not attached because, as I was told, the shako would get ruined on the road. I do not know if I have served you well or not. If not, I am not at fault because about these things I understand absolutely nothing. I am behind the times, my friend.
>
> Now the second question. You ask why I am so late [in replying to you]. But, my dear friend, I have been so very busy that however strange it

may seem to you, I could not find time to fulfill your request. Truly, from sheer negligence, I missed two mailings. I am guilty. Do not be angry.

Now to other things, my friend. Most likely you are reproaching me for not having written to you in such a long time. But I agree completely with Gogol's *Poprishchin:* "A letter is nonsense, letters are written by pharmacists." What could I write to you? If I were to begin to speak as I would like, I would have to fill entire volumes. Every day in my life there are so many new things, so many changes, so many impressions, and so many things that are good and useful for me; there are also many unpleasant and disadvantageous things that even I myself do not have time to think them through. In the first place, I am always busy. I have tons of ideas and I am writing constantly. Do not think that I am lying completely in a bed of roses. Nonsense. In the first place, I have gone through a lot of money, i.e., exactly 4,500 rubles since we parted and 1,000 paper rubles as an advance on my future. Thus, with that tidiness of mine which you know well, I have robbed myself completely, and again am beginning to live as before, without a copeck.

But that is all right. My fame has reached an apogee. In 2 months, according to my calculations, I have been spoken about 35 times in various publications. In some of them I am praised to the skies, in others I am praised with exceptions, and in still others I am cursed to an extreme. What could be better and more noble? But here is what is vile and tormenting: our people, Belinsky, and everyone else are displeased with me over Golyadkin. The first impression was unrestrained delight, clamor, noise, and talk. The second was criticism. Specifically, everyone in the general clamor, i.e., *our people* and the entire public, have found Golyadkin to be so flaccid, boring, and so drawn out that it is impossible to read it. But what is most comical of all is the fact that everyone is angry at me for long-windedness, but also that everyone is reading and rereading me in a frenzied way. The only thing one of our people does is to spend time reading a chapter a day so as not to exhaust himself. All he does is smack his lips from pleasure. Some of the public yell that my work is quite impossible, that it is stupid both to write and to publish such things; others scream that it is taken and copied from their lives; and from still others I have heard such madrigals that it is even embarrassing to speak of them.

As for me, I was even depressed for a while. I have a terrible vice: boundless vanity and ambition. The idea that I had failed expectations and ruined a thing that could have been a great work was killing me. Golyadkin became repulsive to me. Much of it was written in haste and exhaustion. The first half is better than the last. Along with brilliant pages there is foulness and trash. It is nauseating and one does not want to read it. That is exactly what created a hell for me for a time and I fell ill from misery. Brother, I will send you Golyadkin in about two weeks. You will read it. Write me your opinion.

I am passing over my life and my *studies* and will say a bit about our news. The 1st (enormous news) is that *Belinsky* is leaving *The Fatherland Notes*.[38] He has ruined his health terribly and is heading out for the waters and, perhaps, for abroad. He will not take up criticism for about two years.[39] But to support his finances, he is publishing an almanac of *gigantic size* (60 signature pages in all).[40] For him I am writing two stories: the first, "Shaved Sideburns," and the second, "A Tale about Destroyed Offices," both with stunningly tragic interest and—I am already answering [my critics]—condensed as much as possible. These the public are waiting for with impatience. Both stories are short. In addition, I am writing something for Kraevsky and a novel for Nekrasov. All this will take me a year. I am finishing "Shaved Sideburns."[41]

The second piece of news is that an entire horde of writers has appeared on the scene. Some are my rivals. Of them Herzen (Iskander) and Goncharov are especially remarkable. The former has published, the latter is only starting out and has not yet appeared in print anywhere.[42] People praise them terribly. For the time being I am in first place and I hope I stay there forever. Generally speaking, never before has literature begun to be in full swing as now. That is all for the best.

The third piece of news is that I will visit you either very early or very late, or I will not come at all. I am in debt. I will not have any money (without money I will not come for anything), and in the third place, I am swamped with work.

The fourth piece of news is that Shidlovsky has responded. His brother visited me. I am beginning a correspondence with him.

The fifth piece of news is that if you want, my beloved friend, to earn something in the literary field, there is a chance to show off and produce an effect with one translation. Translate Goethe's *Reynard the Fox*.[43] I was even asked to entrust the translation to you, since Nekrasov needs the piece for his almanacs. If you want, translate it. Do not hurry. Even if I do not arrive by May 15th or June 1st,[44] send what you have ready. Everyone is heading off for the summer; but if it is possible,

I, perhaps, will place it somewhere even in the spring and will bring you the money. If not in the spring, then in the fall—but *definitely, without fail*. There will definitely be money. Nekrasov is a publisher, he will buy it. Belinsky will buy it, Ratkov will buy it, and Kraevsky is completely at my disposal. It is a matter of profit. People here have talked about this translation. So start, if you wish, and I will vouch for its success. If you translate roughly three chapters, send them to me. I will *show* them to the gentlemen and they will give you an advance.[45]

I have never been so rich in activity as I am now. Everything is moving along, in full swing.... But what will happen?...

Good-bye, my dear. I kiss you all and wish you all the best. I kiss both Emiliya Fyodorovna's hands. The children too. How are you? Write about yourself. Oh, my friend, I want to see you. But what can I do?

P.S. Verochka has been married 3 months already. They say happily so. Uncle [Kumanin] gave her as much as he gave Varya. She married *Ivanov* (His Excellency). He is 30 years old. He is a professor of chemistry somewhere.

April 1, 1846
Vissarion Belinsky, from a review

> *The Northern Bee* has filled [pages] with not entirely calm and collected proof that Mr. Dostoevsky has not an iota of talent. If you so agree, all the better for you. You will say such a thing and you will be at peace. But others will think that you are not sincere, and that—for whatever reason—you are afraid of a new talent.... But in so doing, you harm only yourself.

April 15, 1846
Faddei Bulgarin, from an article

> Almost all our writers are like spoiled young ladies, suffering from the *vapors*, hysteria, and appetite.

April 26, 1846
Fyodor Dostoevsky, from a letter to Mikhail Dostoevsky

> I have not written to you because up until today I have not been able to take up pen in hand. The reason for that is that I have been sick and near death in the full sense of the word ... with an irritation of the entire nervous system. The illness ... produced a rush of blood and an inflammation of the heart which was remedied barely by leeches and two bloodlettings. I also made myself worse with various concoctions,

drops, powders, and other similar abominations. Now I am out of danger . . . but my recovery will take a long time. My treatment has to be both physical and moral. In the first place, with diet and continual physical deprivations that have been prescribed for me. In the second, with a change of place, abstention from all strong shocks and sensations, a balanced and tranquil life, and finally, order in everything. To this end, a trip to Revel[46] (although not for bathing, since such an activity has been deemed harmful for me) for a change of scene and lifestyle has been prescribed as a drastic remedy. But since I do not have a copeck to my name, and I need huge amounts of money for this trip, not so much for Revel, but for expenses and payments of debt in Petersburg. So practically everything concerning my life and health depends on Kraevsky. If he gives me an advance, I will come; if not, I will not. . . .

I am writing to you in haste and on a business matter. I have a request that you should fulfill with all your energy. Belinsky is going (he left yesterday) to Moscow for the summer. Then together with his friend the actor Shchepkin and a few other people, he is taking a trip to the south of Russia, to Ukraine, and to the Crimea. He is returning in September to take care of his almanac. His wife, however, and her sister and year-old child are setting out for Gapsal.[47] Maybe I will go with them, maybe not. The ship stops at Revel for a few hours. The problem is that their household staff refuses to go to a foreign place, even for the summer. So they are left without a nanny. It is impossible to hire one here . . . except for a huge sum which Mme. Belinskaya is unable to pay. So they ask me most humbly to write . . . that you try with all your might (which I also ask) to find in Revel a nanny, *a German and not a Finn* (that is essential), and if possible an older woman who would agree to go with them to Gapsal until September. The pay will be 15 paper rubles a month. If, however, she agrees to go with them later to Petersburg, then 25 paper rubles. Mme. Belinskaya cannot pay any more than that. It goes without saying that it is quite desirable to find a woman with a good reputation, in a word, a respectable nanny. When you have found her, keep her in readiness from May 5th on, i.e., for departure at a moment's notice because . . . since the ship stops in Revel for four hours, Mme. Belinskaya will come to see you. You will send for the nanny, and the entire business will be taken care of. Everything depends on whether you agree or not. I fall before your knees to do this. I implore you for myself. I like and respect these people. I ask you most humbly that you and Emiliya Fyodorovna try your best.

Mme. Belinskaya is quite weak, aging, and ailing;[48] she is forced to travel all alone, and with a child to boot. No individual could do better than to work for them. They are good people, they live in a contented way, and they treat people superbly. For them a nanny is only a nanny and nothing else. For heaven's sake, brother, please do your best. Also answer me as soon as possible. The Belinskys may be in Revel by the 10th. Write me soon and tell me whether passengers are accepted on the ship that goes from Petersburg to Gapsal via Revel. Otherwise they will not take the nanny on board.

Before my departure I have to finish a short story for the money I borrowed from Kraevsky.[49] Then I will take an advance from him.

The enormous activity in literature is in full swing. . . . I have great hopes. When we see each other, I will tell you all about them, but for now, good-bye.

April 30, 1846
Apollon Grigoriev, from an article

In our humble opinion, *The Double* is a work that is therapeutic and pathological but also literary. It is a story of madness analyzed to an extreme, but also it is as repulsive as a corpse. . . . Having read *The Double*, we think instinctively that the author will pursue this path further. He is fated to play in our fiction the same role that Hoffmann did in German literature. Hoffmann saw . . . German bourgeois life . . . in broken, monstrous, and fantastic forms. In exactly the same way does Dostoevsky delve into the life of a civil servant so that this boring, naked reality assumes a type of raving that is close to madness. . . . We also confess that it will be unfortunate if the goal of Dostoevsky is the same as [that of] the talented but abnormal Hoffmann.

May 1, 1846
An anonymous reviewer, from an article

On Saturday there was again a reading . . . by Mr. Shchepkin. This time we regret to say that the evening was not entirely successful, despite the fact that the audience had filled the room completely. Mikhail Semyonovich was not in his best form. His first piece, Gogol's "Old-World Landowners,"[50] a work that is splendid, full of life, naturalness, and feeling, Shchepkin read in a way that we have never heard from him before. A letter from Dostoevsky's *Poor Folk* went better. But why did Shchepkin read such a thing? Mr. Dostoevsky has inalienable qualities as a writer: a profound view [of life] and a knowledge of the human heart, as well as a masterly brush [to render such things in fiction]. The scene in which Devushkin stands before his kind boss is beyond words! The fact of the matter, though, is that in his faithfulness to life, Dostoevsky comes close to daguerreotype.

May 14, 1846
Nikolai Gogol, from a letter to Anna Vielgorskaya

I have only just started *Poor Folk*. I read three pages and then peeked in the middle to see the makeup and manner of the discourse of the new writer. (You were wrong to tear out only *Poor Folk* and not send me the entire anthology.) . . . In the author of *Poor Folk*, one sees talent. The choice of subject speaks in favor of his spiritual qualities, but also to the fact that he is young. There is much garrulousness and little concentration. Everything [in the story] would have turned out in a much more lively and powerful way if it had been more compressed. Incidentally, my comments draw not from a thorough reading of the work but only from having leafed through it.

Circa mid-May 1846
Stepan Yanovsky, from an 1882 letter to Orest Miller

About ten in the evening, as was our custom, we sat down to tea . . . and Dostoevsky talked about how he was thinking of arranging his life in general . . . about why, not wanting to leave literature, he did not want to be in [state] service, and why he had abandoned his career as an engineer. . . . [He added that he intended] to write and write, and in so doing to defend the humiliated and the injured.

May 16, 1846
Fyodor Dostoevsky, from a letter to Mikhail Dostoevsky

The ladies who have delivered this message to you are Mme. Belinskaya and her most interesting sister. Please receive them well, and if possible, it would not be a bad idea to invite them to dinner. They also asked to be introduced to Emiliya Fyodorovna. As much as possible, nourish their egotism; and, of course, talk about literature as little as possible. But you yourself understand these matters better than I do. Tell them where to stay and what to do. I do not know what is better for them—to stay in Revel or move on to Gapsal.[51]

About myself I will say that I absolutely do not know what is going to happen to me. I do not have a copeck to my name and I also do not know where I can get any money. I cannot leave here unless I have specifically 500 rubles to pay off my debts. So judge for yourself. It is even more than likely that . . . I will not come [to visit you].

I find it boring and burdensome to be here. I am writing but I do not see an end to my work. I send my regards to Emiliya Fyodorovna and ask her graciousness toward the Belinsky ladies. I rely on all her indulgence and kindness. It would also not be a bad idea if for their part, Fedya and Masha[52] showed their cordiality and expressed their opinions openly, to the extent of their well-known solidarity. Well, good-bye, brother, there is no time [to write further]. I absolutely never have had a more difficult time of it [than now]. Boredom, sadness, apathy, and a feverish, convulsive expectation of something better torment me. There is also my illness. The devil knows what it is. If only all of this would somehow pass me by.

After May 16, 1846
Maria Belinskaya, from an 1862 letter to Fyodor Dostoevsky

Fifteen years have passed since the time we last saw each other. Perhaps you have forgotten about my existence, but toward you I have never stopped [having] the most friendly disposition. I have always taken a sincere interest in you.

How often do my sister and I recall you and that time when you were acquainted with my husband. With what attention did my daughter listen to you as you held her in your arms.[53]

After May 16, 1846
Fyodor Dostoevsky, from an 1862 letter to Maria Belinskaya

Your letter made an extremely pleasant impression on me. I so loved and respected your unforgettable husband and [the letter] caused me to recall everything of the best time of my life.

May 24, 1846
Fyodor Dostoevsky, from testimony to the Investigatory Commission for the Petrashevsky affair

My acquaintance [with Petrashevsky] was accidental. If I am not mistaken, I was with Pleshcheev in a candy store . . . and was reading the newspapers. I saw that Pleshcheev had stopped to speak to Petrashevsky, but I had no idea who he was. I left about five minutes later. . . . On the street Petrashevsky caught up with me and asked suddenly, "If I may be so bold as to inquire: what is the subject of your new story?"

Since Petrashevsky had not said a word to me in the candy store, I assumed that he was simply a passer-by . . . not a friend of Pleshcheev. But Pleshcheev, having caught up with us, introduced us. We spoke a bit . . . and parted. So this is how Petrashevsky attracted my curiosity. My first encounter with him was on the eve of a trip to Revel, but I saw him later that winter.

Petrashevsky seemed to [me] a very original individual, not empty. I saw his erudition, his knowledge.

May 24, 1846
Fyodor Dostoevsky, from a letter to Andrei Dostoevsky

Brother. I am leaving right now for Revel. I am sorry that I did not drop by to see you. Recently I have been keeping different apartments, and in general, disorder has overtaken my life because I am uncertain as to whether I will remain in Petersburg. You probably looked for me but did not find me. My health is not bad, but I have not recovered completely. I am leaving to take a cure. I will pass along your regards to our brother. Farewell for now.

June 14, 1846
Vissarion Belinsky, from a letter to Maria Belinskaya

From [Mikhail] Dostoevsky you can find out who are the best doctors in Revel.

June 15, 1846
An anonymous reviewer, from an article

The fabrication of geniuses which the critic of one well-known journal[54] does so successfully must willy-nilly arouse the indignation of well-thinking people. Recently Dostoevsky's prank, his *Poor Folk*, has brought more harm than good to the author of this extremely remarkable but far from brilliant piece.

June 24, 1846
Nikolai Yazykov, from a letter to Nikolai Gogol

Tell me your opinion of Dostoevsky's story [*Poor Folk*]. Piter's[55] critics and scribblers are praising it to the skies. The story is rather long, and I do not feel like reading it for the hell of it. You who are always tormented by a thirst for reading will read it, no matter what. Pletnyov says that Dostoevsky is among your imitators and that the distance between you and him is the same as between Karamzin and Prince Shalikov! That is a devil of a difference!

Circa July 1846 and after
Alexei Pleshcheev, from an 1888 letter to Apollon Maykov

> The distant past breaking into my memory, I, with special pleasure, pause at that time when I, still a beginner, encountered in your family such warm welcome and approval. What a shining time in literature. The usual visitors and friends at your home were I. A. Goncharov and F. M. Dostoevsky, both of whom read their works.

Circa July 1846 and after
Ivan Goncharov, from his memoirs

> The home [of N. A. Maykov] brimmed with life. . . . Young scholars, musicians, and artists . . . crowded . . . in shelter-like rooms. Together with the host and hostess, they were like a family or school in which everyone taught everyone else, exchanging ideas as well as news of science and art that engaged Russian society at the time.

Circa July 1846 and after
Alexander Skabichevsky, from his memoirs

> The members of the Maykov family . . . were severely balanced individuals . . . who housed a private intellectual egoism and, from time to time, an adequate dose of spiritual callousness. [Such shortcomings] they mitigated with societal tact and deportment so that everyone, from the highest to the lowest, found them to be very easygoing and pleasant. Indeed, to us youths, it would have been difficult to find people who were more progressive, idealistic, and humane. Here was the greatest "harmony" of all the elements of human nature . . . the quintessence of a truly enlightened ethics which took the place of the dilapidated, commonplace morality which we had rejected.
>
> To a man [and woman], all the Maykovs were Epicureans, exacting connoisseurs of everything that was graceful and elegant. They were also gourmets who ate and drank in a fairly tasteful way. All the Maykovs were also contemplative types, with a touch of sentimentality. Father Maykov . . . supplied icons for St. Isaac's Cathedral and other churches in St. Petersburg, so much so that he hovered in a world of celestial beings, with eyes that sometimes showed sadness. His eldest son, Apollon, was filled with chaste sounds and prayers. He loved to be

carried away by his own poetic imagination, by classical antiquity and medieval knighthood. He descended . . . into reality only to imitate the love motifs of Heine or to sing the great feats of his world.

The middle son, Vladimir, was also inclined toward introspection. His job as an administrator in the Department of External Trade so seduced him that his wife, who possessed a more lively and passionate temperament . . . ran off to the Caucasus with a nihilist whom Goncharov punished . . . in the person of Mark Volokhov in his novel *The Precipice*. . . .[56]

The younger Maykov brother, Leonid . . . lacked any brilliant or even outstanding gifts. He was a sincere and assiduous researcher-bibliographer . . . who once directed his intellectual gifts at the untalented Tredyakovsky, his prolix *Telemachus*. . . .[57] If he held such visible posts as assistant to the director of the public library, the vice president of the Academy of Sciences, and the chair of the ethnographic division of the Geographical Society . . . it was, for the most part, due to the protection and powerful ties of his brother Apollon . . . who as a youth had achieved glory and fame in the praises of highly placed individuals.

Circa July 1846 and after
Albert Starchevsky, from his memoirs

In all respects, the Maykov family was a model and splendid group, the likes of which people dream about in French novels and stories. . . . It consisted of six people, but almost daily, beginning with dinner until late at night, it embraced a respectful society.

The head of the family, Nikolai Apollonovich Maykov, was the son of Ap. Al. [Apollon Alexandrovich] Maykov, the well-known director of the imperial theaters in the beginning of the century. He was a retired officer, a handsome brunet, with an open and kindhearted disposition. He was married to Yevgenya Petrovna [Maykova] . . . a shapely, beautiful brunette, with an oblong aristocratic face, which was mirrored in her second son, Valerian. After he married, N. A. Maykov retired and lived in Moscow. When the time came to educate his sons, he moved to Petersburg.

While still in Moscow, N. A. Maykov began to take up painting as a lover of art and a self-taught student. In Petersburg he dedicated himself to this undertaking fully. One time he set out for the flea market in Apraksin Court, where formerly masses of ancient small shops housed books, drawings, and pictures in oils, large and small. There he suddenly came across a small picture, cut from a steel form and featuring a well-known Catholic *Virgo immaculata* or something of that kind, with the Most Holy Virgin trampling a snake with her foot. N. A. bought the engraving and from it began to draw a picture in oil colors. Soon there was ready another wondrous image . . . which, with the approval of Tsar Nikolai Pavlovich, was placed behind the altar in the new Troitsky Monastery. . . .[58]

His reputation as an artist solidified . . . N. A. soon painted several more icons for the Troitsky Izmailovsky Cathedral,[59] as well as for the Small Church of the Winter Palace, which had been restored after the famous fire.[60] Finally he completed an order for the left side of the iconostasis for St. Isaac's Cathedral. The colors that N. A. Maykov [used for his icons] were highly singular, and although his drawings and compositions offended many, he was given additional work for St. Isaac's Cathedral.

At that time, all the young Maykovs were students at the university. . . . N. A. Maykov was roughly fifty years old. Yevgenya was about forty. To the highest degree, they were cordial, pleasant, and welcoming. The oldest son, Al. Nik., was still a very young man, a small version of his father. Early in life he showed a poetic talent which later made him famous. The second son, Valerian, was distinguished by a great capacity for sociopolitical journalism, but at that time he was just spreading his wings when accidental death cut short the life of this very gifted and talented youth. The third son, Vladimir Nikolaevich, called the "little old man" because of his quiet and serene nature, was not as gifted and still in high school. The fourth, Leonid Nikolaevich, was still a boy at the time.

The Maykov family also included the younger brother of Nik. Apol., Konstantin Apol., a colonel in the Izmailovsky Regiment[61] and director of the military academy who often visited his brother's home and spent entire evenings with young people there. There was also Natalya Alexandrovna Maykova, the widow of one of N. A.'s brothers[62] . . . the daughter of a well-known writer, poet, and journalist of the twenties,[63] a lady who was superbly educated, well bred, and gifted with superb external features and wit. She was the inspector for the Catherine Institute and was known personally to Empress Alexandra Fyodorovna. . . . There were also people who were engaged in science, art, and literature.

The gentility, openness, humor, and cordiality of the hosts, together with their ability to keep conversations going with lively episodes and digressions . . . greatly affected the young visitors who came to the

> Maykov home. . . . In their circle one heard vulgar talk or anecdotes with double meanings. No one was censured, condemned, or ridiculed. Everyone made merry, and they were free, easy, and engaged. Only unwillingly did regular visitors make for their hats at three in the morning to head home.
>
> Also at the Maykovs' home . . . were readings of prominent individuals in contemporary journalism, together with critical and other comments on matters at hand. . . .
>
> Ivan Alexandrovich Goncharov . . . announced once evening that before he published his first piece, *A Common Story*, he wanted to read it at the Maykovs' home for comments . . . that were precise, open, and unrestrained . . . from close friends and well-wishers.

Circa July 1846 and after
Stepan Yanovsky, from a letter to Anna Dostoevskaya

> At the salon of the Maykovs . . . Fyodor Mikhailovich prevailed . . . with his characteristic atomic analysis, delving into the character of works by Gogol, Turgenev, and his own Prokharchin, which at that time most readers did not understand.

July 1846
Pyotr Bilyarsky, from a review

> Regarding *The Double* by Mr. Dostoevsky . . . never again will we like to see similar abuses of talent and effort. . . . The conversation of the characters in this story transcends all borders of decency . . . a meld of curses and oaths . . . intolerable for educated readers.

July 1, 1846
Valerian Maykov, from a review

> [Dostoevsky's] Mr. Golyadkin Senior is as remarkable and as universal as Chichikov or Manilov.[64] A large number of acquaintances and even yourself, you call Golyadkin.

July 12, 1846
Vissarion Belinsky, from a letter to Maria Belinskaya

> So, your trip to Revel did not bring you any pleasure or advantage because . . . you hoped, mistakenly, to find in Revel a servant and risked going there without one. . . .
>
> The apprehension of [your sister] Agrafena [Orlova] that I babble on to Dostoevsky that his relatives are wishy-washy is completely

unfounded. I would be not a chatterbox but a fool if I did not consider myself correct to laugh at Dostoevsky in the eyes of people who are close to him, and who . . . were kind to you. On this account, I can assure you.

August 15–18, 1846
Ferdinand Loeve, from a review in German

> Russian literature, and contemporary Russian life in general, has this advantage, i.e., it has never followed the model of a single people. From the beginning it has found . . . all the riches of the European spiritual soul. From study and assimilation, Russian literature has acquired something universal, but at the expense of originality.
>
> Other European countries have crossed the marked borders of national life. Gradually they have achieved a degree of spiritual linkage and ethical exchange. They have seemingly risen from the personal to the general. The Russian people, though, the leading light of the Slavic tribes . . . has gone backwards. . . . It has returned to its personal essence. Without singing praises, beloved by so many Slavophiles and Slavomaniacs . . . world history has decided on a new experiment.
>
> [With] the entrance of the Slavic tribes in the community of nations, [we see] . . . works of the Slavic spirit . . . [that] have been successful in informing national creativity with . . . European culture. Pushkin is first in poetry. . . . He has penetrated the secret depths of the Russian genius. . . . He has brought Russian literature, adrift in the waves of the European cultural sea, to the shores of national verse. His cultural talent does not fear comparisons with the greatest names [in art]. . . .
>
> We agree fully with [the people at] *The Fatherland Notes* who champion Pushkin, Gogol, and Krylov. . . . The works of this triumvirate are the core, the truthful source of Russian poetry. . . . The author of the novel that we will discuss does not tap into this source in a complete way. In no way, though, . . . [is he] an imitator. . . . Similar to Goethe's *Werther*,[65] the tone and structure of *Poor Folk* are so original that we, without hesitation, align these two works . . . in their sentimentality.
>
> *Poor Folk* by Dostoevsky is a most successful attempt to represent artistically the [Russian] national character in its current phase of development. . . .
>
> The hero of the novel . . . is a clerk, a titular counselor, a poor individual. . . . The colleagues in his department ridicule him. They pour

papers over his head and so forth. He is for them . . . the symbol of the simple soul, a target for the most coarse witticisms. With touching resignation, this hero has become reconciled to his sorrowful situation. . . . He is a copier of documents. . . . His behavior is undistinguished and unnoticed. His demands do not exceed his finances. His external image is extremely unpretentious. . . . What interest can such an individual attract?

The appeal is found in a belated flowering . . . of a highly forceful spiritual existence. At forty-four years old and thirty years of work . . . in his clerk-like soul, in his scrivener-like heart . . . there shines . . . a creative flame that forces his parched and withered soul . . . to burn with new life. . . .

The idea to portray an individual who is despised by all; who is misunderstood by himself and others; and who, in burdensome and depressing circumstances, has managed to preserve in his heart the full force of emotions . . . [and] the spark of love . . . is truly genius-like . . . [as well as] Christian in universal and historical significance. . . .

Varvara Alexeevna Dobroselova is a young orphan whom Makar, from pure empathy, saves from a depraved woman. . . . [but who] beautiful and innocent . . . becomes the object of courting by one Bykov. . . . Can an individual . . . find sufficient strength . . . to defend herself against an unworthy man?

Is it the complexity of the problem that has so attracted the writer? . . .

The first letter of Makar Alexeevich shows his new mood. He is the philanthropic savior of Varvara Alexeevna. . . . He tries to express his spiritual surge. He rejoices in the splendid morning, the bright sun, the singing of the birds, the smells of the spring air, of all nature. Suddenly he lapses into clerk-like prose: "Well, everything is as it should be; everything is in order, in a spring-like way." He comes up with comparisons: "I liken you to a heavenly bird . . . to an ornament of creation." He admits openly that he has run to a book for his lines. . . .

With joy he moves from a comfortable dwelling . . . to his current noisy and dirty little room . . . [so that] he can look at Varvara's windows to see if she is nearby. Makar Alexeevich . . . has begun to live only for her. In complete selflessness, he asks her about her . . . important and unimportant affairs . . . to drop if only one word about some delight so that he may not rest until he acquires it [for her]. . . . He forgets himself to find his being in her. . . .

But the spark that glows warmly in the ashes of everyday and petty cares . . . cannot burst into youthful flame. The love of our Makar moves to a warm and heartfelt sensitivity, to a simple-souled worship of a beloved entity . . . [whose] spiritual beauty he cannot attain. He thirsts to penetrate into the very depths of this feminine soul. . . . It is better for him to receive than give. . . .

Makar Alexeevich understands that Varvara has been given to him only as a friend. . . . The hundred variants . . . of his gentle unhurriedness, his distinctive tenderness . . . afford him the full and seductive possibility of moving his most passionate feelings to innocent forms of fatherly, kindred attachment. . . . Despite her fleeting requests, he, with most noble delicacy, refuses to meet her other than in a completely innocent place. Such is the modesty of an individual who knows his moral worth. . . .

Makar Alexeevich feels himself to be equal to his friend, although she is the one who helps him to realize such a thing. He expresses this feeling . . . openly and straightforwardly, often with comic pathos. His sole conviction is that he cannot instill passion or offer riches, youth, or rank. . . . He often says that he is an uneducated person, that he has no "style." . . . [Such a view] impedes . . . his declarations of love and his pretenses to marriage to which Varvara would, perhaps, agree if he were not so delicate . . . and remind her that he is her benefactor, her savior. . . .

If Makar Alexeevich had grown up in favorable circumstances, if he had been supported by good people . . . he could have become an excellent poet, an artist who would engage life in a practical way. Now he is only a machine for letters. Such a thing he realizes with bitterness. . . . He begins to ask . . . Why do his colleagues mock him while Varvara respects him, she who is better than them all? Did he ever "jump rank"? Did he not, by the sweat of his brow, earn his own bread? Did he always hold himself a bit more aloof from their liberal ideas? . . .

Varvara deserves a crown for her charming femininity. . . . She is offered a post as a governess . . . but she is too independent, too awkward, too retiring, and too wounded to live among others. Makar is against such an idea. . . . He explains to her how he will feel abandoned, how he will do everything for her so as not to let her go. . . . But he cannot save his Varenka from poverty . . . from shame. . . . His attack against an unjust world order recalls the behavior of the noble knight from La Mancha. . . .

Our poor friend loses courage. His stance toward Varenka moves to suspicion and taunts. He falls into temptation and despair. For the first time in years of irreproachable service and righteous living, he finds himself in the hands of the police. . . . He carouses in a tavern while she suffers. . . .

On his gloomy horizon, there shines still another saving light—none other than his "excellency" who . . . drops a hundred-ruble banknote in the palm of [the clerk's] hand. . . . Makar Alexeevich writes to Varenka that . . . what is important to him is not the hundred rubles but that "his excellency" has pressed the hand of a "blockhead and drunkard." . . .

In his dreams, Makar paints a radiant future. He asks God for forgiveness for all his sins. . . . He promises Varenka that he will be prudent. He reminds her of the possibility of living in harmony and happiness with the exchange of "happy letters" . . . and with reading literature.

But at the very height of his dreams and hopes, the poor man suffers a final terrible blow.

Bykov comes to Petersburg and offers Varenka his hand and heart. Does she ask advice from her friend? No, she decides her fate herself. . . . She writes to her friend that she has given an affirmative answer [to Bykov] and that her decision is final. . . .

What has forced our Varenka to take this decisive step? . . . Continuation of a tie with Makar Alexeevich is impossible. . . . Her nature is ordered so precisely, her emotions are so noble, that they would disappear in the rather effeminate character of Makar. . . .

Poor Devushkin . . . is crushed. . . . His final letter [to Varenka] is a cry of despair, written in bed, in sickness. . . . Our Russian Werther is a splendid sufferer. . . .

Poor Folk is an outstanding book, full of thoughts and reflections. . . . In it a completely new language has entered Russian literature. It is not the variegated style of Pushkin, nor the wise brevity of Krylov, nor the warm . . . and sharp speech of Gogol. It is everyday communication in the very highest sense of this word. The author has appealed to the language of the people as his personal style. He has discovered in it profoundly new aspects. His heroes speak exactly as would Russians of their rank and station. . . .

Reading *Poor Folk*—we hope it will become a national work—Russians will hear themselves. In a most elevated and complete way, they will be uplifted. . . . Surely can . . . Dostoevsky not also be called a national poet, since he infuses his subject with the spirit of his nation?

In a decisive way, we affirm this great contribution of Mr. Dostoevsky to the literature of his land. . . . He has shown that he knows the life of the heart. He can follow the most precise movements of the soul. . . . He puts forward feeling and thinking people in circles that are hidden [from public view]. He has opened our eyes to the eternal core of national morality. . . .

Early September 1846
Konstantin Trutovsky, from his memoirs

Fyodor Mikhailovich once stayed with me at my apartment for a few days. . . . When he was about to go to bed, he always asked me that if he fell victim to his lethargy, he not be buried for at least three days. Thoughts about lethargy always disturbed and terrified him.

September 1, 1846
Valerian Maykov, from a review

What an impression [Gogol's] *Dead Souls* . . . must have made [on Dostoevsky]. . . . Indeed, if the writer of *The Double* had been born eight years earlier, would he be the psychologist he is now?

September 5, 1846
Fyodor Dostoevsky, from a letter to Mikhail Dostoevsky

I hasten to inform you, dear brother, that I somehow made it back to Petersburg and as I had wished, I am staying with Trutovsky. I did not experience any seasickness, but on the way and here in Petersburg I got soaked to the skin and caught one hell of a cold. I have a cough, a head cold and all of that to the highest degree. In the beginning I was depressed terribly. . . . A terrible sadness has taken hold of me.

The Belinskys arrived without any problems and since docking I have not yet seen them. On the next day I dropped by to see Nekrasov. He and the Panaevs live in the same apartment,[66] and thus I got to see everyone. . . .

In the next month's issue of *The Contemporary*, Gogol will publish an article—his spiritual will, in which he rejects all his works and considers them useless and even more than that.[67] He says that he will not take up the pen for the rest of his life because his business is praying. He agrees with all the opinions of his opponents. He orders that his portrait be printed in a huge number of copies and that the profits from them be designated for financial assistance to travelers to Jerusalem and so forth. So that's that. Draw your own conclusions.

I was also at Kraevsky's. He has begun setting "Prokharchin." It will appear in October. So far I have not spoken about money. He is sweet and playful. . . .

It is raining terribly outside and therefore difficult to go out. I am still living at Trutovsky's, but I am moving to an apartment tomorrow. It also has been absolutely impossible to see about an overcoat [for you] because of all the errands and rain. I want to live in a most modest way. I wish the same for you. One needs to accomplish things little by little. We will live a bit and see. And now good-bye. I am in a hurry. I would like to write a great deal, but sometimes it is better not to speak. Write. I am expecting a reply from you in the shortest possible time. Kiss the children. Give my regards to Emiliya Fyodorovna. Also give my regards to anyone whom you should. I will write you more in the next letter. This is just a note. Good-bye, I wish you all the best, my priceless friend—and most important for the time being, patience and health.

September 11, 1846
Pyotr Pletnyov, from a letter to Yakov Grot

On Tuesday I spent the entire day . . . reading *The Fatherland Notes*. There are only wonders in there. Lermontov is already obsolete. . . . and Dostoevsky stands higher than he.

September 17, 1846
Fyodor Dostoevsky, from a letter to Mikhail Dostoevsky

I am sending you an overcoat. Forgive me for being so late. The delay was not my fault. I was looking for my servant and found him finally. I could not buy it without him. The overcoat has its virtues and inconveniences. The virtue is that it is unusually full, in fact, double the normal size; and the color is good, the best for a uniform, gray; the shortcoming is that the material sells for only 8 paper rubles. There was nothing better. But it cost only 82 paper rubles. The remaining money was used for mailing. There was nothing else I could do. There was material at 12 paper rubles, but the color was bright steel-blue. It was excellent, but you would have rejected it. But I do not think you will dislike the one I am sending you. It's still a bit long, though.

Because of the overcoat, I have not written to you until now. I already announced to you that I have rented an apartment. Things are not bad; only I will have almost no means in the future. Kraevsky just gave me 50 silver rubles, and judging from his look, he will not give me any more. I am going to have to endure a great deal.

"Prokharchin" has been disfigured terribly at a certain place. The gentleman of this certain place forbade even the word *bureaucrat* and only God knows why. Even as it was, everything was extremely innocent and things were crossed out everywhere. Anything living in the piece has disappeared. There remains only the skeleton of what I read to you. I am renouncing my story.

I have not heard anything new. Everything is as before. People are waiting for Belinsky.[68] Mme. Belinskaya sends her regards. All ventures . . . seem to have been put on hold; or perhaps they are being kept a secret—only the devil knows.

We are pooling our resources for dinners. Six friends have gathered at the Beketovs', including Grigorovich and me. Each one contributes 15 silver copecks a day, and we have two simple dishes for dinner and are satisfied. As a result, dinner costs me no more than 16 rubles.

I am writing to you in haste. Because I am running late, and the servant is waiting with the package to take to the post office. I have even more nonsense than when your teeth ache. I am very much afraid that the overcoat will come too late for you. But what can I do? I tried as hard as I could.

I am still writing "Shaved Sideburns." The thing is going so slowly. I am afraid that I will be late with it. I have heard from two gentlemen, from the second Beketov and Grigorovich, that *The Petersburg Miscellany* is known in the provinces exclusively as *Poor Folk*. No one wants to know about the other things in the work, although they snatch it up out there like crazy, outbidding each other and paying a high price from people who have been lucky enough to get a copy. In the bookstores, for instance, in Penza and Kiev,[69] it officially costs 25 and 30 paper rubles. What a strange fact: here it just sits and there you cannot get it.

Grigorovich has written an amazingly good story,[70] through my efforts and those of Maykov, who, by the way, wants to write a long article about me by January 1st,[71] the story will be published in *The Fatherland Notes*, which also, by the way, has become completely impoverished. The people there do not have a single story in reserve.

I am seized by a most terrible angst. . . . Give me something good and with my character I will make it worse. I wish Emiliya Fyodorovna happiness and, most important, health. I want that sincerely. I think about all of you a great deal. Yes, brother, money and security are great things. I kiss my niece and nephew. Well, good-bye. I will write more in the next letter. And now, for God's sake, do not be angry with me. And be healthy and don't eat a lot of beef.

P.S. Try to eat as healthily as possible, and please without mushrooms, mustard, and other similar junk. For God's sake, do not eat so much.

September 17, 1846, and after
Dmitri Grigorovich, from his memoirs

Everyone, in equal degree, was drawn to Alexei Nikolaevich [Beketov]. He was goodness and straightforwardness incarnate, with a developed mind and passionate soul that was outraged by any injustice and that was open to any noble and honest striving.

For the most part, gatherings [at the Beketovs' home] were in the evening. Among the many guests (sometimes as many as fifteen individuals) . . . rarely did the conversation focus on a single subject. Rather, as soon as someone raised a question, everyone touched upon it in his own way. For the most part, people broke up into groups, each with separate conversations. But no matter who spoke, or what the topic was, or whether it concerned events in Petersburg, in Russia, or abroad, or a literary or artistic question, one felt in everything a burst of fresh power, the living nerve of youth, and the appearance of enlightened thought which was borne suddenly, in an enlarged passionate brain. Everywhere one heard an indignant, noble onrush against oppression and injustice. The arguments were heated, but never wound up in fights, thanks to the older Beketov, who managed immediately to reconcile opposing individuals or groups, to being about peace and agreement. Youth, flaring with singular lightness and carried away with liveliness, added much to the meetings. Often, when people had had their fill of talking and exclaiming to the extreme, someone suggested a walk, a recommendation to which everyone agreed gladly.

One time, we as a group . . . set out on foot to Pargolovo and spent the night on Parnassus Hill overlooking a lake.[72] Everyone had to provide some kind of provisions. . . . Even now I find it pleasurable to recall the trip. All along the way and throughout the night . . . merriment rained down in a stream; happiness was in everyone's heart. . . . One heard songs, witticisms, amusing stories, and incessant laughter. The lake at Pargolovo, I think, never saw such exuberance.

[In our discussions] personal pride always served as the prime motivator. Constantly to keep one's mind on guard, not to appear dumber than others, to pursue a thought, to support or dispute it publicly—all this, to a significant degree, aroused the consciousness, sharpened the mind, and "shook up the brains."

September 17, 1846, and after
Dmitri Grigorovich, from his memoirs

> Until I became a regular member [of the Beketov circle], my intellectual capacities had developed in a fog. Conversations with Dostoevsky never had gone beyond the boundaries of literature; all the interests of life had been focused on that alone. . . . I had never thought about anything at all seriously; social questions had not interested me in the slightest. . . . Many things that had never entered my mind previously now began to concern me: the living word, sobering up the mind from frivolity, I first heard only here, in the Beketov circle.

September 17, 1846, and after
Dmitri Grigorovich, from an 1853 letter to Mikhail Dostoevsky

> Truly, the Beketov home will be the same fulfilling corner for you as it was for many of our acquaintances.

September 17, 1846, and after
Stepan Yanovsky, from an 1882 letter to Anna Dostoevskaya

> A salon to which everyone [came] . . . to talk . . . about literature . . . to discuss what they considered necessary to develop fictional writing . . . to direct the thoughts of individuals to sober and salutary paths . . . to polish talent and creativity . . . was found in the family of Yevgenya Petrovna and Nikolai Apollonovich Maykov. . . .
> Among its regular visitors were individuals who, in our present time, are known not only in Russia but also in Europe. In the group were first the accomplished and *do nec ultra* human and attractive hosts with their richly talented family, and then I. A. Goncharov, St. Sem. Dudyshkin, M. A. Yazykov, or unforgettable Fyodor Mikhailovich, M. M. Dostoevsky, N. A. Nekrasov, and an entire pleiad of friends, contemporaries, and colleagues who all at the time worked in our best periodical editions and who were developing their talents and gifts and which I have already said without thinking were polishing them precisely in this salon.
> I learned of the salon of Yev. P. and N. Ap. Maykov in the forties, but as people told me, it had existed in Petersburg much earlier. When I became acquainted with the Maykovs—the parents—they at that time had just lost their elder son Valerian. The sudden and recent passing of this especially gifted and still quite young son had such a shattering effect on the parents, and especially on the tender and extremely delicate organism of his mother, so much so that family and friends feared for her life.

136 PART II

September 17, 1846, and after
Vasily Bervi-Flerovsky, from his memoirs

> [The Beketovs] were extremely serious people who later became well-known scholars. Like Petrashevsky, they propagated the study of Fourier.[73]

September 17, 1846, and after
Vasily Bervi-Flerovsky, from his memoirs

> The Beketovs were an extremely capable family. One of them was a botanist and a well-known rector of Petersburg University. Another was a chemist and a member of the Academy of Sciences. A third . . . having graduated from the institute of communications entered [state] service. One time someone brought him money and said, "This is in addition to your salary." "What addition?" he asked. It seems that the engineers had a general cashbox which contained bribes paid by various people. The funds were dispersed among the engineers, according to rank and occupation. Beketov refused the money, thereby ruining his career.

September 17, 1846, and after
Nikolai Beketov, from an 1877 letter to Fyodor Dostoevsky

> I have not forgotten you, although I was only nineteen years old when we went our separate ways. Since that time, you have continued your tireless study of the human soul. To read your works is to converse with one's conscience . . . [to] discern a universal and all-embracing meaning. How splendid to share with the public your spiritual understanding of all that is going on around you.

September 17, 1846, and after
Nikolai Beketov, from an 1878 letter to Fyodor Dostoevsky

> How delightful to receive a letter from you and to know that the tie between us has not been broken. Like you, I recall . . . in our time together . . . your personality standing out in a clear and definite way.

Between September 21 and 26, 1846
Nikolai Nekrasov, from a letter to Vissarion Belinsky

> Dostoevsky has given a story to Kraevsky, but I do not know when he will give one to you.[74]

PART THREE

The Psycho-Spiritual Turn
The Double, *"Mr. Prokharchin," "The Landlady,"* and *"A Novel in Nine Letters"*

Fyodor Dostoevsky wrote *The Double* in 1846 and "Mr. Prokharchin," "The Landlady," and "A Novel in Nine Letters" in 1847. Sadly, not one of these works met with the success of his first piece, *Poor Folk*. Indeed, to readers and reviewers, Dostoevsky seemed to have regressed as a writer and perhaps to have lost his fictional touch altogether. There were valid reasons for disenchantment. If the hero and heroine in *Poor Folk* had captivated audiences with groundbreaking depictions of Russian urban life, the lead characters in *The Double*, "Mr. Prokharchin," "The Landlady," and "A Novel in Nine Letters" confused them with timeworn portrayals of mania and madness, roguery and romance that related little to contemporary life. Readers and reviewers moved from a clerk, Golyadkin, who, à la E. T. A. Hoffmann, invokes a maddening double; to another clerk, Prokharchin, who, à la Dickens, is a miser with visions of the past; to a young man, Ordynov, who, à la fairy tales and courtly novels, seeks to rescue a maiden, Katerina, from a wizard, Murin; and finally to two cardsharps, Ivan Pyotrovich and Pyotr Ivanovich, who, à la Pushkin and Gogol, scheme against everyone including each other.

Making matter worse, readers and reviewers of *The Double*, "Mr. Prokharchin," "The Landlady," and "A Novel in Nine Letters" had to slog their way through fractured plots, tortured prose, and bizarre thoughts and deeds. Readily did they join with Belinsky and company to consign Dostoevsky to oblivion.

It is only when they are measured against Dostoevsky's later works that the value of *The Double*, "Mr. Prokharchin," "The Landlady," and "A Novel in Nine Letters" becomes clear. Each in its own way was a significant exercise in which Dostoevsky probed minds, hearts, and souls to understand human faults and failings. Each in its own way was a link in the admittedly long and weighty chain that brought Dostoevsky to greatness. With apologies to Belinsky and company, Dostoevsky, in these four works, asserted that it was not political, social, and economic injustices that wreaked havoc on society but rather the psychological and spiritual traumas of individuals that, like the steady drop of Chinese water torture, eroded humankind, if not overwhelmed it in biblical floods.

At the basis of *The Double*, "Mr. Prokharchin," "The Landlady," and "A Novel in Nine Letters" are heroes who are alone, adrift, and ambivalent about their place in society. The first three stories are particularly striking vis-à-vis self and other. Golyadkin, Prokharchin, and Ordynov personify paranoia, anxiety, and guilt. They view the world as conspiracy, not community. They rage that they, the meek, do not inherit the earth so much as consume it. They want love, attention, and respect from without to assuage the pain and emptiness from within.

The heroes of *The Double*, "Mr. Prokharchin," and "The Landlady" believe in a good defense as the best offense. Their armor is diverse and intriguing. Money and mask, pose and posturing, camouflage and charade take their place among idées fixes, delusions of grandeur, and aggression, active and passive. Speech is a particular weapon of mass destruction. Ceaseless orations, convulsive outbursts, and numbing repetitions move in sync with syntactic jumbles, lexical breakdowns, and telegraphic ellipses and dashes. Furthermore, the heroes of the four works after *Poor Folk* slash and burn with impunity. They feel no remorse for their sins. They also commit mayhem from bloodlust, without recourse to the theories, manifestos, and ideas that promoted "extraordinary beings," justified ends, and challenged God and creation that moved their counterparts in Dostoevsky's mature fiction to crime and punishment.

Unsurprisingly, the heroes of *The Double*, "Mr. Prokharchin," and "The Landlady" fail miserably at mastering their fates. Not knowing whether they want to be in or out of society, at war or at peace with the world, they fall somewhere in between. Physically, socially, and spiritually, they never find a place to call home. They are their own worst enemies. They live lives of noisy desperation. They tilt at windmills and bite hands that feed them. They count and discount what others say about them. They spurn the very people and things they say they desire.

The heroes of these stories come to bad ends—or dead ends. Never do they know a moment's peace. They experience fevers and trances, nightmares and hallucinations. They encounter thunderbolts and bombshells and see specters and ghosts. They engage in sadomasochism and commit sins of omission and commission. They offer brazen excuses, false confessions, and *apologiae pro sua vita*. Hysterics and hyperbole negate sensibility and sense. Eros and fantasy void affection and love.

On good days, the heroes in the next four works after *Poor Folk* engage in endless monologues; on bad days, they drown in streams of consciousness. They die, go insane, or return to their pain and distress, sadder but dumber for their experience. Indeed, they never learn from their mistakes.

The heroes of *The Double*, "Mr. Prokharchin," "The Landlady," and "A Novel in Nine Letters" may have been done for in life but not in literature. Rather, they reappear in Dostoevsky's later fiction. Golyadkin, in his verbal sputtering between Senior and Junior, rants and raves of the hero in *Notes from the Underground*. Prokharchin prefigures Alexei in *The Gambler* and Arkady in *A Raw Youth* in his idea that money conquers all, as well as Raskolnikov in *Crime and Punishment* in his stance as Napoleon, and in his tortured dreams of accusers, real and imagined. Ordynov presages Ivan Karamazov as a philosopher cum "system." He also competes with Murin for Katerina in much the same way Fyodor contends with Dmitri for Grushenka in *The Brothers Karamazov*. Murin, as the first epileptic in Dostoevsky's fiction, sets the stage for the seizure-prone Prince Myshkin in *The Idiot* and Alyosha in *The Brothers Karamazov*. He again comes to the fore in Stavrogin in *Devils* as a dark, demonic figure who destroys all in his path. Ivan Petrovich and Pyotr Ivanovich foretell Luzhin in *Crime and Punishment* and Pyotr Verkhovensky in *Devils* as solid citizens with squalid schemes. Equally important are the narrators in these early stories who portend the tellers of later tales in that they—flippant and fickle, ridiculing and rambling—exacerbate the chaos in the narrative.

It is to be regretted that Belinsky and company, together with other readers and reviewers of "The Double," "Mr. Prokharchin," "The Landlady," and "A Novel in Nine Letters," did not live to see Dostoevsky achieve greatness. If they had, they would likely have set aside their differences with the writer and understood, even applauded, what he had done in his early writing. They would have seen that in these four works, the young Dostoevsky, however slowly and awkwardly, was moving from empiricism to epistemology, from physics to metaphysics, from the terra firma of political, social, and economic concerns to the muck and mire of human anger, rebellion, and despair. They would again have put him on a pedestal not as a creature of their own making but as one of the greatest writers of their land and time.

October 1, 1846
Ivan Panaev, from a letter to Nikolai Ketcher

> Belinsky's anthology (*Leviathan*) will not come to be. . . . Simply, without ceremony, the local gentlemen have announced that they cannot give to Belinsky the articles they promised to him (Dostoevsky, Goncharov, and others). They say that they are poor and need the money right away, but from Belinsky they have only distant hopes for funds.[1]

October 5–8, 1846
Alexander Herzen, from a letter to Nikolai Ogaryov

> Today I saw Dostoevsky. He was here. I cannot say that the impression was a particularly pleasant one.

October 7, 1846
Fyodor Dostoevsky, from a letter to Mikhail Dostoevsky

> Last time I wrote you to say that I am planning to go abroad.[2] The booksellers are offering me four thousand paper rubles for everything. Nekrasov was going to give me 1,500 rubles . . . but it seems that he will renege. . . . So if my price seems low (judging by my expenses) . . . I myself will publish the volume, perhaps even by November 15th. That is even better because the business will take place right before my eyes and others will not mess up the volume. . . . In a word, such an undertaking will have its own advantages. Then by January 1st, I will sell all the copies to booksellers wholesale. Perhaps I will earn 4,000 [rubles], and although that is the same that the booksellers are offering, I will not publish everything in my volume. As a result, if I add a little bit, a second volume will come out after my return from Italy, and I will arrive to money straightaway.
>
> I am going not for a good time but to take a cure. Petersburg is hell for me. It is burdensome, so burdensome to live here! And my health is noticeably worse. Moreover, I am terribly afraid. What will October bring, for instance? So far the days have been clear. I am very much looking forward to your opinion. But for the time being . . . help me, brother, until December 1st at the very latest. Because until that time, I absolutely

do not know where I can get any money. . . . Kraevsky is throwing some at me, but I have already borrowed 100 silver rubles from him; and now I run away from him. . . . In Italy, at my leisure, in freedom I want to write a novel[3] and finally be able to raise my price. But the system of continual indebtedness that Kraevsky fosters is the system of my slavery and literary dependence. So give me some money if you can. In leaving for abroad, I wrote to you that I would repay the 100 rubles; but if you can send me 50 silver rubles now, I will give that money back too. Everything will be straightened out by January 1st. Figure out if you can lend me money until January 1st. Then give it to me. As regards repayment, count on me as if I were a stone mountain. . . .

I need this money for an overcoat. I no longer have people make clothing for me. I am taken up entirely with my system of literary emancipation, and . . . my clothing is already indecent. I really need an overcoat. I will use 120 rubles for one with a collar, and the rest I want to use to get by until publication. Kraevsky himself has offered to help me. Ratkov and Kuvshinnikov publish things upon his recommendation. They have offered 4,000 rubles for a manuscript.

By January 1st I intend to write some kind of trifle for Kraevsky and then to get away from everyone. In order to get to Italy, I need to pay various debts (including what I owe you) to the tune of 1,600 paper rubles. Thus, I will have about 2,400 paper rubles left. I have asked about everything. The trip costs 500 (at most). In Vienna, I will have clothes and linen made for 300 rubles, things are cheap there. That means that 1,600 rubles will remain. I will get by for eight months. To *The Contemporary* I will send the first part of a novel,[4] get 1,200 [rubles], and from Rome go to Paris for two months and then back. When I arrive, I will publish the second part right away. I will be writing the novel until fall of 1848 and then publish its third or fourth parts. The first part will be published in *The Contemporary* in the form a prologue. I have both the plot and the idea in my head. I am now in almost a panicky fear over my health. Just like during the first part of my illness, the palpitations of my heart are terrible.

The Contemporary is being published by Nekrasov and Panaev on January 1st. The critic is Belinsky. Various journals and the devil knows what else are coming to the fore. But I am fleeing from everything because I want to be healthy to write something healthy. Nekrasov's shop is declining.[5] But Yazykov and company are flourishing. He also has commissions and books. I have already spoken to him about depositing copies with him for their management and dissemination.

Give my regards to everyone, especially to Emiliya Fyodorovna. The children, too, and for God's sake, answer me by the first mail. I am waiting for your letter. Write as soon as possible, because if you do not send money, then at least say so (for which, honest to God, I will not hold it against you), so that I can look elsewhere.

P.S. I will be writing letters very often now.

It will be a long time before we see each other now. But when I return from abroad, I will visit you directly, no matter where you are.

By October 20th, the time of finishing the raw material, that is, "Shaved Sideburns," my situation will become apparent in the clearest way, since on October 15, there will be the printing of *Poor Folk*.

October 14, 1846
Alexei Pleshcheev, from a review

> This year is remarkable in our literature for the appearance of a new and bright star on its horizon—talent in the full artistic sense of the word: we are speaking about Mr. Dostoevsky, the author of *Poor Folk*, *The Double*, and "Mr. Prokharchin." Such talents appear rarely, and for this one can forgive the inadequacies of our fictional writing.

Before October 16, 1846
Avdotya Panaeva, from her memoirs

> A particular master at jesting [in the salon] was Turgenev. On purpose, he dragged Dostoevsky into arguments and irritated him to the highest degree. In response, Dostoevsky often crawled over to the wall and defended in a passionate way absurd views about things he had blurted out in anger and which Turgenev seized upon to ridicule.

Before October 16, 1846
Avdotya Panaeva, from her memoirs

> Belinsky, sometimes hearing how a flushed Dostoevsky argued with Turgenev, said quietly to Nekrasov . . . "What's with Dostoevsky! He is saying such absurdities, and with passion to boot." When later Turgenev told Belinsky about Dostoevsky's sharp and inaccurate judgments of some Russian writer, Belinsky responded:
>
> "Well, you are one to talk! You pick on a sick individual, you egg him on as if you yourself do not see that he is irritated and does not understand what he is saying."

Before October 16, 1846
Agrafena Orlova, from her memoirs

> How passionately Belinsky . . . scolded Turgenev for irritating Dostoevsky, for egging on a sick man whom he loved, valued, and pitied.

Circa October 16, 1846
Isaak Pavlovsky, from his memoirs

> One time guests had gathered at Turgenev's home: Belinsky, Ogaryov, Herzen, and others. They were playing cards. Someone said something stupid just at the very moment when Dostoevsky entered. Everyone started laughing uproariously. Dostoevsky, turning pale, stopped on the threshold; then, without saying a word, he left the room.
> When Turgenev asked the valet about Fyodor Mikhailovich, he answered, "He has been pacing the courtyard for about an hour but without a hat on."
> It was terribly cold out. Turgenev ran into the courtyard.
> "What's with you, Dostoevsky?" he asked.
> "Good God! But this is impossible!" he answered. "Anywhere I go, people everywhere laugh at me. Unfortunately, I saw from the threshold how you had begun to snicker when you saw me. Are you not blushing now?"
> Despite Turgenev's assurances that no one had taken it into his head to laugh at Dostoevsky, the young man did not want to hear anything and, taking his hat, departed.

Circa October 16, 1846, and after
Avdotya Panaeva, from her memoirs

> Once in Dostoevsky's presence, Turgenev was describing his meeting in the provinces with one individual who imagined himself to be a genius and a masterly writer of human life. . . . Dostoevsky turned as white as a sheet and trembled all over. He ran out of the room without hearing Turgenev's story to the end. I said to everyone: What was the point of tormenting Dostoevsky so? But Turgenev was in the most merry mood and had so entertained the others that no one attached any significance to Dostoevsky's hasty departure. Turgenev then began to compose a humorous ditty on Devushkin, the hero of *Poor Folk*, as if grateful to Dostoevsky for having informed all of Russia of the work's existence and with lines that often included the word "mother."[6]

> From that evening on, Dostoevsky no longer appeared at our place and even on the street avoided meetings with anyone from our circle.

After October 16, 1846
Avdotya Panaeva, from her memoirs

> One time Panaev, having met Dostoevsky on the street, wanted to stop him and ask why he had not seen him in such a long time, but Dostoevsky ran quickly to the other side. He was seen with only one friend, who, when he visited the circle, reported that Dostoevsky was abusing everyone . . . as heartless, insignificant, and jealous of his success.[7]

After October 16, 1846
Dmitri Grigorovich, from his memoirs

> After the scene with Turgenev there occurred a final break between Dostoevsky and the members of the Belinsky circle. He no longer visited them. About him there were scattered witticisms and caustic epigrams. He was accused of monstrous pride, as well as envy of Gogol, to whom he should have gone on his knees because in his much-celebrated *Poor Folk*, one felt the influence of Gogol on every page.

After October 16, 1846
Lyubov Dostoevskaya, from her memoirs

> Father found it very painful that he had to bury his illusions of friendship. . . . Naively he assumed that his friends would be happy over his success, as he would have been over theirs. Especially painful to Father was the malice of Turgenev, who, beside himself over the success of *Poor Folk* . . . invented all kinds of things to harm him. . . . The enmity continued throughout their lives.

After October 16, 1846
Fyodor Dostoevsky, from his 1849 *Netochka Nezvanova*

> Talent needs sympathy and understanding. But as soon as you have achieved the slightest success, you will see what kind of people flock to you. But they will not give [you] a second thought. They will look at you with contempt for what you have gained through hard work, self-denial, hunger, and sleepless nights. These future friends will neither encourage nor comfort you. They will not show what is good and true in you. Rather, with spite and glee, they will spot every one of your

mistakes. They will point out all your faults and failings. With cold-blooded scorn, they will declare a holiday over every slip and blunder (as if anyone was perfect)!

October 17, 1846
Fyodor Dostoevsky, from a letter to Mikhail Dostoevsky

I hasten to inform you, dear brother, that I received your money, for which I am inexpressibly grateful, since I no longer feel the cold and other unpleasant things. I also hasten to tell you that all my hopes and calculations are seemingly postponed until a more convenient time.

At the very least, I myself still do not know very much. The conditions that people keep offering me are the likes of which one cannot accept. Either the money is too little; or the money is decent, but you do not get it all at once, but have to wait. It goes without saying that if I am to sell, I can do so only for cash. Finally, I am being advised to wait. That is both good and bad. It is bad for my health. It is good given the fact that if I wait, I can get a more significant sum. In the latter case, there is no chance of publishing before Christmas. Since I have to live on something, I need to sell stories to journals; and then I will have to wait. Therefore the earliest that the publication can occur is perhaps by May 1st. Moreover, I will have to exert myself to arrange everything. And publish two thick volumes and not for two rubles, fifty copecks as I had presumed. But for three, and perhaps more. And so, perhaps, we will see each other this summer, and the trip will not take place until the fall, if I have a lot of money.

All of this distresses me, brother, and I am like a crazy person. Oh, how much labor and difficulties of all kinds one has to endure at first in order to establish oneself. My health, for instance, I have to leave it to *luck*, and the devil knows whether I will have any security. I am writing you a short letter because I do not know anything certain for myself. But I am not entirely downcast. How are you getting along? You write that you are expecting a new guest in the family. God grant that all go well.[8] And may your circumstances also right themselves. I, brother, do not stop thinking about our goals. Our association can become a reality. I keep dreaming about it. I, brother, need to have a *complete success*, without which there will be nothing and I will be just barely getting by. All of this depends not on me but on my energy.

"Shaved Sideburns" is not quite finished. "Prokharchin" is being praised highly. I have been told a lot of judgments.[9] Belinsky still has not arrived yet. The gentlemen at *The Contemporary* keep on hiding.

So I am still hanging on to "Shaved Sideburns" and have not yet promised it to anyone. Perhaps Kraevsky will publish it. I do not know how I will manage with that, however. I will take advantage of circumstances and enter the story into the fray. Whoever fights harder for it will get it. Then I will surely pull down some decent money. But if it happens that I publish it separately, so that I am given a certain sum in advance, I will not give it to the journals.

Brother Andrei sends his regards to both you and Emiliya Fyodorovna. I visit them every so often. How they play cards! I kiss the children and I often think about them. If I do well in selling the story, I will without fail send them candy and various sweets for Christmas. Emiliya Fyodorovna can be assured of all my devotion. Let us be patient, brother, perhaps we will get rich. We need to work. But for God's sake, take care of your health. And I would advise and ask you not to work a great deal. Send it to the devil! Please take care of yourself. And most important, eat more healthily. Less coffee and meat. They are poison. Good-bye, brother. I will write again soon. It is so dark out.

P.S. October here is dry, clear, and cold. There have been few illnesses. Do not forget me and write.

October 18, 1846
Fyodor Dostoevsky, from a letter to Andrei Dostoevsky

Dear brother, I have long since arrived from Revel, and every Saturday circumstances of one sort or another prevent me from getting in touch with you. Forgive me. Come see me tomorrow about 10 a.m.

Late October 1846
Fyodor Dostoevsky, from a letter to Mikhail Dostoevsky

I want to write you a word or two, but no more, because I am running about and flapping about like a fish on ice. The problem is all my plans have collapsed.... The edition will not come to be. Because not a single one of the stories I told you about has become a reality. I am not writing "Shaved Sideburns" either. I have given up on everything: because it is all nothing but a repetition of old things that I have said long ago. Now more original, lively, and bright thoughts are begging to be put down on paper.... In my situation, monotony is ruin.

I am writing another story,[10] and the work is going as it did with *Poor Folk*, crisply, easily, and successfully. I intend it for Kraevsky. Let the folks at *The Contemporary* be angry with me. I do not care.[11]

Meanwhile, after finishing the story by January 1st, I will cease publishing entirely until next year and write a novel that is even now giving me no peace.[12]

But in order to live, I have made up my mind to publish *Poor Folk* and a revised *The Double* as separate books.[13] I will not put Part 1 and Part 2 on them, for instance, it will simply be *Poor Folk* separately and *The Double* too—all my work for the year. With my future novel I hope to do exactly the same thing. And finally, perhaps in 2 years or so I will put together a complete edition and in that way I will really luck out because I will get money twice and create renown for myself.

I will start to publish *Poor Folk* tomorrow or the day after. I will do this through Ratkov; he promises. Now I only curse fate that I do not have 700 paper rubles to publish it at my own expense. Publishing at your own expense is everything. With someone else means taking a risk; you can perish. Booksellers are scoundrels. They have scads of tricks which I do not know about and with which they can swindle you. But their most barbaric thing is the following: they publish an edition at their own expense, and for that they receive from me 350 or 400 copies (the price covering their expenses), they take 40 percent, i.e., 40 silver copecks per copy (I am selling them at a ruble each). That is for *the turnover of their capital* and for *the risk*. Let's say that a bookseller has in his hand 300 rubles. He is the one who sells them. I, however, do not have the right to sell a single copy until all of his are sold because I would be underselling him. He will sell them all and tell me that the public does not want any more and that the books will not sell. It is impossible to verify what he is saying. So that means quarreling with him. Such a thing is done only in extreme cases. I have copies lying around. I need money. Finally, after having made me starve, he will buy a couple hundred copies or so from me at half price.

Finally, there are rascals who hold back requests from other cities and do not release copies even to the Petersburg public who is asking for them. Now, if I publish myself, I suddenly sell to all the booksellers in Petersburg for hard cash. They take a certain percentage. Each one gives more than the other, trying to undercut each other if the book sells well, and finally, the main stockpile is set up in Yazykov's office.

Listen, brother: I request an immediate reply and here is what I propose. Only if you have the money, send me *200 silver rubles*. (I need more, but I can go slightly into debt.) Don't you want to do some speculation? If you are just saving money, then it is just lying around to no avail. I propose that you give me some money for the edition. I can have it published by November 15th. The edition will pay for itself by January 1st. I will send you your 200 silver rubles right away. Later, 1/4 of all the profits. The edition will pay for itself with 350 copies. There will then be 850 left at 75 silver copecks each = 635 paper rubles. I will give the profit to a bookseller. But I would be prepared to share it with you. My money will not be lost. Then, if there is a whiff of success, we would publish *The Double*. Finally, in any event, your money will be returned to you by January. I give you my word of honor that I will not drag you into a false position. Finally, I expect success even if it be slow in coming. It will take at least a year for the *entire* edition to sell out.[14] Here is an example: Osnovyanenko's *Mr. Kholyavsky* was published in *The Fatherland Notes* three years ago.[15] Then it was published separately, and now they want to do a third printing.

If you want, brother, answer me right away and with money. I will correct a few things, go to the censorship, and make arrangements with the printer. If you do not have that much, then for starters send at least 120 silver rubles, no less, for a deposit, and then the remaining 80 silver rubles without fail by November 15th.

Finally, if you cannot do all of this, you will not put me in straitened circumstances, at least as far as time. I will go to the booksellers, and we will publish *The Double* later.

In this matter cast aside all fraternal love, tactfulness, and other such things. Look at this matter as speculation. Do not rob yourself of the desire of doing me a good turn, even if only for a short time. You have a new child on the way. Good-bye, kiss everyone. Give my regards to everyone you should. I am still sick all the time. But after all, you know me.

P.S. Good-bye, dear brother. I await your reply immediately. For God's sake, do not put yourself in a false position, that is, if, for example, you will be giving me the last of your money. Then it is better not to. After all, I am only making a proposal to you. But if you are rich and *willing*, send the money by the first mail, for instance, by the 2nd or 3rd of this month.

Well, listen to me. I have written everything to you and I am saying for the last time: if you have money, do not be afraid and agree. If you do not have money or very little, for God's sake, do not enter into this venture. Answer right away.

Give my regards to Emiliya Fyodorovna. I wish you all happiness, my friends. Gogol died in Florence two years ago.[16]

November 1, 1846
Valerian Maykov, from a review

> With their masterly stories. . . . Pushkin, Lermontov, Gogol, and Dostoevsky . . . these self-seducers have stepped forth boldly into the field of novellas . . . to create works that are truly artistic!!!

November 9, 1846
Faddei Bulgarin, from a review

> The Cossack Lugansky is much higher than Gogol in education, his view on subjects, his exposition and his language, and we could not forgive ourselves if we dared to place Cossack Lugansky alongside Mr. Dostoevsky, whom [the people at] *The Fatherland Notes*, filling in the vacancy left by Gogol, have pronounced a genius!

November 17, 1846
Apollon Grigoriev, from a letter to Nikolai Gogol

> Have you read *The Double* by the talented Dostoevsky? Here for you is the realization of the fantastic basis of "The Portrait." From the work, one becomes oppressed spiritually, so exceedingly burdened as from "The Overcoat." Getting a grasp on this monstrous creation, you find yourself diminished and destroyed. You merge with its exceedingly insignificant hero, and you become sad that you are becoming such a person as well as amused that a person is and can only be that way. What guilt and responsibility are there here? What verdict hangs over you? A man lives likes a worm and dies like a worm, and the deal is done. *Une fois mort, on est bien mort.*[17]

November 23, 1846
Faddei Bulgarin, from a review

> Our honorable colleague[18] has, by mistake, placed Lermontov alongside Gogol, having named them as founders of a natural, that is, antigraceful school! *A Hero of Our Time* and all the fictional writings of Lermontov are much higher than *Dead Souls*, *Taras Bulba*, and all the fairy tales and old wives' stories of Mr. Gogol, as Eugène Sue, Victor Hugo, Alexander Dumas, and Pushkin are higher than the author of

"The Petersburg Corners,"[19] the author of *Poor Folk* . . . and other young writers who do not respect the literature of high art.

November 26, 1846
Fyodor Dostoevsky, from a letter to Mikhail Dostoevsky

Well, how could you, my priceless friend, write that I was seemingly angry with you for not having sent money and thus was silent? How could such an idea enter into your head? And finally, how could I have given you such a pretext to think that about me? If you love me, do me the favor of renouncing such ideas once and for all. Let us try to have everything between us be simple and direct. I will tell you aloud and straightforwardly that I am obliged to you for so much that for my part, not to admit such a thing would be ridiculous, swinish, and base. Now, enough about this. I will do better to write about my circumstances and try to make everything a bit clearer.

In the first place, all my editions have burst and come to nothing. It was not worth it, it took too much time, and it was too early. Perhaps also the public might not have gone for such a thing. I will do the edition toward next fall. By that time the public will have become better acquainted with me, and my position will be clearer. Furthermore, I am expecting several advances. *The Double* is already being illustrated by a Moscow artist. *Poor Folk* is being illustrated in two places here—whoever does the better job.[20]

Bernardsky[21] says that he is not opposed to beginning negotiations with me in February and to giving me a certain sum for the right to publish an illustrated edition. Until then he is busy with *Dead Souls*.[22] In a word, for the time being I have become indifferent to the edition. Besides, I do not have the time to bother with it. I have heaps of work and orders. I will tell you that I had the unpleasant experience of quarreling decisively with *The Contemporary* in the personage of Nekrasov. Annoyed at the fact that I am still giving my stories to Kraevsky, to whom I am in debt, and that I refused to declare publicly that I do not belong to *The Fatherland Notes*, and despairing of receiving a story from me in the future, he made a number of rude remarks to me and demanded money in an impudent way. I took him at his word and with an acknowledgment of debt, I promised to pay him a sum by December 15th. I want them to come to me themselves. They are all scoundrels and envious people. After I hauled off and let Nekrasov have it, he could only mince and try to escape, like a Jew who is having his money stolen. In a word, it is a dirty story. Now they are claiming that I have been infected by vanity, that I have conceived a high opinion of myself, and that I am going over to Kraevsky because Maykov praises me. Nekrasov is planning to criticize me. As for Belinsky, he is such a weak person that even in his literary opinions, he keeps changing his mind. It is only with him that I have kept my previous good relations. He is a noble person. Meanwhile Kraevsky, rejoicing over the chance, gave me some money and also promised to pay off all my debts for me by December 15th. In return I am working for him until the spring. You see what, brother: Out of all this, I have extracted a very wise rule. The first disadvantageous thing for a beginning talent is to be friends with proprietors of publications, from which, as an unavoidable consequence, proceed favoritism and then various obscenities. Then independence of position, work for Holy Art, work that is sacred and pure in the simplicity of a heart that has never before so trembled and moved in me as now before all the new images that are being created in my soul.[23]

Brother, I am being reborn, not only morally but also physically. Never before has there been in me such an abundance of clarity, such equilibrium in my character, such physical health. In this I am much obliged to my good friends the Beketovs . . . and others with whom I am living. They are practical, intelligent people, with an excellent heart, with nobility, with character. They have cured me with their company. Finally, I proposed that we all live together. A large apartment was found, and all the expenses for all the parts of the household do not exceed 1,200 paper rubles a year. How great are the boons of an association! I have my own room and I work days on end. . . .

I congratulate you, my dearest friend, on the arrival of my third nephew. I wish every blessing for both him and Emiliya Fyodorovna. I love you all now three times as much. But do not be angry at me, my priceless friend, for writing a scribbled-over wad of paper instead of a letter. There is no time, and people are waiting for me. But I will write again on Friday. Consider this letter unfinished.

December 17, 1846
Fyodor Dostoevsky, from a letter to Mikhail Dostoevsky

What has happened to you, dear brother, that you have fallen silent completely? With every mail I have been expecting something from you and not a word. I am worried, I think of you often, about the fact that you sometimes fall sick, and I am afraid to draw conclusions. For God's sake, write me at least a few lines. Please write and set my mind at ease. Perhaps you have been waiting for the continuation of my recent letter. Do not be angry at me for keeping my word so inaccurately. I am swamped with work now and I have pledged by January 5th to give Kraevsky the first part of the novel *Netochka Nezvanova*, about the publication of which you have read in *The Fatherland Notes*.[24] I am writing this letter in fits and starts because I am writing day and night except from 7 p.m. on, when, for entertainment, I go to the gallery at the Italian opera to listen to our incomparable singers. My health is good, so there is nothing more to write about it. I am writing with fervor. I keep feeling that I have started up a lawsuit against all of our literature, journals, and critics, and with the three parts of my novel in *The Fatherland Notes*, I am establishing my primacy for this year despite my ill-wishers. Kraevsky is discouraged.[25] He is almost perishing. *The Contemporary*, however, is performing brilliantly. They have already started up a crossfire.[26]

And, so, brother, I will not go abroad either this winter or summer, but will come again to see you in Revel.[27] I can hardly wait for the summer. In the summer I will redo my old things and prepare an edition for the fall. Then we will see what happens. Is your family well, brother? By any chance, is Emiliya Fyodorovna ill? I ask for an immediate response to this letter. As I have already written to you, brother, I am living with the Beketovs on Vasilievsky Island. It is not boring; it is also good and economical. I visit Belinsky sometimes. He is ill all the time, but he has hope. Mme. Belinskaya has given birth.

Thanks to Kraevsky, I am paying off all my debts. My entire task is to work and repay him everything over the winter and not owe a copeck for the summer. Sometime I will get out of debt. It is a bad thing to work as a day laborer. You will destroy everything, including talent and youth and hope, grow disgusted with work, and in the end become a pencil-pusher, not a writer.

Good-bye, brother. You have torn me from the most interesting page in my novel, and there is still a mountain of things ahead. Oh, my dear, if only you are successful. I would love to see you and, before I do, to settle and resolve my situation. I have bound myself with entrepreneurs hand and foot. Meanwhile, on the side, I am receiving brilliant offers. *The Contemporary*, which in the person of Nekrasov wishes to criticize me, will give me 60 silver rubles per signature page, which equals the 300 rubles at *The Fatherland Notes*. *The Library for Reading*—250 paper rubles per signature page, and so on, but I cannot give the people there anything. Kraevsky has taken everything for his 50 silver rubles given as an advance. By the way, Grigorovich has written a physiology, titled *The Village*, which is creating a furor here.[28] Well, good-bye, dear brother. Give my regards to Emiliya Fyodorovna, Fedenka, Mashenka, and Misha. Have the children forgotten me or not? . . . Regards to all the old friends.

P.S. Now, brother, here's what [to do]: come to Petersburg this year for Shrovetide. Even if it be for only two weeks. But definitely come. Room and board will not cost you anything. Nor will tea, sugar, and all your keep. You will not have to spend any pocket money at all. The entire trip will cost only a trifle. Well? What do you think? Think about it. Why not? I would be so glad to see you. And it would be pleasant for you to live while in Petersburg too. You do not need to take any money with you when you come here. I owe you and I will pay for everything. We will get hold of some money. For God's sake, brother, come. You are a stay-at-home. Can you really want to get to the point where you will have to be pulled out of Revel with tongs? Joking aside, come visit at Shrovetide.

Late 1846 and after
Stepan Yanovsky, from his memoirs

Since by this time I was now close friends with Fyodor Mikhailovich, our conversations were most candid, familiar, and intimate. . . . . We were almost the same age: I was twenty-eight; Fyodor Mikhailovich was twenty-four.[29] By nature I was a voracious reader and an individual who was extremely curious and enthusiastic about things. I was also a patriot to the marrow of my bones, as well as someone who believed in the Book of Revelation. Fyodor Mikhailovich was a similarly intense being, a profound thinker and observer. Perhaps it would be more accurate to say that he was a restless scientist-analyst, an extremely proud writer, a believer, and a patriot among patriots.[30] Fyodor Mikhailovich needed a friend who could understand his constantly analyzing mind, and who could esteem and empathize with the value of his work. In this, I as a doctor, together with the small circle of my colleagues and friends, satisfied him completely.

From the very beginning, Fyodor Mikhailovich trusted me. He told me that he was an extremely poor individual who made his living as a writer.

Late 1846 and after
Stepan Yanovsky, from his memoirs

The first illness for which Fyodor Mikhailovich appealed to me for help was purely local. In the course of treatment, though, he complained of a mental nausea or faintness that is commonly associated with paralysis or strokes. After having examined him thoroughly, and taken into account his physical build and temperament, and listened to him about his symptoms since childhood, I diagnosed that he was suffering from a nervous disorder.

Late 1846 and after
Stepan Yanovsky, from his memoirs

> Dostoevsky was a hypochondriac in the extreme (though undoubtedly he had symptoms of such well-known brain dysfunctions . . . as "fainting sickness"). He also so feared strokes and paralysis that he did everything he could to shield himself from upset and distress. To outsiders, Dostoevsky's hypochondria often appeared laughable, and he often took great offense when people thought or told him that he was not sick. To tell the truth, there were times when one could not help but laugh at Dostoevsky's imagined illnesses. When someone happened to say, "What wonderful, fragrant tea!"—Fyodor Mikhailovich, who did not usually drink tea but warm water, would suddenly jump up from his chair, walk over to me, and whisper in my ear: "Will such a thing affect my pulse, doctor? After all, tea is made from leaves!" Each time I had to hide a smile, and to calm him in a serious way, assuring him that his pulse was fine, that his tongue was good, and that his head was clear.

Late 1846 and after
Stepan Yanovsky, from an 1884 letter to Anna Dostoevskaya

> Poverty in Fyodor Mikhailovich expressed itself in a way that was completely analogous to his whining and complaints about his health. It often happened that after two or three comforting words, he himself pronounced himself completely well.

Late 1846 and after
Sergei Yanovsky, from an 1881 letter to Apollon Maykov

> The deceased Fyodor Mikhailovich Dostoevsky suffered from falling sickness when he was still in Petersburg, three or even more years before his arrest in the Petrashevsky affair and his exile to Siberia. The fact of the matter is that this burdensome enemy, called *Epilepsia*—the falling illness—was observed in Fyodor Mikhailovich in 1846, '47, and '48 on an occasional basis.[31] [During that time] observers did not notice anything, but the sick man himself was aware—in truth, vaguely—of his illness and usually called it apoplexy with an aura or

a breeze.³² (Notice this word aura or breeze.) To the extreme hypochondriac Fyodor Mikhailovich, it served to herald an attack, about which he said later, "I always manage to get to Haymarket Square, to my apartment"—even though such anticipation is a key characteristic of *Epilepsia*.³³

For me, as a doctor, it was clear that my dear friend suffered from falling illness. Several times during those years his illness was seen not only in its indubitable form but also to a life-threatening degree.

Late 1846 and after
Fyodor Dostoevsky, from an 1872 letter to Stepan Yanovsky

> You loved me and looked after me, with my great *spiritual illness* (after all, I understand that now).

Late 1846 and after
Lyubov Dostoevskaya, from her memoirs

> Doctor Yanovsky, who loved my father very much and often invited him to his place for consultations about his health, recalls that long before Dostoevsky's exile to Siberia, he suffered from a nervous illness akin to epilepsy.

Late 1846 and after
Yevgenya Rykacheva, from an 1881 letter to Andrei Dostoevsky

> Anna Grigorievna [Dostoevskaya] expressed her displeasure that Maykov published Yanovsky's letter without having shown it to her first, so that she could advise making several omissions regarding the family life of uncle [Fyodor].

Late 1846 and after
Andrei Dostoevsky, from an 1881 letter to Alexei Suvorin

> From 1843 to April 1849 (the time of his arrest), I, with rare exceptions, saw my brother [Fyodor] almost daily;³⁴ but never, in our protracted conversations, did I hear from him about this illness.
>
> One should also note that my brother did not hide his illnesses from me and often complained that he was feeling poorly.
>
> It is true that in this period (I do not recall the precise year), he was somewhat irritable and, it seems, suffered from some kind of nervous illness. I often came across notes which he had left behind for the night with this approximate content: "Tonight I might fall into a lethargic sleep, but do not bury me for several days."

I repeat: my brother never mentioned a "falling" [sickness] in this period. Finally I recall that I heard from him that he had acquired this illness when he was in Siberia.

Late 1846 and after
Stepan Yanovsky, from his memoirs

Not only did Dostoevsky not play cards, but also he did not understand a single hand of any game. In fact, he hated cards altogether. He was also a decisive enemy of wine, binges, and bouts.

Late 1846 and after
Stepan Yanovsky, from his memoirs

Fyodor Mikhailovich loved to arrange dinners at the Hôtel de France . . . with a group of close friends. Such gatherings usually cost less then two rubles each; but the merriment and fond memories of each affair lasted almost right up until the next. . . .

Before dinner everyone had a thimble-like glass of vodka (the sight of which always made Yakov Petrovich Butkov grimace wildly). There were also several bottles of champagne during the meal. At this time, Fyodor Mikhailovich did not drink vodka; and he usually took only a quarter of a glass of champagne, which he downed in one gulp after addresses to his guests, whom he loved to toast with great delight. Everyone also drank tea until late into the night.

Fyodor Mikhailovich enjoyed these dinners very much; and with his guests, he conducted the most sincere and intimate conversations. Indeed, the affairs were like a holiday for him. Fyodor Mikhailovich once told me the reason why he so loved these gatherings. "One's soul becomes light when one sees a poor proletarian, sitting in a nice room, eating a nice dinner and drinking both something fizzing and the real stuff." ("Proletarian" was what Fyodor Mikhailovich called anyone who did not have a regular income from a job, but who earned money on a daily basis.) At the end of a festive meal, a very pleased Fyodor Mikhailovich went up to each diner, shook his hand, and said, "The dinner was all right, but the fish and sauce were particularly good." He even sometimes kissed Yakov Petrovich Butkov.

Late 1846 and after
Stepan Yanovsky, from his memoirs

Fyodor Mikhailovich's love for society was so strong that even when he was sick or engaged in urgent work, he could not stay alone and invited one of his friends over to his place.

Late 1846 and after
Stepan Yanovsky, from an 1884 letter to Anna Dostoevskaya

> From 1846 to 1849, Fyodor Mikhailovich loved an audience and the couch upon which he spoke . . . as a teacher-virtuoso. We listened to him in a reverential way.

Late 1846 and after
Stepan Yanovsky, from an 1882 letter to Anna Dostoevskaya

> You cannot imagine how much I loved and respected your husband. He was not an unforgettable friend—no—this word is far from expressing the feelings which I nourished and nourish toward him. No, Fyodor Mikhailovich was my spiritual father. Every time he said sometime like "Ech, no, old man, Stepan Dmitrievich, that is not so or that is truly not so"—even now such things resound in my entire being as if am hearing them in real life. . . .
>
> I have had many good and honest friends . . . but no one was like Fyodor Mikhailovich. . . . To him went not only my heart but also my soul, both sustained by a profound humanity and by a striving for truth with which he himself had been endowed by God.

Late 1846 and after
Stepan Yanovsky, from an 1882 letter to Anna Dostoevskaya

> Here the image of Fyodor Mikhailovich rises up before me and my eyes, and I see his lips compressed from moral anguish. I notice the movement of his right hand first to smooth his hair and then curl his mustache. I even hear his voice, saying—"Ech, pal, how false it is, how bad it is"—and I also become truly burdened and sad.

Late 1846 and after
Stepan Yanovsky, from his memoirs

> Even as a joke, Fyodor Mikhailovich never allowed himself to lie. In fact, he also expressed disgust for the untruths that others uttered unexpectedly. I remember once an entire circle of individuals close to Fyodor Mikhailovich had gathered in the evening at the home of A. N. Pleshcheev. As usual, Fyodor Mikhailovich was in a good frame of mind and spoke a great deal. At dinner, though, the conversation focused on how one could ascertain that such publishers as Grech, Bulgarin, and P. I. Chichikov (our name for another editor) would never lie to us. During the discussion, someone began to defend Chichikov in a joking way.[35]

> "Well, we can excuse him," this individual said, "since even though he squeezes our brother writers financially, he pays us and does not make mistakes with money. True, Chichikov lies sometimes, but what is the fault in that? After all, even the Gospels say that a lie can sometimes ensure one's salvation."
>
> When Fyodor Mikhailovich heard these words, he grew quiet immediately. He also became withdrawn and he kept repeating to those who were sitting closest to him: "Isn't this something? He is even relying on the Bible. But it is not true what he is saying![36] After all, when one hears someone else lying, that is repulsive enough, but when this person lies and *slanders Christ at the same time, such a thing is repulsive and base.*"

Late 1846 and after
Stepan Yanovsky, from an 1884 letter to Anna Dostoevskaya

> Truly Fyodor Dostoevsky was not a wealthy man, and before the publication of *Poor Folk*, he was so poor that he did not have a ruble for sugar and shoes, but when he retired [from state service] and set out on the literary enterprise, precisely when I first became acquainted with him and later became friends, Fyodor Mikhailovich not only was never hungry but also was never without tea or shoes. I know for sure that he helped many individuals who were close to him . . . although he himself talked constantly about his material needs and also constructed various fanciful plans for getting rich and to help the poor, not with pennies or tickets to a free dinner but with grandiose sums and schemes. And where is this in biographies of Fyodor Mikhailovich?

Late 1846 and after
Stepan Yanovsky, from an 1884 letter to Anna Dostoevskaya

> Fyodor Mikhailovich complained about his lack of money, first because, being by birth a rentier, that is, an individual provided with a stable income from an estate—or as he loved to call himself, a person with a living labor—he throughout his entire life was not able to manage money; and second because by nature he was endowed with a heart that was so kind, empathetic, and generous that at the time he considered himself happy only when he could help a close friend. Furthermore, he forgot himself in a decisive way; and third, it is also important to note that in his very character was something exaggerated, as a result of which it seemed to him that he was very poor, although there was no extreme need.

Late 1846 and after
Stepan Yanovsky, from his memoirs

> Fyodor Mikhailovich was constantly in need of money. When one recalls, though, that he was very well paid for his work and that his life, especially as a bachelor, was extremely modest and without pretension, one has to ask the question: *What did Fyodor Mikhailovich do with his money?*
>
> This question I can answer truthfully, since, regarding monetary matters, Fyodor Mikhailovich was more open with me than with anyone else. Almost always he gave his money to someone who was poorer than he. Kindhearted soul that he was, though, he also gave money to people who were better off than he: individuals who swindled money from the infinitely good-natured individual that he was.

Circa 1847 and after
Vsevelod Solovyov, from his memoirs

> [Dostoevsky said]: "My nerves have been shot since youth. Two years before Siberia, during my various literary difficulties and quarrels, I was afflicted by some sort of strange and unbearably torturing nervous illness. I cannot tell you what these hideous sensations were; but I remember them vividly; it often seems to me that I was dying, and the truth is—real death came and then went away again. I also feared a lethargic sleep."

Circa 1847 and after
Fyodor Dostoevsvky, from *The Insulted and Injured*

> I must confess everything openly. At the beginning of dusk, first little by little and then gradually, whether from an upset in my nerves, or from impressions in a new apartment, or from a recent bout of depression, I began to descend into that condition of the soul which comes to me now in my sickness and which I call *mystical terror*. It is a most oppressive, agonizing illness of something that I myself cannot define, something that is ungraspable and immaterial in the natural order of things, but also something that may yet take shape without fail, this very minute, something which mocks all the conclusions of reason and which stands before me as an undeniable fact that is terrible, horrible, and relentless.
>
> Usually, despite all the protests of reason, this illness becomes more and more powerful, so much so that although . . . the mind sometimes

acquires great clarity, it also loses all power to resist such sensations. It is unheeded, it becomes useless, and this division, this split intensifies the fearful angst of suspense. It [is] . . . something like the anguish of people who are afraid of the dead. But in my distress the vagueness of the danger intensifies my torment.

Circa 1847 and after
Lyubov Dostoevskaya, from her memoirs

Dostoevsky began to doubt his gifts. His health started to shatter and he became nervous and hysterical. Epilepsy had already taken hold of his organism, and although he still had no attacks, he felt himself oppressed. He now avoided visiting salons, locked himself up in his home for hours on end, or wandered through the darkest and most remote streets in Petersburg. During these walks, he talked with himself and gesticulated so that passers-by stared at him. His friends thought he was mad.

Circa 1847
Fyodor Dostoevsky, from an 1859 letter to Mikhail Dostoevsky

[*The Double*] had a splendid idea, a very great and socially important type, of whom I was the first to discover and be its proclaimer.

1847
Dmitri Grigorovich, from his memoirs

In the accusation [of Dostoevsky's imitation of Gogol]—if one could call it that, given that here was a beginning young writer—there was a grain of truth. Unwittingly, the face of the old man Devushkin in *Poor Folk* brings to mind the clerk Poprishchin in *Diary of a Madman*; the scene in which the director's daughter drops her handkerchief and Poprishchin, rushing to pick it up, slides and falls on the parquet floor and almost breaks his nose recalls the scene in which Devushkin, in the presence of his boss, has a button torn from his coat, and he, beside himself in distress, tries to pick it up. Not only in the frequent repetition of one and the same word but also in the construction of the very phrases, in their spirit one sees the remarkable influence of Gogol. . . .

Such influence, though, cannot serve as a great reproach to Dostoevsky. After all, for such a thing one could also indict the entire young literary generation of the time. In one and the same way, all were carried away by Gogol. Almost everything that was written in the narrative mode was a reflection of Gogol's stories, primarily "The Overcoat."

January–February 1847
Fyodor Dostoevsky, from a letter to Mikhail Dostoevsky

Again I beg your absolution that I did not keep my word and write to you by the next mail. But . . . it has been impossible to write. I have thought about you a great deal and agonizingly so. Your fate is a burdensome one, dear brother! With your health, with your thoughts, without people around, with depression instead of a holiday mood, and with a family that, although a sacred and sweet worry, is still a heavy burden—life is intolerable. But do not lose heart, brother. The time will brighten. You see, the more spirit and inner content we have in ourselves, the better is our corner and life. Of course, terrible are the dissonance and disequilibrium that society presents to us. The *external* must be balanced with the *internal*. Otherwise, with the absence of external phenomena, the internal will move too dangerously into ascendancy. Nerves and fantasy will occupy too much space in a being. For want of habit, any external phenomenon seems colossal and somehow frightening. You begin to fear life.

You are fortunate that nature has provided you abundantly with love and a strong character. You also have great common sense and flashes of brilliant humor and happiness. All of these things save you too. I think about you a lot. But good God, how many repulsive, vilely limited, and gray-bearded sages, authorities, and Pharisees of life are there who *pride themselves* on their experience, that is, their lack of individuality (because they are all cut from the same cloth), useless people who preach eternally about contentment with fate, belief in something, limitation in life, and satisfaction with one's place, without penetrating into the essence of these words—a contentment resembling monastic torture and limitation, and with the inexhaustibly petty malice of those who condemn the strong, ardent soul of one who cannot bear their banal daily schedule and calendar of life. Such individuals are scoundrels with their earthly vaudeville-like happiness. . . . I come across them sometimes and they infuriate me in a tormenting way. . . .

But time is getting away. I wanted to write you a great many things. How irritating it is that everything has been interrupted. Thus I will limit myself and write a thing or two about what I am doing. I am working, brother, but I do not want to publish anything before I finish it. In the meantime I have no money, and if it were not for kind people, I would perish. The decline of my fame in the journals is bringing me more profit than loss. All the more quickly will I need things to be seized upon by my admirers, who seem to be many and who will defend me. I have been living poorly. Since I left you, I have spent only 250 silver rubles; and I used up to 300 rubles on debts. I was clipped most badly by Nekrasov, to whom I returned his 150 rubles because I do not want to tie myself to him. Toward spring I will get a huge loan from Kraevsky and without fail will send you 400 rubles. That is a sacred vow because the thought of you tortures me more than anything else.

I doubt that I will come to Helsingfors early.[37] Because perhaps I will try to cure myself completely with Priessznitz's method of cold water.[38] Therefore I will not arrive any earlier than July 1. But I still do not know anything, my dear. My future lies ahead. But even if thunder were to crack over me, I will not move now. I know everything that I can do. I will not spoil my work, and I will correct my financial circumstances with the successful sale of my book that I will publish in the fall. . . .[39]

Take care of yourself, brother. Especially your health. Amuse yourself and wish me well in finishing my work quickly. After that I will have money right away and I will visit you. I have Priessznitz's cure on the brain. Perhaps the doctors will talk me out of it. How I would love to see you. Sometimes I am tormented by such depression. Sometimes I recall how awkward and difficult I was with you in Revel. I was ill, brother. I remember that you once told me that my treatment of you excluded mutual equality. My dear man, that was absolutely unjust. But I do have such a vile and repulsive character. I have always valued you higher and better than myself. I am ready to give my life for you and your family; but sometimes when my heart is swimming in love, you cannot get a tender word from me. In such moments my nerves do not obey me. I am laughable and disgusting and because of that I suffer constantly from an unfair conclusion about me. People say that I am callous and lack a heart. How many times have I been rude to Emiliya Fyodorovna, the most noble of women, who is a thousand times better than I. I recall how purposely spiteful I was sometimes to Fedya,[40] whom at the same time I loved even more than you. I can only show that I am a person with a heart and love when the very exterior of a circumstance, an incident, extracts me violently from my usual banality. Until that point I am disgusting. That inequality I attribute to illness. Have you read *Lucrezia Floriani*, take a look at *Carl*.[41] But soon you will be reading *Netochka Nezvanova*. That will be a confession, like *Golyadkin*,[42] although in a different tone and form.

On the sly (and from many people) I hear such rumors about Golyadkin that it is simply horrible. Some say straight out that the work is a *wonder* and that it is has not been understood. . . . What if I had written only Golyadkin? That would have been more than enough for me. For some it is more interesting than Dumas. Well, now my vanity has come gushing forth. But, brother! How nice it is to be understood. Brother, why do you love me so! I will try to embrace you soon. We will love each other passionately. Wish me success. I am writing "The Landlady." It is already turning out better than *Poor Folk*. It is in the same style. My pen is being guided by a well of inspiration that springs forth directly from my soul. Not like "Prokharchin," with which I suffered all summer long. How much I would like to help you soon, brother. But, brother, rely on the money which I promised you as on a wall, as on a mountain. Kiss your family for me.

P.S. Will we get together in Petersburg sometime, brother? What would you say about a civilian job with a decent salary?

I do not know if Mme. Belinskaya gave birth to a son or a daughter, but it seems somehow strange and embarrassing to ask.

January 1847 and after
Lyubov Dostoevskaya, from her memoirs

The Double is far more endlessly valuable than *Poor Folk*. Here is the original, genuine Dostoevsky. Psychiatrists of our country praise this small masterpiece to an extreme; they are astounded how a young writer, who never studied medicine, could describe so well the last days of an insane person.

This second novel, though, did not have the success of the first. It was way too new; such a scrupulous analysis of the human heart . . . was still not understood. Madness still had not come into fashion;[43] and a novel without a hero or a heroine was found to be boring. The critics did not hide their disappointment. "We were mistaken," they wrote. "Dostoevsky's talent is far less significant than we thought."

If my father had been older, he would not have paid any attention to the critics. He would have continued in his new manner, he would have accustomed his readers . . . to an exclusively psychological investigation. But at that time, he was too young. Criticism could deflect him from his path. My father was afraid to be deprived of the splendid success of his first novel; so he returned to the false genre of Gogol.

January 1847 and after
Avdotya Panaeva, from her memoirs

Dostoevsky had not visited us since the time when Belinsky published in *The Contemporary* his criticism of *The Double* and *Prokharchin*. Dostoevsky was offended by his analysis.⁴⁴ He even stopped seeing Nekrasov and Panaev, regarding them in a mocking and derisive way. They were quite surprised by the way Dostoevsky was acting toward them.

After January–February 1847
Fyodor Dostoevsky, from an 1861 article

> Valerian Maykov undertook his task passionately, with enlightened conviction, with the first enthusiasm of youth. But he did not succeed in having his say. He died in the first year of his activities [as critic of *The Fatherland Notes*]. This fine personality promised much, and perhaps his passing deprived us of a good deal.

January 1, 1847
Vissarion Belinsky, from a review

> Turning our attention to the remarkable works of belletristic prose that have appeared in anthologies and journals over the past year, our glance falls, first of all, on *Poor Folk*, a novel that has achieved great fame for an individual who, up until now, has been unknown in our literature. Incidentally, this work has been spoken about to such a great extent in all our journals that new similar opinions cannot be of interest to the public. Thus we will not expand upon it in any great detail.
>
> No one has ever achieved fame so quickly in our literature as Mr. Dostoevsky. The power, depth, and originality of his talent has been recognized immediately by everyone. What is more important, the public has also shown an unrestrained appetite for Mr. Dostoevsky's giftedness, as well as an equally unrestrained impatience with his shortcomings. . . . Unanimously, almost everyone finds in Mr. Dostoevsky's *Poor Folk* the ability to tire the reader. . . . Some see such a thing as long-windedness, others as unrestrained fecundity.
>
> Truly, one cannot but agree that if *Poor Folk* had appeared with only 10 percent fewer pages, and if the author had had the foresight to rid his novel of superfluous repetitions of one and the same phrases, *Poor Folk* would have been an irreproachably artistic work.

January 1, 1847
Vissarion Belinsky, from a review

> Mr. Dostoevsky has submitted to the judgment of his interested public a second novel, titled *The Double. The Adventures of Mr. Golyadkin*. Although the initial debut of the young writer has smoothed his road

to success, one must confess that *The Double* has not been a triumph with the public. But one still cannot judge the second work of Mr. Dostoevsky as unsuccessful or, even less, as not having any [good] qualities; still one must acknowledge that the verdict of the public is not completely unfounded.

In *The Double*, the author displays a great wealth of talent. His hero belongs to that group of the most profound, bold, and genuine conceptions, the type of which only Russian literature can boast. Here also is a deep wellspring of intelligence, truth, and artistic mastery. But together with such things, one can also see a terrible inability to possess and control an excess of personal powers in an economic way. Everything that was forgivable as shortcomings in *Poor Folk* appears as monstrous weaknesses in *The Double* . . . the inability of an extremely rich and powerful talent to determine, in a reasonable manner and within the limits of artistic development, the idea of the piece.

Let us attempt to explain our thought with an example. Gogol focused the idea of his Khlestakov in such a profound and lively way that it would have been easy to make him the hero of an entire dozen comedies in which he would appear as faithful to himself . . . as a fiancé, husband, father of a family, landowner, and so forth. Undoubtedly these comedies would be superb as *The Inspector General* . . . but they would tire the public . . . with one and the same thing. As soon as a poet expresses the idea of his work, he is done. He must leave it in peace, for fear of boring people with it.

Another example: What could be better than the two scenes that Gogol excluded from his comedy since they slowed the pace of his piece? Comparatively speaking, they ceded nothing in quality to any one of the scenes that remained. So why did Gogol exclude them? Because he, to the highest degree, possessed artistic measure. He knew not only with what to begin and when to end but also to develop his subject with no less or more than what was needed.

We know that Mr. Dostoevsky excluded from *The Double* one splendid scene, believing that it was extremely long;[45] and we are convinced that, at the very least, if he had shortened his *Double* by a third, without wondering if he had omitted something that was good, he would have had another success.

In *The Double*, also, there is still another key shortcoming: its fantastic coloring. In our time, the fantastic can have a place only in the homes of the mentally ill, not in literature; under the eye of doctors, not poets. For all these reasons, *The Double* has been valued only by several dilettantes of art,[46] for whom literary works are the subject not only of delight but also of study. The public is different... not thinking why they like a work, and immediately closing a book when it begins to tire them or without thinking why it is not to their taste. A work that is liked by connoisseurs and not the majority can have its strengths. But [what is] truly good is a work that can please both groups, or, at the least, [can be] liked by the first and read by the second. After all, Gogol was not liked by everyone, but he was read by all.

January 1, 1847
Vissarion Belinsky, from a review

> Dostoevsky's story "Mr. Prokharchin" has caught all the admirers of his talent with an unpleasant surprise. The work flashes with bright sparks of great giftedness... but in such thick darkness that its light gives nothing for readers to discern.... Neither inspiration nor free and naive creativity has given birth to this strange story, but rather... how can one say?... something akin to feigned cleverness and pretense.... Perhaps we are mistaken, but why instead of a genuine... poetic creation... is there something so false, mannered, and incomprehensible... [so] muddled and strange?...
>
> We should note in passing that Gogol contains no such contradictions. Of course, we have no right to demand from the works of Mr. Dostoevsky the perfection of the writings of Gogol, but nonetheless we think that it would be useful for a great talent to follow the example of an even greater one.

January 1, 1847
Valerian Maykov, from a review

> Already in November and December 1845, all the literary dilettantes... were bandying about the comforting news about the appearance of a new and great literary talent. Some cried, "No worse than Gogol"; others took up the call, "Better than Gogol"; still others wailed, "Gogol has been killed."...
>
> Having done such a good (or bad) turn to the author of *Poor Folk*, the town criers carried on so that the public expected a work of ideal perfection... but, having read the novel, it was astounded at having met, along with unusual strengths, several failings characteristic of the work of any young gifted writer, no matter how great his talent....

Perhaps no one in this world has been judged so unreasonably harshly as Mr. Dostoevsky. People had assumed that *Poor Folk* would be the crown of literature, the prototype of an artistic work in both content and form, and that authors after him would be deprived even of the possibility of perfection. The result was that a large part of the public, after having read *Poor Folk*, talked primarily about the *long-windedness* of the novel but kept silent about everything else.

The same thing happened when *The Double* appeared. Indeed, one can say with assurance that it was only with a small circle of readers that these two works were a complete success. . . . [The reason why] most readers dislike Mr. Dostoevsky's works is that they are unaccustomed to the original way in which he depicts reality. . . . In vain do people say that novelty always influences the majority in a positive way. In the first place, the majority is not the same everywhere. In the second place, any majority has a well-established routine. There are examples of an immediate success for extremely mediocre literary works . . . a success founded primarily on nothing other than a novel content. Hence the reason why, in various times and places, genuinely original works are often met with coldness, but in time are acknowledged as first-class and praised to the skies! If Gogol was not understood and valued in the first years of his career, it was because he countered the romantic direction reigning in our literature at the time. It is not surprising that the popularity of Mr. Dostoevsky has met an obstacle, his manner opposing that of Gogol. . . .

The *manner* of Mr. Dostoevsky is original to the highest degree. He, less than anyone else, can be called an imitator of Gogol. Indeed, if anyone should tag him with such a name, the same person would have to call Gogol an imitator of Homer or Shakespeare. In this sense, all genuine artists imitate each other, because elegance is always and everywhere governed by the same rules.

Both Gogol and Mr. Dostoevsky depict genuine society as it exists in reality. But whereas Gogol is a poet who is primarily social, Mr. Dostoevsky is primarily psychological. For one, the individual is important as a representative of a well-known society or circle; for the other, society itself is interesting for its influence on the individual. Gogol is inspired by the individual only when he feels the possibility of using him to penetrate one of the wider spheres of society. With Chichikov, he travels all the corners and alleyways of the Russian provinces. The same thing can also be said about all his works, with the notable exception of *Diary of a Madman.* Gogol's collected works one can decisively call an artistic statistics of Russia.

In Dostoevsky one also meets strikingly artistic depictions of society, but they are for him the backdrop . . . drawn, for the most part, in such thin strokes that they are overwhelmed completely in vast psychological interest. Even in *Poor Folk*, the interest, brought about by the analysis of the characters . . . is incomparably more forceful than the sharp depiction of their surroundings. The more time one spends in reading *Poor Folk*, the more one discovers this feature of profound psychological analysis. We are convinced that any work of Mr. Dostoevsky will gain in the extreme if it is read a second or third time. We cannot explain in any other way the wealth of psychological details, the unusual depth and perception. For example, reading *Poor Folk* for the first time, one will wonder why, at the end of the novel, the author takes it into his head to force Varvara Alexeevna, with such cold despotism, to send Devushkin from store to store with repulsive orders. Such an incident, however, has great significance for the psychologist, and informs the work with an unusually faithful snapshot of human nature. It goes without saying that the love of Makar Devushkin cannot but arouse in Varvara Alexeevna a revulsion which she hides constantly and consistently, and perhaps also from herself. Is there anything more burdensome in the world than the necessity of restraining one's dislike of a person to whom for some reason we are obligated and who (God save us!) loves us! Whoever will take the trouble to sift through their past will most likely recall that they have felt the greatest antipathy not toward enemies but toward people who are devoted to them to the point of self-sacrifice and to whom, in the depths of their souls, they cannot respond in similar fashion.

Varvara Alexeevna (we are deeply convinced) is tortured by the devotion of Makar Alexeevich more than by her crushing poverty, but she cannot refuse the right to torture him . . . as a lackey so that she can be freed of his oppressive guardianship. . . . Reread *Poor Folk* after time has given you the chance to value all the details of this work, and you will find in it a wealth of virtues that, on first glance, you, we, and any reader or reviewer could see as faults.

The Double has had less success than *Poor Folk*. . . . In it, though, Mr. Dostoevsky expresses psychological analysis in all its fullness and originality. Here he has penetrated so deeply into the human soul. In fact, in *The Double*, so fearlessly and passionately has Mr. Dostoevsky looked into the treasured workings of human emotions, thoughts, and deeds . . . that he is like a curious person penetrating the chemical makeup of matter. It is a strange thing! What seemingly can be more positive than a chemical view of reality? But a picture of the world, enlightened by such a stance, always shows itself as enveloped also in a kind of mystical light. . . .

Before us *The Double* unfolds as the anatomy of a soul that has perished from being conscious of a lack of coordination of personal interests in a well-structured society. Recall the poor and sickly proud Golyadkin who lives in constant fear of himself, and who strives, tortuously, not to debase himself before anyone in any way; but who also destroys himself even before his rascal servant Petrushka, and who agrees to trim his pretensions to personhood, even to live *in his own right*. Recall how the slightest movement in nature seems to him to be an evil sign arranged by all kinds of enemies . . . who, fully and invisibly, devote themselves to doing him harm, who keep stubborn vigil over his unhappy persona, and who, stubbornly and without pause, undermine his trifling interests. . . .

We cannot help but say a few words about Mr. Dostoevsky's third work, "Mister Prokharchin." . . . Reading this piece, we were perturbed by a suspicion that until now we could not deny. It seems to us that the author has learned of complaints regarding the long-winded quality of his works, and that to please his readers, he is ready to cut out too many things for the sake of valued brevity, the scale of which no one has determined in a successful way. At the very least, we do not know how else to explain the vagueness of the idea of the piece.

January 5, 1847
Eduard Guber, from an article

What is our Russian literature? Where has it come from and where it is going? Where are its books and its writers? What does it demand, what does it want, and does it even want something? In reality, does it even exist, this literature without books and writers, this literature on the off chance, this literature of thick journals and little clerks. We read and write little. The new writer has become a phenomenon which people look at like a minor marvel. A good book becomes an event which enters into the line of careless gossip and our deeply thoughtful conversations, together with a new planet or a new vice.

Everything that is produced in our literature moves to journals. Individual books visit stores or go begging in libraries to be read. A writer who decides on a separate edition for his work does not like to talk about how many copies he has published or how they have been dispersed.

The number is limited to several hundred. From where comes this contradiction between the reader and the writer, between the book and the buyer? How can one reconcile the hungry head of a book concern with the growing number of literate people in Russia?

Poor Folk is a splendid work about the touching story of a poor worker with a pure and loving heart, who is condemned to humiliation, hunger, and sorrow. This is a simple tale from genuine life which is repeated, perhaps, every day in one of the dark back streets and corners of our noisy, cold, and indifferent city. The story is rendered with profound feeling and an accurate knowledge of life, but also with all the mistakes of a first attempt, with long repetitions, overblown diminutive names, and a tiresome monotony.

The new criticism has seized upon this book greedily, showering it with enthusiastic praises, welcoming this young writer into the ranks of first-class geniuses and raising him to such heights, willy-nilly, and as often happens in such a case, as to make his head spin. The blunders, forgivable in a first work, become coarse mistakes in a second. The inadequacies grow. What was at first monotonous has become so excruciatingly boring that, respected readers, it was only from a sense of duty that I finished reading to the end *Messers Golyadkin* and *Prokharchin*. This bitter but honest truth has to sadden an individual with such a decisive talent as Mr. Dostoevsky. Who knows how guilty in these failures is the careless criticism of the young generation? Who knows what influence they have had over the development of a young, powerful, but still unsteady and immature talent?

February 1, 1847
Vissarion Belinsky, from a review

According to Mr. Guber, it is the *new criticism* . . . which has raised the author of *Poor Folk* to head-spinning heights, and which has appeared in print exactly one month after *The Double*.[47] *The Adventures of Mr. Golyadkin* was published. Consequently, the author of *Poor Folk* has had no opportunity to spoil his second story as a result of the head-spinning from praise for his first. . . .

We also now consider Mr. Dostoevsky to be an individual with a decisive talent, and on the basis of this opinion, we think that neither praise nor abuse influences him in any way. . . . And truly, is it worthwhile to call attention to a talent that can be killed by the praise or censure of the critics? When Pushkin appeared, he was praised and abused without moderation; but he still went his own way; he always remained true to his poetic instinct, sometimes even in spite of the assertions of his own personal mind. Without instinct there is no artist, and so deprived, his talent is so insignificant that the sooner nothing comes from him, the better for literature and the public. Childishly unfounded is the opinion that criticism can kill talents, praising or abusing them, but such a view has lived on in our country since the arcadian period of our literature, when it drowned in the tears and sighs of sensitive writers. . . . But now such an opinion is laughable and wild.

February 19, 1847
Vissarion Belinsky, from a letter to Ivan Turgenev

To my surprise, I did not like Dostoevsky's correspondence between cardsharps.[48] I had to force myself to finish it.

By the way, here is an anecdote for you about one fine man. From Kraevsky this individual took more than four thousand paper rubles, being obligated under contract to deliver to him on December 5th the first part of his large novel, on January 5th the second, on February 5th the third, and on March 5th the fourth. December and January go by. Dostoevsky does not appear, and where to find him Kraevsky does not know. Finally one fine morning in February the doorbell rings in the foyer of Kraevsky's home. The servant opens [the door] and sees Dostoevsky. Taking his coat quickly, the servant rushes to inform Kraevsky. Kraevsky, it seems, is overjoyed. The servant rushes out to Dostoevsky to welcome him, but he sees neither galoshes nor overcoat nor Dostoevsky himself. He has vanished without a trace. Now, truly, is that not a point-by-point scene from *The Double*?[49]

February 21, 1847
Konstantin Aksakov, from a review

[In *Poor Folk*], Dostoevsky does not appear as a complete, artistic talent. Of course, this is his first work, but in the initial attempts of a genuine talent, one almost always sees . . . a sincerity of creation which belongs to him alone. But, generally speaking, such a thing we do not see in this work of Mr. Dostoevsky. . . . The pictures of poverty appear in all their randomness; they are neither refined nor extended to the general sphere. The impression is a burdensome one because the work does not remain in your soul forever. . . .

In Dostoevsky's story, though . . . several features of the poor girl [Varvara Dobroselova] are good; there is also much that is splendid in the story of the student Pokrovsky. . . . Also remarkable is Devushkin's opinion about Gogol's "The Overcoat" . . . even if it is drawn out. . . .

[In *The Double*] we do not see the influence of Gogol so much as an imitation of the writer . . . Mr. Dostoevsky does not understand that what in Gogol is splendid, original, and alive . . . is with him intolerably lifeless, dry, boring . . . and tiresome. . . . We simply do not understand how such a story could have come into being. Almost by heart . . . all of Russia knows Gogol. Before all, he stands as a person in his own right. Mr. Dostoevsky refashions and, as a whole, repeats Gogol's phrases. But it seems that these are only phrases, deprived of their own life. There is only the bare imitation of the externals of the great works of Gogol.

In *The Double* . . . there is neither sense nor content nor thought—there is nothing. From the scraps of the brilliant clothing of an artist, Mr. Dostoevsky has sewn a suit and steps out boldly before the public. . . .

Is he amusing himself at the public's expense? Such a thing is difficult to say.

Is this truly talent? What we have here is a pitiful parody [of Gogol]. Indeed, can *The Double* arouse anything other than boredom and repulsion? Does Mr. Dostoevsky really think that seizing another's devices for his own, he has somehow taken hold of this individual's poetic worth? Does he really think that he has rendered some kind of service [to society]?

Speaking about Mr. Dostoevsky's *The Double*, we can repeat the words that Mr. Goldyakin also often repeats:

"Oh, this is bad, bad! Oh, very bad, indeed! Oh, our affairs are bad! Oh, things have caught up with us!"

Yes, that is it exactly! *The Double* has caught up with all bad things and in a poor way at that!

If it were not for Dostoevsky's first story, in no way would we have the patience to read his second. But we did so from a sense of duty, wishing to find something in his piece, but did not. It is so boring that we set the work down many times only to force ourselves to pick it up and read it anew. . . . Where is the talent we saw in Dostoevsky's first piece? Or has he begun to leave it only there?

Circa March 1847 and after
Fyodor Dostoevsky, from testimony to the Investigatory Commission for the Petrashevsky affair

I first visited Petrashevsky's home during Lent 1847. . . . In the first two years of our acquaintance, I saw him rarely. Sometimes three or four months would pass before I came to his place.

March 5, 1847
Apollon Grigoriev, from a review

> Of works of the school of Gogol . . . worthy of attention is Dostoevsky's superb story "A Novel in Nine Letters."

March 5, 1847
Ivan Goncharov, from a letter to Pyotr Yazykov

> As promised, I am being so bold as to send with this letter four copies of *A Common Story* . . . one for your personal library and the other three for the Committee for the Karamzin Library [in Simbirsk]. . . . I am also enclosing one copy of *Poor Folk* by F. M. Dostoevsky.

March 17, 1847
Apollon Grigoriev, from a review

> Writers . . . of the school that rather pitiful opponents call *natural* . . . see Gogol only as justifying and restoring any and all trifling personality, any and all kind of microscopic entity. . . .
>
> In so doing . . . they have fallen into the sentimental generation of Makar Alexeevich Devushkin and Varvara Alexeevna Dobroselova (in the novel *Poor Folk*) . . . or they have focused on the individual to such a degree as to legitimate any and all pretenses in the pathological story of Golyadkin Senior, who appears fully as a slave with no escape from his bondage.

March 27, 1847
Vasily Botkin, from a letter to Vissarion Belinsky

> It is painful for me to recall the mannered, fanciful Dostoevsky, although one must confess that for all his closure and sedition, he has a deep sense of the tragic. But to dig down into such a thing, one has to go through entire piles of manure.

April–June 1847
Fyodor Dostoevsky, from a letter to Albert Starchevsky

> I am sending you your proofs, but I have not looked through them. I am unwell with a rush of blood to the head; on doctor's orders, I absolutely cannot work. When I am capable of doing so, I will start. If there is not any work for me, I will return the advance to you as soon as the *Dictionary* comes out.[50]

174   **PART III**

April–mid-May 1847
Fyodor Dostoevsky, from a letter to Albert Starchevsky

> I have sat down for five hours over the form that is being sent to you. The article about the Jesuits ought to be rewritten completely.

April 1, 1847
Ivan Panaev, from an article

> My glory is secure. People talk about me. They are interested to learn my name and rank. About town are so many anecdotes with me as the hero. One honorable writer grants me a laudatory word. Another, for several evenings in a row, talks about nothing but my lack of talent. A third gives a soiree and people come (although they never came previously) because deftly he wishes it to be known on what day, at what hour, he will show me at his home.
>
> I must confess that I got terribly cold feet when I appeared before a large and unfamiliar crowd; I was so scared that I almost died right then and there. But when I was led into a room and praised for my great talent, I was brought back to consciousness.
>
> Incidentally, I did not show right away that I needed medicine no longer. Having come to my senses completely, I, for a long time, did not show any signs of life, but, with closed eyes, kept listening, like a cat whose is tickled under its throat. . . .
>
> But you cannot imagine what a surprising delight it is when people talk about you, when they praise you so! . . .
>
> But now I am beginning to get angry and depressed when, for a long time now, people are talking about something else. . . . Purposely do I make the rounds of bookstores and taverns, sitting behind a journal, and looking and eavesdropping and choking from agitation. . . . But what is going on? . . . People are praising [me], good God, they are praising. . . . Of course, there are those who censure [me]; but they are envious, undoubtedly envious, or they have a brother or some other relative who writes verse or they themselves do so. How can it be otherwise? You understand why else would they censure [me]? . . . Oh, envy, cursed envy! . . . Oh, pride, which prevents deserving ones [from getting] what they deserve! . . . After all, am I at fault because chance has gifted me with the wings of an eagle but has forgotten to give others those of a raven? . . . What do you think? Guilty as charged!

After all, I have only just set out on my path, and already I have endured from you envy and pride, the zealous enemies of any kind of external success! Already on my heart are bruises (an expression borrowed from one well-known Russian poet) and various heavy sores.... But later, later....

Soon, very soon I will present a complete picture of the horrors visited on me in my battle with human envy and pride.... Now, though, I wanted to present to you a more moving picture: a picture of glory and successes.

A first group, whom I have never seen, boast of their acquaintance with me; a second group gloat about what happened to me in a certain province; a third group, in surprising detail, describe my characters in such a way that when I go out, I resemble them like two peas in a pod; a fourth group are complete strangers to me, but when I meet them, act like they know me, bowing and smiling pleasantly. Finally, a certain publisher runs to my place, spreads his arms and legs, examines me from all sides, lisps, whistles, and at last explains that he wants my "poetry, if you please."

What do you think? Are all these facts seemingly sufficient to show that my glory is secure? Yes! My glory is secure: I am now a great person and no one can surpass me in anything! People should be honored to make my acquaintance. I have every right to put on airs before them—and I will put on airs!

How will I know what I am worth when my glory had already reached the furthermost corners of our country?... Just the other day I received a letter.... And what a letter it was!... From whom?... The hand of a woman.[51] She wrote to me that she was beautiful and young, and that in her earlier years she loved the mountains and valleys, hills and streams, and that I had begun to appear to her as an ideal.... "I am certain (she wrote to me!) that it was you! I knew your features . . . I knew you. Everywhere, for a long time, I felt you unseen alongside me.... Your genius...." But I am telling you only a few words of what she said.

Finishing the letter, she asked for my picture and my verse. She herself wrote poetry, [crediting] an unnamed person who had inspired her inexperienced pen (an obvious reference to me, but again from modesty, I am only saying little). "Publish them," she said, "they are splendid." So I am doing so now. Read on:

In vain do people say I chase after glory
But no one knows what I hide

> Suddenly my black curls are decked with myrtle
> My mind takes all in stride. . . .
>
> Why great thoughts, common sense,
> Are the problems of the day?
> They do not move or shake me
> My fancy in a deadly way.
> I need not the real world
> but poetry, dreams, and fears
> First salons, mazurkas, and polkas,
> Then grottoes, moons, and tears!
> In the blinding light of balls
> Amidst roses of red and cream
> I sit alone under a gloomy birch
> With delight I dream and dream.
> In vain do people say I chase after fame.
> Tricked them have I one and all
> No, in my black curly head, I think
> and repeat: I'm having a ball.

April 12, 1847
Faddei Bulgarin, from a review

> Young people do not understand that speculators denigrate them with their ennobling views. The honorable Mr. Gogol who never rose higher than Paul de Kock or Pigault-Lebrun, they proclaimed a Homer! . . .
>
> After Mr. Gogol reduced these speculators to despair with his silence, they put forth from the mob another young man, Mr. Dostoevsky, and call him a *genius, equal* to Gogol. They did so not to benefit Mr. Dostoevsky but to call the attention of the public to that journal which has published the fairy tales of Mr. Dostoevsky. But their attempts were not successful!

April 13, 1847
Fyodor Dostoevsky, from "The Petersburg Chronicle"

> If you begin to feel like reading, take the two volumes of *The Contemporary* for March and April, and there, as you know, is *A Common Story*. . . . The novel is good. In it is observation and much intelligence. The idea seems to us bookish and belated, but it is done in a deft way. Incidentally, the key wish of the author—to maintain his idea and to explain it in as much detail as possible—imparts to the work some

kind of special dogmatism and dryness; it even stretches and strains it. Such a shortcoming does not also redeem the easy, almost flying style of Mr. Goncharov. The author believes in reality; he shows people how they are. The Petersburg women [in it] come out especially successfully. . . .

Mr. Goncharov's novel is extremely interesting.

April 21, 1847
Leopold Brandt, from a review

[Goncharov] is a worthy successor to both Messrs. Gogol and Dostoevsky, of whom, as is well known, one has refused glory, and the other has been denied such by both readers and reviewers.

April 27, 1847
Fyodor Dostoevsky, from "The Petersburg Chronicle"

Passionately do we love our fatherland, our native Petersburg, our love of play, wherever and whenever it happens. In a word, we have a great many public interests. But *circles* are even more useful in our country. Everyone knows that all of Petersburg is nothing more than a large collection of small circles, each with its own makeup, rules, laws, logic and oracle. . . . Such a thing is the result of our national character which still avoids social life . . . and looks homeward [for company]. For social life, one needs art. . . . Home is more natural and peaceful, there one does not need art at all.

In some circles, you are asked in a rousing way—*what's new?* Quickly the question takes on a personal cast, with answers as gossip, yawns or other things that make you also yawn in a cynical and patriarchal way. In these circles, between gossip and yawns, you can extend your useful life in a most serene and delight way . . . until you leave this pleasant and serene world and enter a better one.

In other circles . . . people talk business with force. With passion, there gather educated and well-intentioned individuals . . . who, cruelly, banish all innocent pleasures like gossip and preference (these are seemingly not literary circles); and who, with incomprehensible enthusiasm, talk about important things. When people in these circles finish talking, postulating, solving social questions, and convincing everyone of everything, they become irritated and unpleasantly tired. Everyone becomes angry with everyone else. Bitter truths are uttered, sharp and sweeping personalities are bared. In the end, all retreat to their corners and settle down . . . [making things] pleasant . . . but in the end, offensively annoying.

April 27, 1847
Fyodor Dostoevsky, from "The Petersburg Chronicle"

Good Lord! Where have they gone—the villains of old dramas and novels? How pleasant it was when they lived in the world . . . and to have alongside a most virtuous individual who defended good and punished evil. . . .

This villain, this *tirano ingrato* . . . was, for some secret and completely incomprehensible reason, predetermined by fate. He was a villain while still in his mother's womb. Even his ancestors . . . sensed his appearance in the world. Purposely, they chose *a family name* which accorded completely with the social situation of their descendant . . . and from which we knew that this individual went about with a knife and slashed people . . . without taking a copeck. . . . God knows why. . . . as if he were some kind of machine. . . . How good it was! At the very least, how understandable!

But now God knows what writers talk about. Now, suddenly, it turns out that the most virtuous person . . . and most incapable of wrongdoing, becomes a complete villain suddenly, without even himself noticing [such a change]. . . . Even more annoying is that no one notices or says [anything] . . . [since] he lives honorably and for a long time before he finally dies amidst such honors and praise that one becomes envious he is mourned so sincerely and tenderly.

April 27, 1847
Fyodor Dostoevsky, from "The Petersburg Chronicle"

Gogol's book created a great stir in early winter. Particularly noteworthy was the unanimous response from almost all the newspapers and journals, even as they contradicted one another constantly in their assessment.[52]

May 1847
Vera Dostoevskaya-Ivanova, from a letter to Andrei Dostoevsky

I do not know why brothers Misha and Fedinka are angry with me. I have sent two letters to them, but they have not answered either one. When you see brother Fedinka, ask him to write at least five lines to me. Such a thing will make me extremely happy.

May 1, 1847
Vissarion Belinsky, from a review

> Perhaps the talent of Mr. Dostoevsky was greeted with exaggerated praise. But why must one invariably put forth the verdict, a cabal, an assemblage, a speculation, and not an exaggeration, a mistake? No one from among people with intelligence and taste will not come to reject Mr. Dostoevsky's talent, even remarkable as it is. It must be that the entire question is the extent and volume of his talent. . . .
> We must avoid such praises as *"Pushkin, Lermontov, Gogol, Dostoevsky."*[53]

Circa May 7, 1847
Fyodor Dostoevsky, from a letter to Mikhail Dostoevsky

> I will write you only two lines because I am very busy. I do not know where my letter will find you. With all my might I will try to finish up my affairs so that I can visit you for a week even if it be in September.[54] As for money, I was a little mistaken in my calculations. I will have to write perhaps even two feuilletons a week,[55] that is, no more than 250–300 paper rubles' worth. Since I have to pay back the Maykovs, from whom I have borrowed a great deal (although they are not even asking for it back), and for the apartment, I do not know how much I will be sending to you. I am in such a state, brother, that if by October 1st I repay you only 100 silver rubles, I will consider myself to be most fortunate. But from the first of October or September (I will come to visit you then, on the last ship), things will change. After finishing my novel, I will take an advance of 1,000 silver rubles from Kraevsky and on no condition other than for *an indefinite period of time.* Since *The Contemporary* is making a go of it and luring contributors away from *The Fatherland Notes* in a fierce way, he, *Andrei Alexandrovich Kraevsky,* is very frightened. He will agree to anything. Furthermore, it is to his good fortune and *mine* that my novel is being published at the end of the year.[56] It will appear during the subscription period, and, most important, if I am not mistaken, it will be the capital thing of the year and will get the better of my friends, the "contemporaries," who are doing everything they can to bury me. But to hell with them. Then after receiving the 1,000 silver rubles, I will come to see you with the money and with the final decision regarding you. You can come to Petersburg even alone, taking a leave of 28 days, to find a position and—or continue to serve in the engineers or leave it forever. . . .

I do not know about a translation. I will work all summer and try to find one. In Petersburg we had a fool named Furmann (he's abroad now). He receives 20,000 a year just on translations! If you had even so much as a year of financial security, you could definitely make a go of it. You are young;[57] you could even make a literary career. Nowadays everyone is making one. In ten years or so you could even forget about translations.

I am writing very zealously; perhaps I will finish. Then we will see each other earlier than planned. What does Emiliya Fyodorovna have to say? I send her my humblest regards, the children also. Good-bye, brother. I have a slight fever. I caught a cold yesterday by going out at night without a frock coat and in just an overcoat, and it was sleeting ice along the Neva. It is as cold here as in November. But I have already caught cold up to six times—it is nothing! Generally speaking, my health has improved greatly.

Good-bye, brother. Wish me success. After the novel I will get down to publishing my three novels (*Poor Folk*, *The Double*, rewritten, and the last one) at my own expense, and perhaps my fate will clear up.

God grant you happiness, my dear.

P.S. You will not believe it. Here is it already the third year of my literary activity and it is as though I am in a daze. I do not see any life, and there is no time to come to my senses. Study disappears for lack of time. I want to establish myself. They have created a dubious renown for me, and I do not know how long this hell will continue. Here is poverty, rush work—if only there were some peace.

May 30, 1847
Apollon Grigoriev, from an article

Akaky Akakievich of Gogol's "The Overcoat" has become the forefather for a multiplicity of microscopic personalities: For a long time, minuscule joys and trifling sufferings and sorrows have entered into the everyday habit of writers, but under the pen of Mr. Dostoevsky and Mr. Butkov, they have been carried to an extreme. . . . Such is "Prokharchin.". . .

Dostoevsky and Butkov delve so deeply into the trifling appearances of an observed or moral disease that, consciously or unconsciously, they set aside any concern about the artistry of their descriptions, trying exclusively to render with all possible faithfulness and accuracy the charm of that corner where [a character like] Mr. Prokharchin lives, without taking hardly great responsibility for their writing.

June 1847
Vissarion Belinsky, from a review

> Mr. Imrek[58] calls *Poor Folk* . . . "an artistic work," and the author a "talent that one cannot doubt." . . . But on that very same page . . . exactly nineteen lines later, he says: "But his (Mr. Dostoevsky's) story *decisively cannot be called an artistic work.*" Simple unhappiness! . . .
>
> From *Poor Folk* Mr. Imrek moves on to *The Double.* . . . The artificial, mannered style of this work is so strikingly manifest that even Mr. Imrek has rendered it with a rather successful parody:
>
> "It is not difficult to seize upon the devices [of the work]. The devices are not at all difficult to seize. It is not at all difficult or a difficulty to seize upon devices such as these. But the matter is not thus done, ladies and gentlemen; the very matter, ladies and gentlemen, is not over; it is still not thus completed, my good people, this very matter. And here, you know, one needs not only this but also that. It, you see, is something else that is demanded, this this, this that, and like it something else, too. And this this and this that is not to be had. Precisely this very this is not to be had; a poetic talent, ladies and gentlemen, such an artistic thing is also not to be had. Yes, here it is, this very thing, that is genuine, so it is; so it really is."

June 1, 1847
Fyodor Dostoevsky, from "The Petersburg Chronicle"

> The study of a city . . . is not a useless thing. We do not recall when we happened to come across a French book which contained a bevy of views on contemporary Russia.[59] Of course, views by foreigners on contemporary Russia are well known; but for some reason, we have resisted measurement by European standards. . . .
>
> This book by a notorious tourist had been read greedily throughout Europe. In it he writes that there is nothing characteristic about Petersburg architecture; that there is nothing particularly striking, or *nothing national* [about it], that the entire city is one ludicrous caricature of certain European capitals; and that Petersburg, in its architecture alone, is such a strange mixture [of styles] that one cannot stop exclaiming "oh!" and "ah!" in surprise at every turn.
>
> Greek architecture, Roman architecture, Byzantine architecture, Dutch architecture, rococo architecture, the newest Italian architecture, our Orthodox architecture—all this, our traveler says, is thrown together in such an amusing way that . . . there is not a truly splendid building [in the city]!

Our tourist also waxes eloquent on Moscow, on its Kremlin. About the latter, he has several ornate, rhetorical phrases. He is proud of Muscovite nationality, but he curses droshkies and cabs for straying from ancient, patriarchal lines. . . . [He also laments] the disappearance of everything that is native and national in Russia. The idea here is that Russians are afraid of their national character and thus do not want to go about as before, fearing justly that somehow their patriarchal carriages will shake their souls.

So writes a Frenchman, that is, an intelligent individual who, like any Frenchman, is superficial and exceptionally stupid. Such an individual does not accept things that are not French whether they be literature, the arts, the sciences, or even native history. He can become angry that there are people who have their own history, ideas, native character, and development. But so adroitly, secretly, even subconsciously . . . does the Frenchman agree with certain—we will not say Russian— armchair, leisure-time ideas of ours. He sees Russian nationality in the same way that many of our time want to see it, that is, as a dead letter, as an idea that has outlived its time, as a heap of stones, as if recalling [the remains] of ancient Rus, and, finally, as a blind, wholehearted appeal to a dreamy native land.

Without a doubt, the Kremlin is an extremely honorable monument to our distant past. It is an antiquarian rarity to be regarded with special curiosity and great respect. But how the Kremlin is absolutely national—this is something we cannot understand! There exist national monuments that have outlived their time and have stopped being national. We will say further: the Russian folk knows the Kremlin . . . [as] a religious [monument] to which flow people from all corners of our country to kiss the relics of Russian miracle workers. Such a thing is good, but nothing special. Crowds of folk go to pray to Kiev, to the Solovetsky Islands,[60] to Lake Ladoga,[61] to Mount Athos,[62] everywhere. But do such individuals know the lives of the prelates, of Saints Peter and Philip?[63] Of course not. . . . They have not the slightest understanding of the most important periods of Russian history.

People will say: our folk venerate the memory of ancient tsars and princes . . . who are buried in the Archangel Cathedral.[64] That is good. But whom among Russian tsars and princes . . . do the folk know before the Romanovs [ascended the throne]? *By name*, they know three: Dmitri Donskoi, Ivan the Terrible, and Boris Godunov (the remains of the last one lying in the Holy Trinity Lavra). The people know Boris Godunov only because he built "Ivan the Great."[65] About Dmitri Donskoi and Ivan Vasilievich they will tell you wonders beyond belief. . . .

People will also say: Who is this folk? The folk is dark and illiterate. They will also point to society, to educated people. But the delight [of such people] for the native land . . . seemed to be airy and cerebral, armchair and romantic, for who in our country knows history?

Historical tales are very well known. But for some reason, history in our time is a most unpopular, armchair affair, the province of scholars who argue, serve up, and compare, but who . . . cannot agree on the most fundamental ideas. They seek to explain facts that, more than ever, remain riddles. We will not argue: Russians cannot remain indifferent to the history of their tribe, in whatever form it may appear. But to demand that everyone forget and reject their present for certain honored antiquarian subjects is, in the highest degree, both unjust and absurd.

June 1, 1847
Fyodor Dostoevsky, from "The Petersburg Chronicle"

Petersburg is not like [Moscow]. One does not move an inch without seeming to hear and feel the contemporary moment, its idea. Truly . . . here everything is chaos, everything is a mix. Many things are food for caricature, but so is all of moving life.

Petersburg is the head and heart of Russia. . . . Everything about its many-faceted character gives witness to unified thought and movement. The rows of Dutch buildings recall the time of Peter the Great. The structures of Rastrelli hark back to the era of Catherine [the Great]; those in the Greek and Roman style, to the present time. They all show the history of European life in Petersburg and in all of Russia.

These days Petersburg is dust and garbage. It is still building and becoming. Its future is still an idea—the idea of Peter I. With each day it is forming, growing, and taking root, not in a swamp but in all of Russia, which lives as one Petersburg. Already everyone has felt the power and the blessings of the Petrine direction. Already all of society has been summoned to realize this great idea. Everyone has begun to live. Everything—industry, trade, science, literature, education—has begun to organize social life. . . . In our contemporary striving, we see not the disappearance of national life but rather the triumph of nationality, which, contrary to what many people think, is not perishing under European influence. As we see it, whole and healthy is that folk which loves the genuine moment in a positive way, and which understands and lives by its principles.

June 1, 1847
Fyodor Dostoevsky, from "The Petersburg Chronicle"

Never have people talked about contemporary ideas and directions so much as now, in the present time. Never has literature, as well as all manifestations of social life, aroused such curiosity. . . .

Almost everyone is beginning to discern and analyze society, each other, and himself. Everyone is examining and measuring one another with curious glances. An overall confession is coming into place. People are talking about, quoting, and scrutinizing one another . . . often in torment and pain. A thousand points of view are opening up to people who never expected [to have] a personal view on anything. . . . They understand and espouse the view that analysis does not spare the analyzers, and that is better to know oneself than to get angry at writers who are a most quiet and submissive lot and who do not wish to offend anyone. . . .

There is nothing more unjust than reproaches as to the emptiness and the inertia of our literature in the past year. Several new stories and novels have appeared in various periodicals and have met with complete success.[66] There have appeared several remarkable articles, primarily in literary criticism.[67] . . . There has come to be an edition of Russian classics by Smirdin which also has enjoyed great success and will continue indefinitely.[68] There also has seen the light of day a complete edition of works by Krylov.[69] The number of subscribers to journals, newspapers, and other publications have increased greatly, and the demand for reading has begun to spread through all levels of society. The pencil and chisel of artists have also not remained idle. The splendid undertaking of Messrs. Bernardsky and Agin—the illustrations for *Dead Souls*—are coming to an end, but one cannot praise enough the conscientiousness of these two artists.[70] Several of their illustrations are so splendid that it would be difficult to want anything more. M. Nevakovich, for now our single best caricaturist, continues his *Jumble* in a constant and tireless way. From the very beginning, the newness and wonder of this publication has attracted fervent and widespread curiosity.[71] Truly it would be difficult to imagine a more convenient time than now for the appearance of a caricaturist-*artist*. Many are the ideas developed and experienced by society. It is nothing to crack heads for subjects [for stories], although we often seemingly hear [people saying]: "What is there to talk and write about?" But the more talented a writer, the richer are his methods for carrying this thought into society. For him there are neither barriers nor everyday difficulties. For him there are themes and subjects always and everywhere. In these times the artist can find food no matter where he wishes to speak about everything. Furthermore, people have the urge to speak their minds. They also have the urge to seize upon and to consider that which has been said.

June 13, 1847
Varvara Dostoevskaya-Karepina, from a letter to Andrei Dostoevsky

If you write to us, let me know if brother Fedinka is well and if he is in Petersburg. I have heard nothing about him regarding his literary activity.

June 15, 1847
Fyodor Dostoevsky, from "The Petersburg Chronicle"

A friend of mine has assured me that we [Russians] do not know how to be lazy, that we find such a thing burdensome, without delight and quiet, since rest for us is somehow feverish, angst-ridden, gloomy, and unsatisfying; and that at the same time, there [reigns] in our country analysis, comparison, skeptical glances, and secret thoughts that always before us is some eternal, never-ending, and mundane task. . . .

Such a claim reminds me of [the story of] the punctual German who, leaving Berlin, noted calmly in his roadbook: "Upon arriving in Nuremberg, don't forget to get married." Of course the German, first of all, always has some kind of system in his head. He never feels the ugliness of facts; he is grateful for such things.

In truth, though, one cannot help but acknowledge that sometimes our actions have no system and that things somehow move along according to some set Eastern order. . . . We drag our life harness by force, with burdensome effort, from responsibility and duty, and we are also ashamed to admit that we do not have the strength to do so and become tired. . . .

Is that why we have in our country a powerfully developed but extremely unpleasant habit (which, we do not deny, can also be somehow useful in our way of doing things) always . . . to believe and consider in an extremely precise way our impressions, to consider . . . a forthcoming future delight . . . [and] to value and enjoy it in advance, in dreams . . . even though it is ill-suited for the present? . . .

We always . . . tear apart a flower to understand it more forcefully and then complain when we have fumes, not scents. But it is difficult to say what will become of us if we do not devote even several days a year to quenching our eternal and endless thirst for immediate genuine life via the various manifestations of nature. . . .

How do we not become tired, how do we not fall into paralysis, always chasing impressions, as if finding rhythm in a poor line of verse; tortured by an external thirst for spontaneous life; and frightened, to the point of illness, of our very illusions, of the hungry chimera, of this very dreaminess, and all those auxiliary measures which in our time try somehow to fill the completely sluggish emptiness of everyday colorless life?

In our country, the thirst for life moves to such an unrestrained passion. Everyone wants a serious activity. Many wish passionately to do good, to be of use. Little by little they begin to understand that happiness consists not in sitting on your hands . . . [waiting] to become a knight when an opportunity presents itself, but in eternal tireless activity, in the development and practice of all our inclinations and talents.

But do we have in our country many who are engaged in such tasks, and who do them with desire, *con amore*?

People say that by nature we Russians are lazy and love to avoid matters at hand, but thrust something upon us and we will do it as never before. But is such a thing entirely true? What evidence is there for such an unenviable national trait? Generally speaking, people have been crying out far too many things about general laziness and lack of action. To one another they have also been talking a great deal about useful activity, although, one must confess, that is all they are doing. Not for anything, though, are they ready to accuse their colleagues, perhaps only because, as Gogol noted, such individuals do not bite.

But, ladies and gentlemen, try to take a first step forward toward a *better and useful activity* and imagine it in some form. You show us a *business or a cause* . . . you begin to interest us in such a thing, you give it to us to do, and you set in motion our personal individual creativity. But are you able to do such a thing, Messrs. Urgers-On? Yes or no? No. So there is nothing to accuse, only that you have wasted words in vain. So it is in our country that a business or cause somehow always happens by itself, that is somehow an external affair, and that it does not evoke a special empathy. Here appears a purely Russian ability: to carry out a business or cause by force is foolish, dishonorable, and, as they say, winds up going completely to pieces. This trait shows clearly our national habit and manifests itself in everything, even in the most insignificant facts of our common life.

For example, in our country, if one does not have the means to begin to live in palaces or to dress as respectable people should, to dress like *everyone* (that is, like the very few), then our corner often resembles a cowshed, and even our clothes lead to unpleasant cynicism. If a person is dissatisfied, and if he lacks the means to articulate and to manifest that which is a bit better in him (not as a matter of pride, but as a consequence of the most natural human necessity to acknowledge, realize, and bring about a personal I in real life), then he will fall immediately into the most improbable state. If one may be allowed to say so, he will drink heavily, yield first to card-playing and card-sharping, next to dueling, and finally go out of his mind from *ambition*. At the very same time, he will despise his ambition fully and even suffer that he has been pained by such trivialities as ambition. You look—and unwillingly come to a conclusion that is almost unjust, even offensive, but also *seemingly very likely* that in us is little sense of personal worth, little essential egoism, and that, finally, we are unaccustomed to do a good deed without some kind of reward.

For example, give a task to an exacting, systematic German, one that is contrary to all his strivings and inclinations, and explain to him that it will set him on his way, feed him and his family, introduce him to society, take him to a desired goal and so forth, and the German will set about the business right away. He will even complete it without question, and even introduce into the new task a special new system. But is this a good thing? In part no, because in this case the individual goes to another, terrible extreme, to phlegmatic immobility and sometimes excluding the individual and, in its place, taking in his system, responsibility, formula, as well as his absolute worship of old world customs even if they do not measure up to the current time.

The reforms of Peter the Great created in Russia free activity, but they would not have been possible with this element in the national character, naively splendid, but sometimes extremely comic.

We have seen that the German, until the age of fifty, remains a bachelor. He teaches the children of Russian businessmen, knocks together a copeck here and there, and copulates via a legal marriage with his Minchen, dried up from a long spinsterhood, but heroically faithful. A Russian will not endure such a situation. He will quit loving such an individual or *go completely to pieces* or do something else. Here one can truly quote the opposite of a well-known proverb: what is health to a German is death to a Russian.

Are there many among us Russians who have the means to carry out their business or cause with love as they should—because such a thing demands desire, love for an agent, the entire person. Have many have found their stride? . . . No, they wave their hands and let the matter slip from them. But in characters who yearn for action, for immediate life, and for reality, but who are also feminine, tender, and weak, there gradually comes to the fore what people call dreaminess, so much so that in the end, people become not people but strange entities of an average type—dreamers.

But do you know what dreamers are, ladies and gentlemen? They are Petersburg tragedies, personified sins, tragedies that are silent, mysterious, gloomy, and savage, with all frenzied tragedies, with all catastrophes, upheavals, beginnings and ends.

We are talking seriously here. You sometimes meet individuals who are absent-minded, with vacant looks and pale, haggard faces; who seem perpetually engaged in something that is terribly burdensome or some skull-cracking business; and who sometimes appear weary and wan from burdensome labors; but who essentially come up with exactly nothing. Such are dreamers from the outside. Dreams are always burdened because they are extremely unbalanced. They are first extremely happy, then extremely gloomy. They are first boors, then attentive and tender. They are first egoists, then capable of the most noble sentiments.

As far as jobs go, these people are not fit for anything. They work, but they accomplish nothing. Rather, they are only *pulled along* by their own business or cause, which, in essence, is almost as bad as doing nothing at all. Such individuals despise formalities . . . but especially because they are submissive, forgiving, and fear that life will pass them by, they themselves are premier formalists.

At home, though, dreamers are completely different. For the most part, they live in complete isolation, as if hiding from people and the world and even rushing off into something melodramatic at a first glance at them. They are gloomy and terse with servants, and withdraw deep into themselves; but they also very much love everything that is idle, easy, and contemplative, everything that affects, in a tender way, emotion or arousing sensations. They love to read, and relish all kinds of books, even serious and specialized ones, but typically, after the second or third page, they drop what they are reading or become dissatisfied with it completely. Their fantasies are lively, fleeting, and even arousing. Their impressions are in sync with their moods, and an entire dreamlike world, with joys and sorrows, with heavens and hells, with the most captivating women, with heroic gestures, with heroic activity, always with some heroic struggle, with crimes and all kinds of horrors, suddenly possesses the entire being of the dreamer. The room disappears. Space, too. Time stops or flies by so quickly that an hour becomes a minute. Sometimes entire nights pass by unnoticed, in indescribable delights. Often in the course of several hours, dreamers experience a paradise of love or an entire existence that is huge, gigantic, unheard of, marvelous like a dream, splendid and grandiose. From some unknown cause, the pulse quickens, tears well up, and pale, moist cheeks burn with feverish fire. When dawn bursts forth with rosy light into the windows of dreamers, they are pale, sick, tormented, and happy. They throw themselves on their bed without recalling anything and, nodding off, they still hear the sensation in their heart, physical and sickly. The minutes of sobering up are terrible. The unhappy ones cannot bear them and accept their hell quickly in new, increased doses. Again a book, a musical motif, some old, distant memory from actual life—in a word, one of a thousand reasons, the most insignificant, and hell rises to the fore. Again a fancy, in a bright and lavish way, stretches out along the patterned and whimsical canvas of a quite mysterious dream. On the street, he walks about, hanging his head, paying little attention to his surroundings, sometimes forgetting reality completely. But he will note that the most ordinary everyday trifle, the most empty mundane thing will quickly assume a fantastic coloring. Already his glance becomes so fixed as to see the fantastic in everything. Closed shutters in broad daylight, an old woman on her last legs, a gentleman off to a meeting, waving his arms and muttering aloud to himself—such types, incidentally, one meets often—a family picture in the window of a poor wooden home—all these things are almost adventures.

The imagination is set on fire. Suddenly there is born an entire story, a tale, a novel. Often reality makes a burdensome, hostile impression on the heart of dreamers. They rush off to take refuge in their cherished, golden corner, which in reality is often dusty, slovenly, disordered, and dirty. Little by little our pranksters begin to shun crowds and societal interests, and gradually, imperceptibly begins to lose the talent for genuine life. Naturally, it begins to seem to him that the delight attained by his willful fantasy is fuller, more lavish, and more alive than genuine existence. Finally, in his delusion, he loses completely the moral sense by which individuals are able to appreciate all genuine beauty. They become unhinged and lost. They let slip moments of genuine happiness. In their apathy, they lay down their hands in a lazy way. They do not want to know that human life is endless self-contemplation of nature and daily being. There are dreamers who even celebrate the anniversary of their fantastic sensations. They often note the days of the month when they are particularly happy and when their fantasies come into most pleasant focus. And if at that time they wander into some street, read some book, or see some woman, they, without fail, try to see them again on the anniversary of their impressions, copying and recollecting the slightest circumstances of their rotten, impotent happiness.

Is not such a life a tragedy! Is it not a horror and a sin? Is it not a caricature? And are we all not more or less dreamers!

June 17, 1847
Apollon Grigoriev, from an article

Mr. Imrek is displeased with Dostoevsky's *Poor Folk* particularly because it "leaves an unpleasant impression which is inadmissible in the creation of great art." . . . We do find faults in its extreme sentimentality, as well as the variations and variants in a single letter—but not because it leave a burdensome impression. Such a thing can arise from anything.

[But] *The Double* . . . Mr. Imrek laughs at in a very witty and, for the most part, accurate way.

Summer 1847
Mikhail Yazykov, from a letter to the editor

Two or three years before his exile, on a splendid summer evening sometime in July or August, F. M. Dostoevsky paid me one of his frequent visits. . . . Among the guests were I. I. Panaev . . . and, it seems, Nekrasov . . . as well as P. V. Annenkov and I. S. Turgenev.

As usual, the lively conversation continued far into the night. Suddenly at around two in the morning, when the room had already become filled with light, Dostoevsky's thoughtful and concentrated expression became somehow agitated . . . his eyes were frightened, and his voice anxious and hollow.

"Mikhailo Alexandrovich, where am I?" he asked.

I had no idea what to do when, suddenly, Dostoevsky jumped up from the couch and ran very quickly through the large room where we sitting and straight to the open window to get some fresh air.

My wife was not feeling well and in an adjoining room. All the other guests were taking their leave. Having seen them off quickly, I grabbed a carafe of water. . . . We were alone.

When I ran to the window, I saw Dostoevsky with a distorted expression on his face. His entire body was shaking, and his head was shuddering and leaning to one side.

Having never seen and not knowing the signs of falling sickness and not suspecting . . . also a mild epileptic attack, I decided to pour cold water over his head. Immediately, in a powerfully aroused condition . . . he ran headlong through the room . . . and, without a hat, onto the Fontanka in the direction of Anichkov Bridge.

Deciding to catch up with him, I ran out of the gates . . . of my home[,] . . . jumped into the first carriage that came my way and ordered the driver to head for Nevsky Prospekt. . . . I caught sight of Dostoevsky running toward Liteinyi Street. . . . Having finally caught up with him . . . I jumped out of the carriage and stopped him.

Dostoevsky had calmed down somewhat. He had come to his senses and began to thank me for my concern, adding, vaguely, that he was still far from his apartment and that it would be better to hurry on over to the Mariinsky Hospital . . . to find a doctor on duty.

Assured that the attack had passed, I seated him in the carriage headed toward my place; but after a few minutes, he was completely at peace, and continued on to his place.

July 7, 1847
Stepan Yanovsky, from an 1881 letter to Apollon Maykov

I ask you, Apollon Nikolaevich, to recall the time when, in July 1847, you found me at home in a complete uproar . . . and Fyodor Mikhailovich sitting on a chair with an uplifted arm from which blood [ran], as black as coal and flowing like a stream, and crying out to us, "I've been saved, pal, I've been saved!"

This was the first serious attack of the illness which was accompanied by a terrible rush of blood to the head and an unusual excitement of the entire nervous system.

Another time I accidentally met Fyodor Mikhailovich on St. Isaac Square. He was coming from Solonitsyn's place and was being led under his arm by some kind of clerk from a military department. Fyodor Mikhailovich was in a terribly aroused state. He was screaming that he was dying and that he be taken quickly to my place. His pulse was more than a hundred beats [per minute] and was extremely strong. His head was arched backward and convulsions had begun.

I sat him down alongside myself and the clerk in the first cab that came my way and took him to my place.

In this letter I will not describe to you more about the course of this illness. But several days after this paroxysm, you, your brother Vladimir Nikolaevich, and the deceased Alexander Ustinovich Poretsky, Pyotr Mikhailovich Tseidler, and Ivan Ivanovich Lkhovsky saw me in my apartment, and I remember well that I called this illness falling sickness and [said that I] had treated the ailing man with the appropriate measures.

July 7, 1847
Stepan Yanovsky, from his memoirs

> Fyodor Mikhailovich and I agreed . . . that we would meet three times a week at my place from three to six in the afternoon. . . . But one time [Dostoevsky] having missed a meeting . . . I, instinctively and for no reason at all, was seized by an anxious feeling. . . . Walking toward Senate Square . . . I saw Fyodor Mikhailovich standing right in the middle of the place! He was not wearing a hat. His tie was loose and his coat and jacket unbuttoned. On his arm was a writer who wrote for the military. With all his might, Fyodor Mikhailovich was crying, "This is one who is saving me," and other things in that vein. . . . Later, whenever Fyodor Mikhailovich recalled our encounter, he always said, "After this, how can you not believe in premonitions?"

Mid-July 1847
Stepan Yanovsky, from his memoirs

> Before his arrest [in 1849] Fyodor Mikhailovich did not write long letters. If and when he did write to someone, he did so on small scraps of paper. Of all the notes I received from Fyodor Mikhailovich, there is an interesting one . . . in which he informed me that, having lived in Pavlovsk,[72] he had been subject to paralysis. He had been very busy taking up a collection for a drunkard who did not have any money for drink, but who, when he did, got drunk . . . and went from cottage to cottage, demanding that someone beat him up for money.
>
> Fyodor Mikhailovich told the story . . . not only with so much humanity for the drunkard that tears flowed down my face but also with the equally great humor and mercilessness that were part of his talent as well.

After July 15, 1847
Stepan Yanovsky, from a letter to Anna Dostoevskaya

> The Maykovs lived in a spacious apartment . . . with rooms that were large, high-ceilinged, and with furnishings that were extremely elegant and comfortable. Every Sunday . . . beginning at seven in the evening, there gathered youths with souls into which the good Lord had inserted a huge dose of talent, as well as with hearts that, from the very beginning, [were filled] with love for those close to them, with goodness and truth, and with minds that searched for light. . . .
>
> Here people read and discussed their articles and put forth projects and plans for works. . . . Everything was done in such an extremely serious and friendly way, without the slightest feeling of envy or malice, that one can say it was precisely here that would come the people who would write *The Frigate Pallada* and *Oblomov*, *Notes from the House of the Dead* and *The Diary of a Writer*,[73] and so many other things . . . works that would make up the treasured essence of Russian literature.
>
> In these groups . . . Fyodor Mikhailovich, with his personal atomic analysis, analyzed the writings of Gogol, Turgenev, and his own Prokharchin, a piece that remained unintelligible to most readers even though it was a subject taken directly from life. . . .
>
> Hosts and guests came together for dinner . . . for good music and singing . . . the gatherings lasting until three and even four in the morning.

After July 15, 1847
Dmitri Grigorovich, from his memoirs

> Once a week . . . in the Maykovs' home . . . one always met the leading lights of literature, many of them appearing with manuscripts.

After July 15, 1847
Stepan Yanovsky, from his memoirs

> From time to time, when the Maykovs hosted dances . . . Fyodor Mikhailovich not only loved to see people dance, but in such activities he also willingly took part. . . .
>
> Fyodor Mikhailovich loved dance as an expression of spiritual worth and a veritable sign of health. He regarded such activities, though, not as opportunities to become close to a woman physically but merely to exchange a lively word or two with his partner.

After July 15, 1847
Anna Dostoevskaya, from her memoirs

> [Dostoevsky] loved [Apollon] Maykov not only as a talented poet but also as the finest and most intelligent of men.

July 25, 1847
Nikolai Nekrasov, from a letter to Ivan Turgenev, Vissarion Belinsky, and Pavel Annenkov

> *Illustrated Almanac* consists of small humorous articles in poetry and prose.... For it we have ordered and prepared articles from Goncharov, Dostoevsky, and Apollon Maykov.

August 1847
Ivan Goncharov, from an obituary

> Valerian Maykov studied history, politics, and economics. He adored philosophy and studied its latest trends, particularly in Germany.... He studied chemistry in spurts, as a person with a soul. He loved art passionately in all its manifestations and studied it in theory and practice, both at home and abroad. Knowing three languages, he had access to all the great works in science and literature. His poor health allowed him to work only a few hours a day, but that did not prevent him from giving himself over to his favorite studies. Gifted with a mind that was enlightened, insightful, and receptive, he, with unusual facility, acquired knowledge unlike anyone else.
>
> When he studied, he did not hide from people or society. He shunned [even] the slightest pedantry and all external signs of erudition. He found knowledge anywhere, anytime, in conversations, in books. Often a serious thought forced him into a friendly circle. There, in an easy and attractive way, he developed an idea, and possessing fully a gift for words, he could expound upon it in a way that was common and accessible to all. It was enough for him merely to latch on to a hint of a notion before he made it his own; subjected it immediately to an innate precise analysis; and from it drew an immediate, brilliant, often unexpected but always severely logical conclusion, avoiding, with unusual skill, paradox and sophistry. It was also sufficient for him to get hold of a bare outline of any system before, by virtue of his mental facilities, subjecting it to his own authority and bringing it to life. An important and profound work of a thinker or philosopher he read with such great enthusiasm, like a work of fiction, where and whenever he could, not hiding in his study or behind closed windows....

Judging by his splendid beginnings [as a critic], his work ethic, his many-faceted education . . . one can say with assurance that he was fated to claim a great place among our genuine recognized talents of the first rank. . . .

Valerian Maykov always found the good in people . . . not with any design or advantage in mind, but even unconsciously . . . from an instinct that was tender, noble, and innate . . . [and] from impulses that were youthful and flowed from his splendid nature. . . .

His precise and observant mind did not overlook the failings of people . . . but the meekness and almost feminine softness of his heart caused him to be patient and indulgent of such things. No one ever heard from him a caustic or bilious word, or a sharp and decisive judgment or verdict at the expense of another. No one ever noticed in him a hostile disposition toward others. He . . . tried to excuse or mitigate a moral failing in a person . . . or to express an unfavorable expression with a regretful smile or a rare ironic word. One had to see his sense of calm . . . when he tried to arouse in himself dissatisfaction with someone, how he worried about how to erase any unpleasant trace from anyone who had offended him! It was also wondrous to see how he could right away call people to himself . . . that he attracted so many friends, and that his death called forth to them the double loss of a gifted, intelligent public figure and a kind, tender, and noble friend.

August 15, 1847
Alexei Pleshcheev, from an article

V. N. Maykov promised to be a critic whom our society awaited and who united in himself soundness, erudition, and aesthetic tact. By chance we have heard that this young critic was reproached for the length of his articles, his long-windedness, and his lack of journalistic liveliness. The first failing, if it existed at all, occurred solely from a desire to utter thoughts as clearly and demonstratively as possible. . . .

What a loss our literature has suffered! What a beneficial public figure society has lost! Such noble strivings and thoughts, so many broad concepts, so many bold and profound ideas have been carried with him to the grave! . . .

It was enough to meet Valerian Maykov only once to see how much love there was in his heart; how passionately it empathized with all that was noble and lofty; and how disturbed it was by the sight of anything that diminished human dignity.

Kindness and empathy incarnate, this man could not have enemies. He never offended anyone even with words, and if someone, in conversation with him, happened to have his pride hurt accidentally, Maykov redoubled his efforts right away to reach out to the offended party and to do anything he could to rectify the wrong.

Such an individual one could not help but love.... Valerian Maykov could find the good in anything.... He was ready to forgive all faults and failings.... He was there for everyone. Anyone who came his way with a confession, an inner doubt, or an unanswered question, he responded to with sympathy and comfort.

August 16, 1847
Mikhail Dostoevsky, from a letter to Fyodor Dostoevsky

I hasten to share with you, my treasured friend, some pleasant news. First of all, I am for the minute secure financially. I have received my salary, so if you still have not sent any money to me, then, at the very least, do not worry or grieve over me. You would not believe how often I think of you, my dear toiler. In the second place, Reingardt was in Helsinki. He dropped by our place but did not find us at home. We were at a summer cottage with acquaintances. The next day I went over to his place . . . and spent a half hour with him, i.e., right up to his very departure for Revel. He still had one or two people to visit, so it was only on the road to the ship that I managed to tell him that I had business with him and that . . . I wanted to write to him immediately. "But what is it? Can you not say it simply, in two words?" he said to me. So I allowed myself time to explain everything to him. This Reingardt is a rare individual. He did not hesitate and promised to send 300 rubles by the first mail. Nonetheless, I wrote to him because in my conversation with him there was much that was left unsaid. So if the Muscovites are swindling us,[74] this resource can be counted on. I say this . . . because I believe only in you and me. If there is money coming from Moscow, it will be addressed by me to repay Reingardt. He told me . . . that he would be glad to help me even more, that he agrees with me completely as to my business, and that there is nothing else for me to do.

So I will have 300 rubles. To his we will add 100 rubles from the sale of furniture and even an additional 100 rubles. So in a very short time, I will have gathered together 500 rubles. That is a significant sum, is it not? And 150 rubles to my wife for the two of us to live on for two months, and 100 rubles for equipment. So I can hope to bring with me about 200 rubles, which can serve for you and me as a deposit in our common bank. This money will be the beginning of that 350,000 rubles that, according to your words, we will be the happy possessors of in ten years....

What kind of apartment do you have? Will it be suitable for both of us? Write and tell me how much you are paying for it. Does it come with wood? We definitely need an apartment with wood so as to spare us any vile fuss....

Why don't you write, my dear? When I don't receive from you any news in a long time, I keep thinking that you are sick and I worry terribly. Just you wait—you will get better once I am there.

Brother, begin to busy yourself about work. We do not want to spend the day without something to do. How great it will be when we are living together....

If you will begin to publish *Poor Folk* in the fall,[75] it will be for me a splendid occasion to strike up an acquaintance with the people who do typography and book production.

I fear that the Muscovites have written to Krivopishin. The fact of the matter is that my retirement will proceed through the Department of Inspection. But they might hold it up under a pretext, for example, that one of the forms is not correct. But you need not follow up on it. I will submit a petition on September 1st.

Late August–early September 1847
Fyodor Dostoevsky, from a letter to Nikolai Nekrasov

Of course the conditions that you were pleased to offer me at our last meeting at Maykov's [home] are quite advantageous. But at the present moment I find myself in such a difficult situation that the money you promised me will not bring me any benefit at all; it will only extend my desperation for no good purpose. Perhaps you may be partly aware of my circumstances.

In order to get on my feet at least a bit, I need 150 silver rubles. Therefore, Nikolai Alexeevich, if you do not wish to give me the money in a lump sum, then to my greatest regret, it will be impossible to deliver my story to you. Because I will not have the material means for writing it.[76] If, however, you agree to give me such a sum in advance,[77] then in the first place, the date by which you will receive the story will be January 1, 1848, no earlier. You probably would find it more pleasant for me to say *for certain, and not about*. Therefore, *for certain, by January 1, 1848*.

In the second place, I will ask you to pay out the money in the following way: 100 silver rubles on October 2, 1847, and 50 silver rubles, right now, that is, with *my* messenger.

Pardon me, Nikolai Alexeevich, for negotiating with you by means of a letter and not personally, as would be more convenient for us. I kept wanting to see you after I had completed my latest work in its entirety.[78] But now, at the present moment, I find myself in such a repulsive position that I decided to begin the business now about which I am writing to you openly.

I cannot leave the house because I caught a cold this morning and now it seems that I will have to stay home for about four days.

P.S. *In any event*, I ask you most humbly to send an answer with my messenger because afterwards I will not need him.

September 9, 1847
Fyodor Dostoevsky, from a letter to Mikhail Dostoevsky

I hasten to answer your letter. Well, do as you wish with your family, as you yourself think best, but you, in regard to yourself, do not change your disposition for anything. You are afraid that they will not grant you an extension; but can't you take a leave for 2 or 3 months? If you cannot, consult the district commander and simply ask him to see that there will be no delay with such a thing. After all . . . I do not think they want to squeeze someone who is retiring. But come anyway. . . . Your retirement may be issued in November.[79] You say that people are shaking their heads. I say to you—do not be upset over such a thing. You write that I have made a slow start too. But after all, that is only right now. Wait a bit, brother, things will improve. We have an association. It is impossible that we should both fail to make our way out onto the road. Nonsense! Just remember what sort of people are shaking their heads! What you are getting now, you will always get in Petersburg, but not without such hard work! I will stay in my apartment and wait for you. I am not well and am finishing a story so that it can be printed in October.[80] Thus I am hurrying.

You do not say on what day you are leaving for Revel. But it does not make any difference. My letter, perhaps, will reach you on the eve of your departure. How will you arrange things for your family there? 125 silver rubles is not a lot of money. I will write to the Muscovites, but you write too from Helsingfors and tell them to send the money to my address. It is clear that Karepin is a son of a bitch and a scoundrel of the first degree.

Come soon, brother. In a fit of terrible need, I can get some money. But do you know how much I need myself? At least 300 silver rubles by October 1st. Out of that sum, 200 rubles will be used for debts and 100 will be spent on me personally, and all of that is only if there is money. Just in case, I will write down for you everything that I can realize by the first days of October if some extreme need should present itself.

From Kraevsky	50 silver rubles
From Nekrasov	100 silver rubles
At a certain place	50 silver rubles
Selling the right to a printing of *Poor Folk*	200 silver rubles
	400 silver rubles

That is a goodly sum but it will ruin me, taking into consideration the sale of *Poor Folk*. I have no time to publish *Poor Folk*. But through a certain printer I hope to publish it without money. If you would turn up here, you could take care of all this; then all winter long we would keep getting money. You will not be making a mistake if you come here as soon as possible. I will tell you that perhaps there is hope that if you are in town, you will have the work about which I wrote you the last time. In addition, there is a certain publication toward the New Year, a colossal one, financed by huge capital, which will be able to furnish you with a great deal of work for translation-compilation. You can also get translations from Kraevsky or Nekrasov, with whom I will enter into a definite arrangement and which he wants awfully much. In addition, there is yet another publication toward the New Year, and still *another one* after that. All of them will come to be.[81] It is too bad that you did not finish translating Schiller's plays. If you had done them all, they could have been sold. Gather together everything you have. A few days ago, when I told Kraevsky that you could translate a book for the Geographic Society (in my last letter to him), and that you knew German and had translated all of Schiller, he suddenly asked rashly, "Where is his translation?" Then thinking the better of it, he fell silent suddenly. Even if it does not appear in *The Fatherland Notes*, Kraevsky could facilitate its acquisition.

Well, good-bye, my dear. I did not write much of what I wanted to. Honest to God, there is no time.

P.S. Do you know what an association means? If we work apart, we will collapse, become timid, and lose heart. But two people [working] together for a single goal—that is another matter. There you have a hearty person, boldness, love, and twice as much energy.

Write me about everything in as much detail as possible. Write me about figures (money, time, and so forth) carefully and precisely.

200   PART III

September 13, 1847
Mikhail Dostoevsky, from a letter to Fyodor Dostoevsky

> The Muscovites are not sending money. . . . We have 125 rubles which is terribly little. . . . Most likely I will arrive at your place without money.[82] But I am not downcast. We are healthy and will not perish. Our association is a matter that is sacred and great. . . .
>
> Do not think of selling *Poor Folk*. Somehow we will manage. . . . If only my retirement will not be delayed . . . this is what worries me.[83] Write to the people in Moscow. I will also write to them.

Fall 1847 and after
Fyodor Dostoevsky, from testimony to the Investigatory Commission for the Petrashevsky affair

> It was through me that my brother, Mikhailo [Mikhail] . . . became acquainted with Petrashevsky when we lived together after his arrival from Revel. He met Petrashevsky for the first time at my place and was invited to gatherings at his place. I took my brother there to meet people and have fun, since he did not know anyone in Petersburg and missed his family.
>
> My brother, though, did not take any part in the conversations at Petrashevsky's place. I did not hear even two words from him. Everyone who came to Petrashevsky's home knows such a thing [to be true]. Mikhail visited there more and more rarely, and when he did turn up there, it was from curiosity and because, being a working family man who was extremely poor . . . he denied himself almost all other pleasures.

Fall 1847 and after
Lyubov Dostoevskaya, from her memoirs

> Uncle Mikhail was also interested in this society [of Petrashevsky's], but since he was married and the father of a family, he considered it more sensible not to visit the gatherings at Petrashevsky's home too often. But he took advantage of the forbidden books from his library. At that time Uncle Mikhail was a great fan of Fourier and studied his utopian theories.

Fall 1847 and after
Lyubov Dostoevskaya, from her memoirs

> Uncle Andrei also visited the gatherings at Petrashevsky's.[84] At that time he was still too young and had begun to study at an institution of

higher learning. Several years younger than his brothers, he saw them more as heads of a family than friends. In their turn, the elder brothers treated him like a young boy. . . .

My father never spoke with his youngest brother about politics. As a result, Uncle Andrei did not suspect the role my father played in the Petrashevsky Circle. . . . He always surrounded himself with educated people. He heard about the interesting society that gathered at Petrashevsky's home and asked one of his friends to introduce him to its leader. . . .

One time there, he ran into my father, whose face was pale and distorted with anger.

"What are you doing here?" he asked Andrei in horror. "Leave right away so I can say that I never saw you here!"

My uncle was so frightened by my father's ire that he left the salon right away.[85]

Circa early October 1847
Stepan Yanovsky, from his memoirs

> Still another incident [in readings with Dostoevsky] occurred with A. N. Pleshcheev, who was still a youth at the time, without a mustache or beard, seemingly no more than eighteen or nineteen.[86] As I now recall, Fyodor Mikhailovich left my place one Sunday, inviting me to a housewarming at his place. At that time, Mikhail Mikhailovich [Dostoevsky] was about to retire [from state service]. He arrived in Petersburg alone without his family and had moved in with Fyodor Mikhailovich. According to the invitation, I arrived at the Dostoevskys' with my friend Vlasovsky at five a.m. There I also found Pleshcheev, Kreshev, Butkov, an engineer-officer (whose name I forget), and Golovinsky. Also, acting as a servant and known to all was a noncommissioned officer named Yevstafy, whose name Fyodor Mikhailovich noted warmly in one of his stories.[87]
>
> After Yevstafy gave each of us a glass of tea, Fyodor Mikhailovich turned to A. N. Pleshcheev and said, "Well, old boy, read to us what you did with the anecdote I gave you." Pleshcheev began to read his work immediately, but his story was so weak that we barely could listen through to the end. Although Pleshcheev was somehow pleased with his piece, Fyodor Mikhailovich said to him in a straightforward way, "In the first place, you did not understand me and came up with something different from what I told you to do; and in the second place, you expressed yourself in a very poor way." After such a verdict, Pleshcheev destroyed the story.

October 1847 and after
Lyubov Dostoevskaya, from her memoirs

> In colorless and limited Petersburg my father's talent burned itself out. . . . He did not have money for travel to Europe, the Caucasus, or the Crimea—travel at the time was very expensive. My father was perishing . . . and was happy only at the home of his brother Mikhail, who had settled in the capital and, having left his soldiering, had decided to devote himself entirely to literature. Mikhail was married to a German woman, Emiliya Ditmar, and they had several children. My father loved his nephews very much; their childlike laughter dispersed his melancholy.

October 1, 1847
Mikhail Dostoevsky, from a letter to Fyodor Dostoevsky

> I am very glad that [brother] Andryusha has left. Beyond the fact that he has a splendid job, he is finally getting accustomed to living with his mind. But you will not believe how weak his heart is.

November 4–8, 1847
Vissarion Belinsky, from a letter to Vasily Botkin

> Kraevsky is facing hard times, not because he does not have good stories in hand, but because he publishes such vile things as . . . Dostoevsky's "The Landlady"—a (nervous expletive) work, and without end to boot.

November 20–December 2, 1847
Vissarion Belinsky, from a letter to Pavel Annenkov.

> Dostoevsky did a really bad turn to Kraevsky, who published the first half of one of his stories [only to learn later] that he had not written the second half, nor would he ever do so. . . . The story is so extremely vulgar, stupid, and talentless. It starts off with absolutely nothing (and no matter how hard he tried) goes nowhere. The hero is a nervous (expletive deleted). No matter how the heroine looks at him, he flops down into a faint. Truly!

Conclusion

In 1846 and 1847 Fyodor Dostoevsky was decidedly not on the straight and steady path that Pushkin and Gogol, Turgenev, and Tolstoy appeared to travel to glory and fame. Nothing was going right for the young writer. Indeed, the wrong turns were so manifest, multiple, and menacing that they threatened not just creative impasse but the end of his literary career. To everyone, including himself, Dostoevsky was not simply moving down slippery slopes; he was going off the rails in literature and life.

The threats were external and internal. The four works after *Poor Folk*—*The Double*, "Mr. Prokharchin," "The Landlady," and "A Novel in Nine Letters"—were seen as failures by readers and reviewers. Disturbed and deranged characters, complex and convoluted plots, and winding and windy prose caused former admirers and fans to lose faith in the young writer and to look elsewhere for solutions to national problems. Also, with his antics and shenanigans, Dostoevsky had so alienated the admittedly problematic and fickle members of the Belinsky circle that he soon found himself persona non grata, if not the laughingstock of the Russian literary world.

From within, Dostoevsky was beset by dark shadows of ongoing doubt. More than ever, he wondered if he had the stuff to be a writer. Anxiety and angst turned to depression, despair, even flirtations with death.

CONCLUSION

To be sure, there were bright spots for Dostoevsky in 1846 and 1847. There was Stepan Yanovsky, who assured him that he had a long while to live. There was brother Mikhail, who, more than ever, was ready to sacrifice everything for his younger sibling. There was Valerian Maykov, who understood what Dostoevsky was trying to do in his art. There were the other Maykovs, who, along with the Vielgorskys and the Beketovs, gave him friendship and family. There were dinners with Butkov, Pleschcheev, and other new acquaintances. At best, though, such people were temporary fixes for what ailed Dostoevsky. They were lulls in the gathering storm of his life.

With hindsight, it is tempting to posit numerous what-ifs for Dostoevsky during 1846 and 1847. What if he had handled the success of *Poor Folk* in a more humble and judicious way? What if he had gotten along with Nekrasov, Turgenev, and Panaev? What if he had taken Belinsky's advice and focused on sociopolitical themes? What if he had given readers and reviewers what they wanted in fiction? What if he had been more disciplined in his writing? What if he had had a more structured way of life? What if he had been faithful to his family and friends? What if he had adhered to the virtues and values of his childhood, adolescence, and youth? What if he had prayed to God? What if he had kept company with the philosophical and literary masters of the past?

Admittedly, if Dostoevsky had done all or any of these things, he would have had an easier time of things. In truth, though, the price the young writer would have paid for conformity would have been even higher than what he paid for going his own way. If Dostoevsky had listened to anyone but himself at this time, he would not have become the national and international figure he would be twenty years later. Most likely he would have been a footnote in Russian literature, a minor realist, akin to Grigorovich and Panaev, who wrote about "poor folk" in cities and villages throughout his homeland.

During this period, though, Dostoevsky was learning three valuable lessons. First, he was experiencing firsthand the perils of seeing himself as a genius, an extraordinary man. On good days, he soared on the success of *Poor Folk*. He was the self-appointed successor of Pushkin, Lermontov, and Gogol. No one could tell him anything. He knew it all. On bad days, he crashed with the failures of *The Double*, "Mr. Prokharchin," "The Landlady," and "A Novel in Nine Letters." Indeed, he seemed to be regressing as an artist. In response, Dostoevsky retreated into physical and spiritual "undergrounds," into self-canceling dualities. He was lord and louse. He was master and man.

Second, the young Dostoevsky was discovering the human penchant for putting idols and man-gods on pedestals one moment but tearing them down, suddenly and viciously, the next. It was a painful if invaluable lesson for the young writer to see that mobs made the man. The young Dostoevsky had been carried aloft by Belinsky and others who proclaimed him the savior of Russian literature. He was slammed against rocky shores when he failed to meet their expectations as a critic of national life. Even more shocking for the young Dostoevsky, perhaps, was not only how quickly he was abandoned by former friends and fans but also how he became the object of their relentless ridicule and scorn. Belinsky and company would not leave him in peace. Rather, among themselves and in poetry and prose, they took every opportunity to berate the young writer as a huckster and a fraud. Equally instructive, Belinsky and his circle were angrier with themselves than they were at him. No one, he learned, wanted to look foolish.

Third and most important, Dostoevsky was progressing as a writer. In *The Double*, "Mr. Prokharchin," "The Landlady," and "A Novel in Nine Letters," he was sketching heroes and heroines, images and ideas that would become mainstays of his later fiction. Indeed, in 1846 and 1847 Dostoevsky's topics and themes poured forth in a lava-like flow. If Belinsky and others censured the young artist for writing that was undisciplined, prolix, and repetitive, it was in part because he could not rein in the streams of impressions and observations that swept over him. Boldly he was transcending romantic and realist models to create his own poetics, his own rationale for his tortured path through existence. One wonders if in 1846 and 1847 the line between Dostoevsky and his heroes was too close for comfort. In the four works after *Poor Folk*, was Dostoevsky writing about himself or about others? Was he, in the depths of his soul, also a miser, a madman, a dreamer, a pervert, a huckster? In truth, he feared he was all of them.

In the long run, the blunders and slips that Dostoevsky made in 1846 and 1847 were minor and forgivable. He can be excused for vainglory and arrogance, as well as for anger and spite. He was, after all, only in his midtwenties. Let others recall their sins in this period of their lives and cast the first stones.

Sadly, though, Dostoevsky did not learn from his mistakes. Within two years he would make a bad situation worse, committing such egregious errors that he descended into a personal and professional abyss. Refusing to indict himself for his ills, the young artist blamed the world. It was political, social, and economic systems, he believed, that caused human unhappiness. External not internal reform was the answer. A member of the Petrashevsky circle, Dostoevsky ran afoul of officialdom. The crime of seditious activity led to the punishment of exile in Siberia.

CONCLUSION

It may seem mere truism to say that if people did not make mistakes, there would be no literature. It is, perhaps, an even greater verity to note that if writers did not make mistakes, they would not be able to write about people who did. If Pushkin and Gogol, Turgenev and Tolstoy advanced slowly and steadily in their craft, Dostoevsky did not. He had more—a great deal more—living to do.

Directory of Prominent Names

Agin, Alexander Alexeevich (1817–1875), artist and illustrator
Aksakov, Konstantin Sergeevich (1817–1860), critic, writer, and Slavophile
Alexander III (1845–1894), tsar of Russia from 1881 to 1894
Alexandra Fyodorovna (1798–1860), wife of Nicholas I
Anna Ioannovna (1693–1740), empress of Russia from 1730 to 1740
Annenkov, Pavel Vasilievich (1813–1887), critic and memoirist
Babikov, Konstantin Ivanovich (1841–1873), poet, prose writer, and journalist
Bakunin, Mikhail Alexandrovich (1814–1876), revolutionary and anarchist
Balzac, Honoré de (1799–1850), French writer
Baratynsky, Yevgeny Abramovich (1800–1844), poet
Beketov, Alexei Nikolaevich (1823–?), classmate of Fyodor Dostoevsky and brother of Andrei and Nikolai Beketov
Beketov, Andrei Nikolaevich (1825–1902), botanist, rector, publicist, brother of Alexei and Nikolai Beketov, and grandfather of Alexander Blok
Beketov, Nikolai Nikolaevich (1827–1911), professor, academician, chemist, physicist, social figure, and brother of Alexei and Andrei Beketov
Belinskaya, Maria Vasilievna (1812–1890), wife of Vissarion Belinsky
Belinskaya, Olga Vissarionova (1845–1904), daughter of Vissarion Belinsky
Belinsky, Grigory Nikiforovich (1784–1835), doctor and father of Vissarion Belinsky
Belinsky, Vissarion Grigorievich (1811–1848), critic
Belinsky, Vladimir Vissarionovich (1846–1847), son of Vissarion Belinsky
Bellini, Vincenzo (1801–1835), Italian composer
Bernardsky, Yevstafy Yefimovich (1819–1889), engraver and illustrator
Bervi-Flerovsky, Vasily Vasilievich (1829–1918), writer, sociologist, publicist, and economist
Bilyarsky, Pyotr Spiridonovich (1817–1867), critic
Blanc, Louis (1811–1882), French politician, historian, and socialist
Blok, Alexander Alexandrovich (1880–1921), poet and grandson of Andrei Beketov
Bonaparte, Napoleon (1769–1821), French statesman and military leader
Botkin, Vasily Petrovich (1812–1869), essayist, critic, translator, and publicist

DIRECTORY OF PROMINENT NAMES

Brandt, Leopold Vasilievich (1813–1884), writer and critic
Bulavin, Kondraty Afanasievich (1660?–1708), revolutionary
Bulgarin, Faddei Veneviktovich (1789–1859), writer, journalist, and publisher
Butashevich-Petrashevsky, Mikhail Vasilievich (1821–1866), revolutionary and theorist
Butkov, Yakov Petrovich (1821–1856), writer
Byron, George Gordon (Lord) (1788–1824), English poet
Cabet, Étienne (1788–1856), French philosopher and socialist
Calderón de la Barca, Pedro (1600–1681), Spanish dramatist, poet, and writer
Catherine the Great (1729–1796), empress of Russia from 1762 to 1796
Cervantes, Miguel de (1547–1616), Spanish novelist
Custine, Marquis de (1790–1857), French aristocrat and writer
Dal', Vladimir Ivanovich (1801–1872), writer and lexicographer
Dickens, Charles (1812–1870), English writer
(von) Ditmar, Emiliya. See Emiliya Dostoevskaya
Donskoi, Dmitri (1350–1389), grand prince of Moscow from 1363 to 1389
Dostoevskaya, Anna. See Anna Snitkina-Dostoevskaya
Dostoevskaya, Emiliya Fyodorovna (1822–1879), wife of Mikhail Dostoevsky
Dostoevskaya, Lyubov Fyodorovna (1869–1926), daughter of Fyodor Dostoevsky
Dostoevskaya-Ivanova, Vera Mikhailovna (1829–1896), sister of Fyodor Dostoevsky
Dostoevskaya-Karepina, Varvara Mikhailovna (1822–1893), sister of Fyodor Dostoevsky
Dostoevskaya-Vladislavleva, Maria Mikhailovna (1844–1888), daughter of Mikhail Dostoevsky and niece of Fyodor Dostoevsky
Dostoevsky, Alexander Andreevich (1857–1894), son of Andrei Dostoevsky and nephew of Fyodor Dostoevsky
Dostoevsky, Andrei Mikhailovich (1825–1897), architect, engineer, and younger brother of Fyodor Dostoevsky
Dostoevsky, Fyodor Mikhailovich (1821–1881), novelist and short-story writer
Dostoevsky, Fyodor Mikhailovich (the Younger) (1842–1906), son of Mikhail Dostoevsky and nephew of Fyodor Dostoevsky
Dostoevsky, Mikhail Andreevich (1788–1839), father of Fyodor Dostoevsky
Dostoevsky, Mikhail Mikhailovich (1820–1864), writer, critic, journalist, translator, and older brother of Fyodor Dostoevsky
Druzhinin, Alexander Vasilievich (1824–1864), writer, translator, and editor
Dudyshkin, Stepan Semyonovich (1820–1866), critic and journalist
Dyadkovsky, Yustin Yevdokimovich (1784–1841), doctor

Fénelon, François (1651–1751), French archbishop, theologian, poet, and writer
Feuerbach, Ludwig von (1804–1872), German philosopher and anthropologist
Fonvizin, Denis Ivanovich (1744?–1792), dramatist
Fourier, Charles (1772–1837), French philosopher
Gagarin, Grigory Ivanovich (1782–1837), prince and brother of Sergei Gagarin
Gagarin, Ivan Sergeevich (1814–1882), Jesuit and son of Sergei Gagarin
Gagarin, Sergei Ivanovich (1777–1862), prince, brother of Grigory Gagarin, and father of Ivan Gagarin
Gall, Franz (1758–1828), German physiologist
Godunov, Boris Fyodorovich (1551–1605), tsar of Russia from 1598 to 1605
Goegg-Pouchoulin, Maria (1826–1899), Swiss feminist
Goethe, Johann Wolfgang von (1749–1832), German writer
Gogol, Nikolai Vasilievich (1809–1852), dramatist, novelist, and short story writer
Golovinsky, Vasily Andreevich (1829–1875), lawyer
Goncharov, Ivan Alexandrovich (1812–1891), writer
Granovsky, Timofei Nikolaevich (1813–1855), medievalist, professor, and Westernizer
Grech, Nikolai Ivanovich (1787–1867), grammarian and journalist
Grigoriev, Apollon Alexandrovich (1822–1864), poet, critic, translator, memoirist, and author
Grigorovich, Dmitri Vasilievich (1822–1899), writer
Grot, Yakov Karlovich (1812–1893), philologist
Guber, Eduard Ivanovich (1814–1847), poet and translator
Guizot, François (1787–1874), French historian, orator, and statesman
Hegel, Georg (1770–1831), German philosopher
Herzen, Alexander Ivanovich (1812–1870), writer and thinker
Hoffmann, E. T. A. (1776–1822), German writer, composer, and critic
Hugo, Victor (1802–1885), French writer
Ivan IV (the Terrible) (1530–1584), tsar of Russia from 1533 to 1547
Ivanov, Alexander Pavlovich (1813–1868), husband of Vera Dostoevskaya
Izler, Ivan Ivanovich (1811–1877), confectioner
Izmailov, Alexander Yefimovich (1779–1831), fabulist, poet, novelist, and publisher
Kalita, Ivan Daniilovich (Ivan I) (1288–1340?), grand duke of Moscow and Vladimir
Karamzin, Nikolai Mikhailovich (1766–1826), writer, poet, historian, and critic
Karepin, Pyotr Andreevich (1796–1850), husband of Varvara Dostoevskaya and guardian of the Dostoevsky children after the death of Mikhail Andreevich Dostoevsky

DIRECTORY OF PROMINENT NAMES

Katkov, Mikhail Nikiforovich (1818–1887), journalist
Kavelin, Konstantin Dmitrievich (1818–1885), historian, lawyer, and sociologist
Ketcher, Nikolai Khristoforovich (1809–1886), writer and translator
Khanykov, Nikolai Vladimirovich (1819–1878), historian, orientalist, ethnographer, and diplomat
Kirillov, Nikolai Sergeevich (dates unknown), captain and editor
Kock, Charles Paul de (1793–1871), French novelist
Koltsov, Alexei Vasilievich (1809–1842), poet
Kraevsky, Andrei Alexandrovich (1810–1889), editor and journalist
Kreshev, Ivan Petrovich (1824–1859), poet, translator, essayist, and journalist
Krivopishin, Ivan Grigorievich (1796–1867), general and lieutenant
Krylov, Ivan Andreevich (1769–1844), fabulist
Kukolnik, Nikolai Vasilievich (1809–1868), playwright and prose writer
Kumanin, Alexander Alexeevich (1792–1863), uncle of Fyodor Dostoevsky
Kuvshinnikov, Nikolai Ivanovich (1819–1893), publisher
Kvitka-Osnovyanenko, Hryhory (1778–1884), Ukrainian writer, journalist, and playwright
Lambert, Yelizaveta Yegorvna (1821–1883), countess
Lamennais, Robert de (1782–1854), priest and philosopher
Lermontov, Mikhail Yurievich (1814–1841), writer and poet
Leroux, Pierre (1797–1871), French philosopher and economist
Lichtenberg, Georg (1742–1799), German physicist and satirist
Lkhovsky, Ivan Ivanovich (1829–1867), collegiate assessor
Loeve, Ferdinand (1809–1899), German teacher and editor
Lomonosov, Mikhail Vasilievich (1711–1765), polymath, scientist, and writer
Louis Philippe I (1773–1850), king of France from 1830 to 1848
Lugansky. See Dal'
Maykov, Apollon Alexandrovich (1761–1836), father of Nikolai and Konstantin Maykov, and grandfather of Apollon, Valerian, and Leonid Maykov
Maykov, Apollon Nikolaevich (1821–1897), poet
Maykov, Konstantin Apollonovich (1811–1891), colonel and brother of Nikolai Maykov
Maykov, Leonid Nikolaevich (1839–1900), historian, bibliographer, ethnographer, and academician
Maykov, Nikolai Apollonovich (1794–1893), artist, academician, and father of Apollon, Valerian, and Leonid Maykov
Maykov, Valerian Nikolaevich (1823–1847), publicist and critic
Maykov, Vladimir Nikolaevich (1826–1885), journalist, translator, and editor
Maykova, Natalya Alexandrovna (1809–1871), daughter of Alexander Izmailov and wife of Valerian Maykov

Maykova, Yevgenya Petrovna (1803–1880), poet, prose writer, wife of Nikolai Maykov, and mother of Apollon, Valerian, and Leonid Maykov
Melgunov, Nikolai Alexandrovich (1804–1867), writer, publicist, translator, and critic
Meyerbeer, Giacomo (1791–1864), German composer
Miller, Orest Fyodorovich (1833–1889), folklorist, professor, and first biographer of Fyodor Dostoevsky
Mozart, Wolfgang Amadeus (1756–1791), Austrian composer
Nechaev, Sergei Gennadievich (1847–1882), revolutionary, terrorist, and nihilist
Nekrasov, Nikolai Alexeevich (1821–1878) poet, writer, critic, and publisher
Nevakovich, Mikhail Lvovich (1817–1850), artist, caricaturist, dramatist, and publisher
Nicholas I (1796–1855), tsar of Russia from 1825 to 1855
Odoevsky, Vladimir Fyodorovich (1803–1869), philosopher, writer, critic, philanthropist, and pedagogue
Ogaryov, Nikolai Platonovich (1813–1877), poet, historian, and activist
Orlova, Agrafena Vasilievna (1818–1901), sister-in-law of Vissarion Belinsky
Orlova-Belinskaya, Maria Vasilievna (1834–1902), wife of Vissarion Belinsky
Ozerov, Vladislav Alexandrovich (1769–1816), dramatist
Panaev, Ivan Ivanovich (1812–1862), writer and journalist
Panaeva, Avdotya Yakovlevna (1820–1893), writer and memoirist
Pavlov, Nikolai Filippovich (1803–1864), writer, dramatist, translator, publisher, and editor
Pavlovsky, Isaak Yakovlevich (1852–1924), journalist, dramatist, translator, and revolutionary
Peter (?–1326), metropolitan and saint
Peter the Great (1672–1725), tsar of Russia from 1682 to 1725
Petrashevsky. See Butashevich-Petrashevsky
Philip II (1507–1569), metropolitan and saint
Pigault-Lebrun, Charles (1753–1835), French novelist and playwright
Pleshcheev, Alexei Nikolaevich (1825–1893), poet
Pletnyov, Pyotr Alexandrovich (1792–1866), writer, poet, and critic
Pogodin, Mikhail Petrovich (1800–1875), historian and journalist
Poretsky, Alexander Ustinovich (1818–1879), writer, journalist, and undercover agent
Priessnitz, Vincenz (1799–1851), farmer and proponent of alternative medicine
Proudhon, Pierre-Joseph (1809–1865), politician and philosopher
Pushkin, Alexander Sergeevich (1799–1837), dramatist, novelist, poet, and short story writer
Pyat, Felix (1810–1889), French socialist, journalist, and politician

Pypin, Alexander Nikolaevich (1833–1904), academician and historian of literature
Rastrelli, Francesco (1700–1771), Italian architect
Ratkov, Pyotr Alexeevich (dates unknown), bookseller and publisher
Reingardt, Nikolai Ivanovich (dates unknown), friend of Mikhail Dostoevsky
Renan, Ernest (1823–1892), French linguist, philosopher, historian, and writer
Rossini, Gioachino (1792–1868), Italian composer
Rubenstein, Anton Grigorievich (1829–1894), pianist, composer, and conductor
Rykacheva, Yevgenya Andreevna (1853–1919), daughter of Andrei Dostoevsky and niece of Fyodor Dostoevsky
Saint-Simon, Henri de (1760–1825), French theorist and philosopher
Saltykov-Shchedrin, Mikhail Yefgrafovich (1826–1889), writer
Sand, George (1804–1876), French novelist and memoirist
Schelling, Friedrich (1755–1854), German philosopher
Schiller, Friedrich (1759–1805), German writer and poet
Scribe, Eugène (1791–1861), French dramatist and librettist
Senkovsky, Osip Ivanovich (1800–1858), orientalist, journalist, and entertainer
Senyavina, Alexandra Vasilievna (?–1862), society figure
Shakespeare, William (1564–1616), English dramatist
Shalikov, Pyotr Ivanovich (1767?–1852), writer and journalist
Shchepkin, Mikhail Semyonovich (1788–1863), actor
Shevyryov, Stepan Petrovich (1806–1864), literary historian, critic, and poet
Shidlovsky, Ivan Nikolaevich (1816–1872), friend of Fyodor Dostoevsky
Skabichevsky, Alexander Mikhailovich (1838–1910), historian, critic, and memoirist
Smirdin, Alexander Filippovich (1795–1857), publisher and editor
Snitkina-Dostoevskaya, Anna Grigorievna (1845–1918), second wife of Fyodor Dostoevsky
Socrates (470–399 BC), Greek philosopher
Sollogub, Vladimir Alexandrovich (1813–1882), writer
Solonitsyn (dates unknown), friend of Fyodor Dostoevsky
Soloviev, I. G. (dates unknown), bookseller
Solovyov, Vsevelod Sergeevich (1849–1903), writer
Starchevsky, Albert Vikentievich (1818–1901), Polish historian, journalist, editor, philologist, lexicographer, and encyclopedist
Stasyulevich, Mikhial Matveevich (1826–1911), writer, scholar, historian, journalist, editor, and publisher
Strakhov, Nikolai Nikolaevich (1828–1896), philosopher, publicist, and critic
Strauss, David (1808–1874), German theologian and writer

Studitsky, Alexander Yefimovich (1817?–?), journalist and translator
Suvorin, Alexei Sergeevich (1834–1912), publisher and journalist
Tissot, Samuel-Auguste (1728–1797), Swiss physician
Tolstoy, Lev (Leo) Nikolaevich (1828–1910), novelist and short story writer
Totleben, Eduard Ivanovich (1818–1884), engineer and general
Tredyakovsky, Vasily Kirillovich (1703–1769), poet, essayist, and playwright
Trutovsky, Konstantin Alexandrovich (1826–1893), painter and friend of Fyodor Dostoevsky
Tseidler, Pyotr Mikhailovich (1821–1873), pedagogue and writer
Turgenev, Ivan Sergeevich (1818–1883), novelist, short story writer, and playwright
Vielgorskaya, Anna Mikhailovna (1822–1861), daughter of Mikhail and Luisa Vielgorsky
Vielgorskaya, Luiza Karlovna (1791–1853), wife of Mikhail Vielgorsky
Vielgorsky, Mikhail Yurievich (1788–1856), author, composer, and musician
Vlasovsky, Nikolai Yefgrafovich (1818–1854), captain and friend of Stepan Yanovsky
Voltaire (1694–1778), French philosopher
Vyazemsky, Pyotr Andreevich (1792–1878), poet
Yanovsky, Stepan Dmitrievich (1815–1887), doctor
Yazykov, Mikhail Alexandrovich (1811–1875), friend of Fyodor Dostoevsky
Yazykov, Nikolai Mikhailovich (1803–1846), poet
Yevstafy (dates unknown), retired officer and Dostoevsky's servant in 1847
Zhukovsky, Vasily Andreevich (1783–1852), poet

Notes

Introduction

1. Claims as to Dostoevsky's alleged epilepsy had been made twice previously, also giving rise to suspicion and doubt.

The first was made by Dostoevsky's daughter Lyubov in her notoriously unreliable account of the writer's life. It was "family legend," she wrote, that "news about the death of Dostoevsky's father had brought about the first attack of his epilepsy."

The second claim was by Grigorovich circa 1844. "Intense work and constant sitting at home had been extremely harmful to Dostoevsky's health," he noted. Grigorovich continued: "Several times during our rare walks he experienced attacks. One time . . . we came across a funeral procession. Dostoevsky turned away quickly. He wanted to return home, but before we managed to take a few steps, he had an attack so powerful that with the help of passers-by, I carried him to the nearest bench. We brought him back to consciousness by force. After such attacks, Dostoevsky showed a usually oppressive spirit which lasted about two or three days."

Such a charge Grigorovich made in 1892, eleven years after Dostoevsky's death. Furthermore, given the fact that Grigorovich was a notorious gossip and scandalmonger who delighted in joining Belinsky, Turgenev, and others in poking fun at Dostoevsky, one wonders why he did not disclose this episode earlier, when he could have caused considerable harm to the writer, if not vanquished him completely.

See L. Dostoevskaia, *Dostoevskii v izobrazhenii svoei docheri*, 2nd ed. (St. Petersburg: Andreev i synov'ia, 1992), 39; and D. Grigorovich, *Vospominaniia* (Moscow: Zakharov, 2007), 71.

2. It should be noted that Nekrasov also claimed that Dostoevsky suffered from fainting spells, but in a little-known and unpublished document, titled *The Stone Heart*, thought to have been written in 1846–47 or 1855–56 but found among his papers long after his death and first published in 1917 (see the discussion later in the chapter).

3. I. Turgenev, "Vospominaniia o Belinskom," in *Polnoe sobranie sochinenii i pisem v dvadtsati tomakh. Sochineniia*, vol. 14 (Moscow: Nauka, 1967), 35. Turgenev also saw Maykov as Belinsky's successor. See Annenkov's letter to Alexander Pypin, dated July 12, 1874, in K. Bogaevkaia, "P. A. Annenkov o V. G. Belinskom," in *Literaturnoe nasledstvo. Revoliutsionnye demokraty. Novye materialy*, ed. V. Vinodradov et al., vol. 67 (Moscow: Izdatel'stvo Akademii nauk, 1959), 550.

Part One. Pride before the Fall

1. P. Annenkov, "Zamechatel'noe desiatiletie," in *Literaturnye vospominaniia* (Moscow: Pravda, 1989), 320–21.

2. See Belinsky's letter to K. Kavelin, dated November 22, 1847, in Belinskii, *Polnoe sobranie sochinenii v tridnadtsati tomakh*, vol. 12 (Moscow: Izdatel'stvo Akademii nauk, 1956), 433.

3. Ibid., 222 and 304.

4. Ibid., 128 and 257.

5. Ibid., 25, 128, and 252–53.

6. Ibid., 344 and 321.

7. Balzac wrote both *Cousin Pons* and *Cousin Bette* in 1846 under the collective name *Poor Relations*.

8. Dostoevsky's *Poor Folk* appeared in Nekrasov's anthology *The Petersburg Miscellany*, which went on sale in the imperial city on January 24, 1846.

9. *Leviathan*, an almanac of almost five hundred pages, was also to include prose by Turgenev, Panaev, and Herzen; poetry by Apollon Maykov; and criticism by Timofei Granovsky and others. Although *Leviathan* never came to be, most of the planned works appeared in *The Contemporary*.

10. Sologub has erred here. Kraevsky was editor of *The Contemporary*. As already noted, Dostoevsky's *Poor Folk* was published in Nekrasov's *Petersburg Miscellany*.

11. Brandt, of course, is referring to Belinsky and Nekrasov.

12. Makar's surname, Devushkin, is rooted in the Russian word *devushka*, or "girl."

13. That is, "without connection to anything."

14. Again, Belinsky and Nekrasov.

15. Brandt is quoting the Russian proverb "The first pancake is a lump" (*Pervyi blin komom*).

16. Sadly, the piece was never published. Anna Dostoevskaya writes: "The article suffered a mournful fate. Fyodor Mikhailovich had been asked to do the piece for an anthology [titled *The Chalice*] by the writer K. I. Babikov, who paid him an advance of two hundred rubles. The article was done by autumn and mailed to Hotel Rome in Moscow.

"Fearing that Babikov might have moved to another apartment, Fyodor Mikhailovich asked [Apollon] Maykov . . . to send the manuscript to the Moscow bookseller I. G. Solovyov to give to Babikov. In a letter dated November 3, 1867, Maykov informed us that he had carried out my husband's intentions.

"Living abroad, we did not know whether the article had appeared in print. It was only in 1872 that Fyodor Mikhailovich received a request from some bookseller to let him have the article . . . since Babikov had died and the volume had never been published.

"My husband was very upset over the loss of the article, all the more so because he had worked on it a great deal, and although dissatisfied with the piece, he valued it greatly. We began inquiring as to where it could have wound up, even asking the Moscow bookseller for help, but without any result. The article vanished without a trace.

"I still regret its loss. . . . It was a skillful and very interesting piece." See A. Dostoevskaia, *Vospominaniia* (Moscow: Khudozhestvennaia literatura, 1971), 159–60.

17. Znamensky Church, or the Church of the Sign, was built between 1794 and 1804 and is located in central St. Petersburg.

18. The Nikolaevsky station was completed in 1849. It is also likely that it is the station from which Tolstoy's Anna Karenina made her first trip to Moscow.

19. Dostoevsky's description is untrue for both men.

20. In an 1861 piece titled "Famous European Writers before the Judgment of Our Criticism," Grigoriev wrote: "Belinsky was, first of all, open—even sometime excessively open—to any new direction of truth. One can say without any special daring that in 1856 he would have become a Slavophile." See A. Grigoriev, "Znamenitye evropeiskie pisateli pered sudom nashei kritiki," *Vremia*, no. 3 (1861): otdeleniia 2, 47.

21. Maria Goegg-Pouchoulin was a founder of a women's boarding school in Geneva as well as editor of the journal *The United States of Europe* and secretary of the League of Peace and Freedom.

22. Dostoevsky is referring to Sergei Gagarin, grand master of the court, a member of the Council of the Empire, and a knight of Saint Alexander Nevsky and Saint Vladimir, first class; his brother Grigory Gagarin, prince, poet, diplomat, and patron of the arts; and Sergei's son Ivan, who converted to Catholicism and became a Jesuit.

23. Ernest Renan was the author of the enormously popular 1863 work *Life of Jesus*, in which he infused race into the theology and personhood of Jesus, specifically Renan's claim that Jesus had purified himself of his Jewishness and had become a Christian Aryan.

Also, by rejecting both Jesus as God as well as His miracles, Renan claimed not only that he was restoring Jesus to greater dignity as a human but also that Jesus's life should be written in the same way as any historical person's. He also insisted that the Bible could and should be subject to the same critical scrutiny as other historical documents.

Needless to say, with *Life of Jesus*, Renan angered many Christians. In particular, the work outraged Jews, since in it Renan depicted Judaism as foolish, illogical, and inferior to Christianity.

24. Belinsky reserved his vilification of Christ for a select few, but in letters to friends, he disparaged immortality, religion, and believers.

He wrote Botkin on September 5, 1840: "You say that you believe in immortality. But what is it really? One thing then another, anything you like—a glass with kvass, an apple, a horse. I congratulate you on your faith, but it is not for me." On June 27–28, 1841, he continued to Botkin that religion was a "strange idea that could arise only in the heads of cannibals."

To Herzen, Belinsky noted on January 26, 1845, "In words such as 'god' and 'religion,' I see obscurity and darkness, the chain, and the knout." And in his famous letter to Gogol, penned on July 15, 1847, Belinsky proclaimed that the "Russian utters the name of God when he scratches his ass." See Belinskii, *Polnoe sobranie sochinenii*, vol. 10 (1956), 215; vol. 11 (1956), 553; and vol. 12 (1956), 53 and 250.

25. In his 1867 *Literary and Life Reminiscences*, Turgenev wrote: "Belinsky's knowledge was not vast. He knew little and there is nothing surprising about this. Even his enemies did not accuse him of any lack of industry or laziness; but the poverty surrounding his childhood, his poor upbringing, his unfortunate circumstances, his early illnesses, and the necessity of earning a living by hurried work—all this prevented Belinsky from acquiring sound knowledge [of things]." See I. Turgenev, *Polnoe sobranie sochinenii v dvadtsati vos'mi tomakh. Sochineniia*, vol. 14 (Moscow: Akademiia nauk, 1967), 29–30.

26. Dostoevsky is referring to himself in the third person here.

27. The friend is thought to be Vasily Botkin, the young writer Turgenev.

28. George Sand, Belinsky wrote to Nikolai Bakunin on November 7, 1842, was "decidedly the Joan of Arc of our times, the star of salvation and prophetess of a great future." See Belinskii, *Polnoe sobranie sochinenii*, vol. 12, 115.

29. Annenkov recalled circa fall 1843: "In front of my eyes, Belinsky took up reading a history [of the French Revolution] . . . one that was remarkable for its complete lack of any verifications of the people and events, namely, Cabet's work *The People*, which found signs of a vast collective intelligence in all instances when the masses of the people took up action; and which explained . . . even the fall of the Republic in the moving and blessed unselfishness of these same masses who had sustained a victory over the foes, not for themselves, not for any immediate benefit to be derived from the event, but for the glorification of their principles—liberty, equality and fraternity."

The book in question is Cabet's 1841 *My Right Line or the True Path for the Salvation of the People,* in which Cabet argued that proletarians and bourgeoisie together establish both fellowship and communism. See Annenkov, "Zamechatel'noe desiatiletie," 185.

30. Doubtless Belinsky knew Pierre Leroux's 1837 essay "Cult," which, forbidden in Russia, argued for a national religion without spiritual despotism and theocracy. That said, Belinsky called Leroux an "insurgent Catholic priest." See Annenkov, "Zamechatel'noe desiatiletie," 213.

31. Belinsky was hardly alone in his passion for French socialists. Mikhail Saltykov-Shchedrin recalled in 1880: "From France—of course, not the France of Louis Philippe and Guizot, but the France of Saint-Simon, Cabet, Fourier, [and] Louis Blanc . . . —there flowed to us a *belief in humanity* . . . a shining conviction that the golden age was not behind us but before us." See M. Saltykov-Shchedrin, *Polnoe sobranie v dvadtsati tomakh*, vol. 14 (Moscow: Khudozhestvennaia literatura, 1972), 112.

32. Most likely, what appealed to Belinsky was Feuerbach's conception of men, women, and children as objects of their own worship. He took comfort from the fact that Feuerbach argued not only for the destruction of God but also for a theological foundation for a religion of humankind.

Belinsky knew Feuerbach's 1841 work *The Essence of Christianity*, a defense of materialism and of the anthropological essence of faith. No doubt he admired Feuerbach's claim that God did not create humankind in His own image and likeness so much as the opposite. It was humankind who had attributed its highest and most sublime attributes to a godhead, thereby alienating its very essence. Belinsky also had to applaud the task that Feuerbach outlined ahead: men and women were to reclaim from an imagined God or gods all the qualities that rightfully belonged to them and to incorporate such virtues and strengths into the very fabric of social life.

Annenkov recalled: "One of the almost inflammatory materials . . . [was] Feuerbach's famous work [*The Essence of Christianity*] which was then in everyone's hands. . . . No other work made such a powerful impression in our Western circle . . . obliterating so rapidly the remnants of all preceding outlooks."

"Herzen . . . was a fervent expositor of its propositions and conclusions . . . connecting the upheaval it revealed in metaphysical ideas with the political upheaval heralded by the socialists, and in which he once again coincided with Belinsky."

Annenkov adds: "One of Belinsky's friends had made a translation for him of a few chapters and crucial passages in Feuerbach's book. Belinsky was thus able to make . . . a palpable acquaintance with the process of criticism which overthrew his old mystical and philosophical idols. . . .

"Belinsky was so stupefied by [*The Essence*] that he remained completely mute in the face of the work and lost the ability to pose questions of his own, a feature that had always distinguished him." See Annenkov, "Zamechatel'noe desiatiletie," 250.

33. In his 1835 work *The Life of Jesus*, a popular "forbidden" book in Russia, David Strauss criticized Christian dogma and denied both the authority and authenticity of the Gospels. In his view, the New Testament was the stuff not of divine revelation but of mythopoetic aspirations of the Jewish community during the time of Christ.

An early pioneer in the "quest for the historical Jesus," Strauss concluded that knowledge of a real-life Son of Man was buried hopelessly under layers of legend and myth, and that Jesus Christ, if He existed at all, was merely one of many self-proclaimed prophets of the period.

34. The French Commune was a radical socialist and revolutionary government that ruled Paris from March 18 to May 28, 1871. Felix Pyat was one of its most colorful members. He was also editor of *Avenger*, a widely read revolutionary journal.

In the first days of the Commune, Pyat advocated the end of national conscription, as well as the separation of church and state. Lies and missteps, the execution of enemies, the demolition of historical sites, and his stances as a firebrand revolutionary forced Pyat to flee France in late May and to be condemned to death in absentia by officials of the national government.

In 1880, however, Pyat was amnestied and allowed to return. Eight years later, he helped to prevent the overthrow of the Third Republic.

35. See the discussion of Pushkin later in this part of the book.

36. Gogol first published *Dead Souls* in 1842.

37. Dostoevsky has a point. In Gogol's works, Belinsky wrote, a "different definition of Art applies—that of a representation of reality in all its truth. Here everything is in types. The ideal is understood not as an embellishment (and consequently a lie), but as the relationships in which the author places the types he has created, along with the idea he wishes to express in his works." See Belinskii, *Polnoe sobranie sochinenii*, vol. 10 (1956), 294–95.

38. Pushkin published *The Tales of Belkin* in 1830. About this work, Belinsky wrote in 1846, "there is absolutely nothing good. . . . They are unworthy of Pushkin's talent and name. They are akin to stories by Karamzin, but with this difference. Karamzin's tales had a great significance in their day, but the *Tales of Belkin* are beneath their time. Especially pitiful is 'The Squire's Daughter,' untruthful and vaudeville-like in its portrayal of gentry life from an idyllic point of view." See Belinskii, *Polnoe sobranie sochinenii*, vol. 7 (1955), 577.

39. Gogol's "The Carriage" appeared in 1836. That same year Belinsky wrote, "'The Carriage' is nothing other than a joke, done in an extremely masterly way." See Belinsky, *Polnoe sobranie sochinenii*, vol. 2 (1953), 179–80.

40. Pushkin wrote *Eugene Onegin* between 1825 and 1832. As Belinsky wrote in his 1844 article titled "Eugene Onegin": "The novel ends with Tatyana's rebuke and the reader parts forever with Onegin in the most evil moment of his life. . . . But what is going on here? Where is the novel? What is its idea? What kind of novel lacks an ending? . . .

"What happened next to Onegin? Did he revive his passion for a new suffering, one that conforms better to human dignity? Or did he kill it with all the forces of his soul, his cheerless angst having turned into deadly, cold apathy? We do not know . . . since it is a *novel without an ending*." See Belinskii, *Polnoe sobranie sochinenii*, vol. 7 (1955), 469.

41. As Belinsky wrote in his famous 1847 "Letter to N. Gogol," "Pushkin . . . had to write only two or three loyal letters and to take on the livery of a chamber-Junker to lose suddenly the love of the people." See Belinskii, *Polnoe sobranie sochinenii*, vol. 10 (1956), 217.

42. Turgenev penned "Three Portraits" in 1846. If Belinsky rejected "Three Portraits" in private, he extolled the work in public. "With its deft and lively exposition," he wrote in 1846, "Turgenev's 'Three Portraits' has the charm . . . of remembrances of the good old days." He added a year later, "With 'Three Portraits,' it is apparent that Turgenev has found his genuine path in prose." See Belinskii, *Polnoe sobranie sochinenii*, vol. 9 (1955), 566, and vol. 10 (1956), 345.

43. In the ninth article in his cycle on the *Works of Alexander Pushkin*, Belinsky used Tatyana's faithfulness to her husband to oppose despotism in families and to defend the rights of women.

In his 1880 speech at the unveiling of Pushkin's statue in Moscow, Dostoevsky saw Tatyana as a "pure Russian soul" who discerns that she cannot realize happiness at the expense of another.

44. Since the 1830s, preference has been a popular card game in Russia.

45. Both Belinsky and Panaeva begged to differ. "In the evening, around ten," Panaeva recalled, "Belinsky visited us to play preference, for which he had a wild passion. Talking forcefully throughout the game, he often sat next to me so that I could see the game.

"'It would be much better to play preference with us than always reading your George Sand,' Belinsky said. . . .

"'You and I always quarrel so, but at cards we simply will come to blows,' I responded. 'Furthermore, it is harmful for you to play preference: you get way too excited and then you need to rest.'

"'My excitement over cards is nothing; what really harms me is when, for example today, I got upset when I was brought a page of my article which had been bloodied by the censor. How can I allow [my editors] to publish such a repulsive piece! From such distress the chest aches, and it is difficult to breathe.'" See A. Panaeva, *Vospominaniia* (Moscow: Gosudarstvennoe izdatel'stvo khudozhestvennoi literatury, 1956), 90.

About Belinsky and preference, Turgenev also remembered, "Belinsky played cards poorly, but with the same sincerity and the same passion with which he did everything." See Turgenev, *Polnoe sobranie sochinenii*, vol. 14, 47.

46. As has been noted, Dostoevskaya's assertion is incorrect.

47. This is not true. Before *Poor Folk*, Dostoevsky was a stranger to the Russian literary world.

48. Gioachino Rossini's *William Tell* appeared in 1829, Wolfgang Amadeus Mozart's *Don Giovanni* in 1787, Vincenzo Bellini's *Norma* in 1831, and Giacomo Meyerbeer's *Huguenots* in 1836.

49. Dostoevskaya is wrong again. *The Double* appeared in Kraevsky's *Fatherland Notes* on January 30, 1846, two weeks after the appearance of *Poor Folk* in Nekrasov's

Petersburg Miscellany. Furthermore, the lie about borders concerned *Poor Folk*, not *The Double*.

50. The individual was Grigorovich.

51. Panaev's claim is suspect. As will be seen, Belinsky never believed that Dostoevsky would supersede Gogol.

52. Interestingly, Turgenev omitted the remark on Belinsky's failing powers as a critic in later editions of his memoirs.

53. The full text of this verse appears later in this part of the book.

54. Nekrasov's *The Stone Heart* is also known as *How Great I Am!* and *On That Day at Around Eleven O'Clock in the Morning*. In the piece, Mertsalov bears affinities to Belinsky, Glazhievsky to Dostoevsky, Trostnikov to Nekrasov, Balakleev to Grigorovich, Reshetilov to Turgenev, Razbegaev to Panaev; Sputnik to Annenkov, the Journalist to Kraevsky, and the All-Around (and Also Embracing) Nature to Botkin and Alexander Druzhinin.

55. Apparently Nekrasov knew that "to descend into nothingness" (*stushevat'sia*), was one of the young writer's favorite terms. As Dostoevsky wrote in *A Writer's Diary* in November 1877:

> "The verb *stushevat'sia* means to disappear, to perish, *to descend to nothingness*, so to speak. But *stushevat'sia* means to perish not immediately, not to be wiped off the face of the earth with thunder and crashing . . . but to sink gradually into nothingness. It is like a shadow on a drawing done in shaded lines that gradually moves from black into white until it disappears completely, *to nothingness*.
>
> "Although I was the first one to use the verb *stushevat'sia* . . . I was certainly not the one who invented it. The term was thought up by my classmates when I was at the Main School of Military Engineering. Perhaps I also took part in its invention . . . but somehow it came into being all by itself. In all six classes at the school, we had to draw various plans—fortifications, structures, and military buildings. The ability to draw a plan freehand and well was a strict requirement so that, like it or not, even students who had no inclination for drawing still had to attain a certain level in this art. . . . You might graduate . . . as an excellent mathematician, a builder of fortifications, or an engineer, but if your drawings were poor . . . you were deprived of such significant advantages as promotion to a higher rank. As a result, everyone tried hard to draw well.
>
> "All plans were drawn and shaded in India ink . . . and everyone tried to learn how to shade a given surface well, from dark to light to white—to nothingness; a good shading gave to the drawing a stylish look.
>
> "Suddenly people began to ask: 'Where's so-and-so?' 'Ah, he's disappeared [*stushevalsia*] somewhere.' Or, say, two friends were talking and one would say to the other that he had to get to work: 'Well, now you'd better disappear [*stushshiusia*].' Or a senior student would say to a new student, 'I called you; where did you manage to disappear to [*stushevat'sia*]'?
>
> "'Stushevat'sia' . . . was used only in our class . . . and when we graduated, it seemingly did so as well. Some three years later I remembered it and used it in my tale." See F. Dostoevskii, *Dnevnik pisatelia za 1877 god* (Berlin: Izdatel'stvo I. P. Ladyzhnikova, 1922), 456–59.

56. In truth, Dostoevsky had begun *Poor Folk* in early 1844—a year before its publication—and wrote no more than two redactions of the work.

57. The claim is wrong on both counts. Byron wrote *Manfred* from summer 1816 to winter 1817. He began *Don Juan* in July 1818, working on the piece until his death in 1824.

58. Such a piece is unknown.

59. Staraya Russa, famous for its mineral springs, is a town in northwest Russia, roughly sixty miles south of Novgorod.

60. This is not true. See Panaeva's excerpt from February 1846.

Part Two. Havens from the Storms

1. V. Sollogub, *Povesti. Vospominaniia* (Leningrad: Khudozhestvennaia literatura, 1988), 436 and 493.

2. Ibid., 435.

3. L. Dostoevskaia, *Dostoevskii v izobrazhenii svoei docheri*, 45.

4. St. Isaac's Cathedral is the largest Russian Orthodox cathedral in St. Petersburg. It is also the largest Orthodox basilica and the fourth-largest cathedral in the world.

5. V. Komarovich, "Iunost' Dostoevskogo," *Byloe*, no. 23 (1924): 17.

6. Maykov became the lead critic for *The Fatherland Notes* after Belinsky left the journal for *The Contemporary* in 1847.

7. The *Pocket Dictionary of Foreign Words*, edited by Mikhail Petrashevsky and Nikolai Kirillov in 1846, popularized materialist, democratic, socialist, and utopian views, and was thus, by the end of the decade, banned by the tsarist government.

8. The Catherine Institute was a school for girls of the nobility. Founded in 1798, it was closed after the October Revolution.

9. For whatever reason, Pavlov did not write the review.

10. Most likely Dostoevsky is referring to his final proofing of his story, *The Double*, which was published in *The Fatherland Notes* in February 1846.

11. Again, the work in question is *The Petersburg Miscellany*.

12. *Illustration* was a newspaper published weekly in St. Petersburg from 1845 to 1849, with Nikolai Kukolnik as its first editor.

13. *The Northern Bee* was a newspaper published in St. Petersburg, first three times a week and then weekly, and edited by Faddei Bulgarin, who, among others, attacked Pushkin, Gogol, and Belinsky.

14. *The Library for Reading* was a conservative monthly of literature, science, the arts, industry, news, and fashion published in St. Petersburg from 1834 to 1865. (Osip Senkovsky was its first editor.) It published works by Vasily Zhukovsky, Ivan Krylov, Vladimir Odoevsky, Yevgeny Baratynsky, and Pyotr Vyazemsky, as well as by Pushkin, Gogol, and Lermontov.

The Library for Reading reviewed and sometimes published in translation the works of such French writers as Honoré de Balzac, Victor Hugo, George Sand, and Eugène Scribe.

15. Neither Odoevsky nor Sollogub wrote an article about *Poor Folk*.

16. Dostoevsky is referring to Maykov's review, published in January 1846.

17. *The Fatherland Notes* was a literary and sociopolitical journal published in St. Petersburg from 1839 to 1867. It favored the ideas of the Westernizers, with Belinsky

playing a prominent role as editor of the literary, critical, and bibliographical sections of the publication. At this time, *The Fatherland Notes* had a huge circulation of some 2,500 copies monthly.

18. From 1769 to 1849, the tsarist officials allowed so-called assignat paper rubles to exist alongside silver rubles, with free convertability from paper to silver guaranteed by decree but limited to copper coins. By keeping silver in the state treasury and copper in circulation, they hoped to circulate money more rapidly, thereby strengthening the finances of government.

19. After having seen her fiancé only three times, the seventeen-year-old Vera Dostoevskaya married the thirty-three-year-old Alexander Pavlovich Ivanov, a professor at the Konstantinovsky Landmark Institute in Moscow, on January 7, 1846.

About Ivanov, Andrei Dostoevsky wrote: "I found Alexander Ivanov to be a very kind, merry, and sympathetic individual. From our first meeting, we got along well. I liked him a great deal and what feelings I had for him lasted to the end of his life."

Also, according to Anna Dostoevskaya, Dostoevsky loved Vera and her entire family in a special way. See M. Volotskoi, *Khronika roda Dostoevskogo, 1506–1933* (Moscow: Sever, 1933), 190; and Dostoevskaia, *Vospominaniia*, 126–27.

20. Bulgarin is referring to the so-called Natural School in Russian literature, a movement that embraced the youthful writings of such authors as Nekrasov, Dostoevsky, and Turgenev, which, beginning around 1840, sought to establish in native soil the content and form of European urban realism and which, as did Western writers of the city at this time, made everyday people the new heroes and heroines of literature.

21. Nekrasov's "On the Road" appeared in 1845.

22. About "Shaved Sideburns," see the discussion later in this part of the book.

23. Most likely Pletnyov is referring, tongue in cheek, to the so-called Nekrasovetsy, a religious sect of Old Believers who, as descendants of fugitives, Cossacks, runaways, and the participants in a civil uprising known as the Bulavin rebellion (1707–8), raided areas in southern Russia until 1737, when they resettled in territories of the Ottoman Empire.

24. Gogol wrote *Diary of a Madman* in 1835.

25. Gogol published "Nevsky Prospekt" in 1835.

26. *The Muscovite* was a monthly literary and historical journal published in Moscow from 1841 to 1856. Headed by Mikhail Pogodin and Stepan Shevyryov, *The Muscovite* espoused "official nationality," that is, conservative nationalism rooted in autocracy and monarchy.

27. Again, Belinsky, Nekrasov, and company.

28. Gogol's Popryshchin is the hero of his 1835 *Diary of a Madman*, Akaky Akakievich Bashmachkin of his story "The Overcoat."

29. Tatyana Larina is the heroine of Pushkin's *Eugene Onegin*.

30. The reference is to Ivan Krylov's 1813 fable "Demyan Fish Soup." When the "hot and red" Foka flees his host Demyan after repeated helpings of fish soup, Krylov concludes, "Author, if you have many gifts but do not know when to quit . . . then know that your verse and prose are more sickening than too much fish soup."

31. Eugène Sue wrote *The Mysteries of Paris* in 1842 and *The Wandering Jew* (not *Eternal*) in 1844; Alexander Dumas père wrote *The Count of Monte Cristo* also in 1844.

32. Izler's café-restaurant featured some thirty types of ice cream. In 1845 its owner, Ivan Izler, who was Swiss, was the first confectioner in Russia to receive a patent to make ice cream by machine. It exists today.

33. Robert Lovelace is the villain in Samuel Richardson's 1748 *Clarissa, or the History of a Young Lady*.

34. Chichikov, Petrushka, and Selifan are characters from Gogol's 1842 novel *Dead Souls*.

35. The Table of Ranks was established by 1722 by Peter the Great as a system for establishing equivalencies in titles and positions in the military, civil service, and court bureaucracy. It also provided a system of promotion for all governmental servitors vis-à-vis fourteen levels or steps.

The lowest or fourteenth rank included the army rank of ensign, the navy rank of ship commissar, and the civil service rank of assistant councilor. At the first or highest rank were such positions as field marshal, admiral general, and chancellor. Similar listings of ranks existed in both Denmark and Prussia.

36. Franz Joseph Gall was a physiologist and a pioneer in studying the localization of mental functions in the brain. He was also the founder of "cranioscopy" (later renamed "phrenology"), in which the external shape of the skull is seen as determining both the personality as well as the mental and moral faculties of the individual.

Needless to say, Gall's ideas were pronounced as invalid by both church and state in Germany and France. They were accepted in England, though especially among the ruling classes, who appealed to Gall to justify the presumed inferiority of colonial subjects. Gall's ideas were also popular in the United States from 1820 to 1850.

It should be noted, though, that Gall contributed significantly to the study of neurology. He was the first to suggest the then revolutionary idea that character, thoughts, and emotions were located in the brain, not the heart.

37. Khlestakov is the rogue hero of Gogol's *Dead Souls*.

38. In truth, Belinsky had notified Kraevsky of his move from *The Fatherland Notes* to *The Contemporary* on February 6, 1846. He did so not only because of his friendship with Nekrasov, editor of *The Contemporary*, but also because of the more radical political and social stance of the journal.

39. On May 12, 1846, Belinsky left for a two-week stay in Odessa to improve his failing health. The following year he traveled to cities in Germany, Belgium, and France to continue medical treatments.

40. The work in question is the already noted *Leviathan*.

41. Both stories remained unfinished. Sections from "A Tale about Destroyed Offices" appeared in Dostoevsky's 1846 story "Mr. Prokharchin" and echoes of "Shaved Sideburns" in his 1859 novel *The Village of Stepanchikovo and Its Inhabitants*.

42. Herzen had published "Dilletantism in Science" in 1842–43, "Letters on the Study of Nature" in 1845–46, and also during this time period *Who Is to Blame?* in *The Fatherland Notes*.

Goncharov made his literary debut with a translation of two chapters of Eugène Sue's novel *Atar-Gull*, in 1832; a story, titled "A Bad Ailment," in 1838; and another, named "A Lucky Error," in 1839.

43. Goethe wrote *Reynard the Fox* in 1793.

44. In fact, Dostoevsky visited Mikhail in Revel on May 25, 1846.
45. Mikhail Dostoevsky's translation of *Reynard the Fox* appeared in *The Fatherland Notes* in 1848.
46. Revel was the Russian name for Tallinn, the capital of Estonia.
47. Gapsal, more commonly known as Haapsalu, is a city in Estonia, roughly fifty miles southwest of Revel and 250 miles southwest of St. Petersburg.
48. Maria Belinskaya was thirty-four years old at the time. She died in 1890.
49. The story in question is "Mr. Prokharchin," which was published in *The Fatherland Notes* later that year.
50. Gogol wrote "Old-World Landowners" in 1835.
51. Maria Belinskaya, together with her daughter Olga and sister-in-law Agrafena Orlova, remained in Revel for the summer, where they were treated cordially by Mikhail Dostoevsky and his family. The two women, though, saw their hosts as highly impractical people.
52. Mikhail's children Fedya (Fyodor) and Masha (Maria) Dostoevsky would later become pianists and students of Anton Rubinstein, one of the great keyboard virtuosos of the nineteenth century.
53. The child in question is Olga Belinskaya, born on June 13, 1845. A son, Vladimir, died in infancy in 1847.
54. The reference is to Belinsky.
55. "Piter" is the affectionate name of the citizens of St. Petersburg for their city.
56. Goncharov published *The Precipice* in 1869.
57. Vasily Tredyakovsky published *Telemachus*, a translation of François Fénelon's 1669 *Adventures of Telemachus*, in 1766.
58. See the next note.
59. The Troitsky Izmailovsky Cathedral, also known as Trinity Cathedral, the Trinity-Izmailovsky Cathedral, and the Cathedral of the Holy Primary-Life Trinity of the Imperial Guard of the Izmailovsky Regiment, was built between 1828 and 1835. Dostoevsky married his second wife, Anna Grigorievna Snitkina, there in 1867.
60. The Small Church of the Winter Palace was built in 1768. Destroyed by fire in 1837, it was rebuilt in 1839.
61. The Izmailovsky Regiment was founded by Empress Anna Ioannovna on September 22, 1730, to support the throne. The regiment was particularly crucial during the Battle of Borodino against Napoleon Bonaparte on September 7, 1812.
62. Natalya Maykova was the wife of Valerian Maykov.
63. The individual in question is Alexander Izmailov.
64. Manilov is also a character in Gogol's *Dead Souls*.
65. Goethe wrote his loosely autobiographical epistolary novel *The Sorrows of Young Werther* in 1774.
66. In truth, Nekrasov was in a peaceful ménage à trois with Panaeva, who, for the next ten years, was his common-law wife.
67. Gogol's "Will" appeared in 1847 as part of his *Selected Passages from a Correspondence with Friends*.
68. Belinsky had left St. Petersburg for Moscow on April 26, 1846, and, after a trip to southern Russia, returned to the imperial capital around October 20.

69. Penza is a city located about four hundred miles southeast of Moscow. Kiev, capital of Ukraine, is about five hundred miles to the southwest of the Russian capital.

70. The work in question is Grigorovich's *The Village*.

71. The article in question is Valerian Maykov's article "Something about Russian Literature in 1846," published in *The Fatherland Notes* in January 1847.

72. Pargolovo is a municipal settlement, located roughly eleven miles north of St. Petersburg. Parnassus Hill, at a height of roughly 140 feet, is the highest point in the city.

73. Briefly, Fourierism is a philosophy of utopian reform that sought to recast society into independent, self-sufficient "phalanges" (phalanxes).

Fourier's phalanges were to consist of roughly 1,500 individuals of varying ages, aptitudes, intelligence, and wealth who would live and work harmoniously in rural settings, as well as in massive and sumptuous palace- and hotel-like structures, without government intervention.

Work was to be apportioned on a rational and rotating basis; goods produced were seen as the property of the group. Members of phalanges would receive hourly wages, scaled to the difficulty or disagreeableness of tasks; they could also lay claim to private property and inheritances.

The result, Fourier claimed, would be increased industry, social and sexual equality, as well as the end to indigence, fraud, oppression, and war.

74. The piece was "Mr. Prokharchin."

Part Three. The Psycho-Spiritual Turn

1. Panaev fails to note that Nekrasov did not wish to publish *Leviathan* but that he had offered to print all the materials in the anthology in *The Contemporary*.

2. At this time Dostoevsky did not realize his wish to go to France and Italy.

3. The work in question is *Netochka Nezvanova*.

4. Dostoevsky may be alluding to *Netochka Nezvanova*.

5. Dostoevsky may be referring to the sales of *The Petersburg Miscellany*.

6. Such a verse is unknown.

7. Again, the individual in question is Grigorovich. Consider Turgenev's remark in a letter to Yelizaveta Lambert, written on November 28, 1860, that Grigorovich was a "heartless gossip and liar." See I. Turgenev, *Polnoe sobranie sochinenii. Pis'ma*, vol. 4 (Moscow: Akademiia nauk, 1962), 166.

8. Mikhail Mikhailovich Dostoevsky was born on November 5, 1846.

9. What Dostoevsky fails to tell his brother Mikhail is that the reviewers were sharply critical of "Mr. Prokharchin."

10. Most likely the story in question is "The Landlady," which was published in the October–December 1847 issue of *The Fatherland Notes*.

11. Dostoevsky has in mind both Nekrasov and Panaev.

12. Most likely *Netochka Nezvanova*.

13. Dostoevsky was unable to publish *Poor Folk* as a separate book until 1847 and a revised edition of *The Double* until 1866.

14. Dostoevsky's plans were not realized.

15. Hryhory Kvitka-Osnovyanenko wrote *Mr. Kholyavsky*, a humorous portrait of life among the Ukrainian gentry, in 1839.

16. This is not true. Gogol died in Moscow on February 21, 1852. Dostoevsky may be referring to Gogol's death metaphorically, as the writer was no longer writing fiction.

17. "Once you're dead, you're really dead."

18. Bulgarin, of course, is referring to Belinsky.

19. "The Petersburg Corners" was written by Nekrasov in 1845.

20. As has been noted, Dostoevsky's revision of *The Double* was not published until 1866. Also, the edition of *Poor Folk* that appeared in November 1847 lacked illustrations.

21. Yevstafy Bernardsky was a wood engraver who began publishing illustrations for Gogol's *Dead Souls* in 1846.

22. Also, in his feuilleton "A Petersburg Chronicle," written on June 1, 1847, Dostoevsky wrote: "The splendid undertaking of Messers Bernardsky and Agin—the illustrations for *Dead Souls*—are coming to an end, and one cannot praise enough the conscientiousness of both artists. Several of their drawings are done so splendidly that it is difficult to want anything better." See Dostoevskii, *Polnoe sobranie sochinenii*, vol. 18, 28.

23. Dostoevsky was working on "The Landlady."

24. The publication of *Netochka Nezvanova* was announced in *The Fatherland Notes*, no. 12 (1846), but the work did not appear in print until issues 1, 2, and 5 of the journal in 1849.

25. As will be seen, Dostoevsky had not fulfilled his contractual obligations to Kraevsky, a situation that led Belinsky, for one, to conclude that the writer had taken advantage of the publisher.

26. Dostoevsky is referring to the polemic between Belinsky in *The Contemporary* and Maykov in *The Fatherland Notes* in 1846 and 1847, in part over the poetry of Koltsov.

27. Dostoevsky did not go to Revel in 1847.

28. As well it should have. Akulina, the heroine of Grigorovich's work, suffers an "education" of beatings and abuse by her husband, Grigory; but she retains her dignity and self-worth even as she dies in the process.

In the final scene, Grigory drives through a blinding snowstorm to bury his wife's body, accompanied by their distraught daughter, Dunka, who runs through deep snowdrifts to keep up with her father.

Grigorovich's *The Village* was praised by reviewers and readers because it showed not only a peasant woman with human emotions but also the changing tenor of serf life. (Grigory is corrupted by the idle life of a village factory.) It also garnered praise for depicting peasant mores, folklore, and vernacular language in a realistic way.

29. Yanovsky claims that he met Dostoevsky in 1846; if so, he was thirty-one, and the writer, twenty-five at the time.

30. As has already been noted, Yanovsky's claims as to Dostoevsky's religious and patriotic beliefs are without evidence in this period.

31. Doctors had called epilepsy "the falling sickness" for almost a century. Samuel-Auguste Tissot, in his 1771 work *Treatise on Epilepsy or the Falling Sickness*, saw the affliction as caused by brain tumors, head injuries, metabolic disturbances, or hypersensitivity of the brain. For victims of "falling sickness," valerian drops were a common remedy.

32. The Russian here is *kondrashka s veterkom*. At the time, *kondrashka* was a colloquial term for apoplectic stroke or even sudden death—a darkly humorous expression derived, supposedly, from Kondrati (Kondrashka) Bulavin, who staged an uprising—the previously mentioned Bulavin rebellion—against tsarist forces in 1707–8. (The hero in Dostoevsky's "Mr. Prokharchin" also suffers from *kondrashka*.)

Russian textbooks of the 1840s translated "aura," the classic warning symptom for epilepsy, as "breeze," which conveys the literal meaning of the phenomenon. For instance, Yustin Dyadkovsky, in his 1847 work *Practical Medicine: Lectures*, noted, "Suddenly there appears a special sensation of rising hot or cold steam, well known as *epileptic breeze*, which runs through one nerve ending to the entire nervous system, immediately causing attacks." . . .

"[Such a condition] ends in *death* or a hemorrhage in the brain or a weakening of strength, the result of repeated attacks." See Iu. Diadkovskii, *Izbrannye sochineniia* (Moscow: Medgiz, 1958), 431.

Since Dyadkovsky's *Practical Medicine* appeared in early 1845, it is more than likely that Dostoevsky knew of the publication and even self-diagnosed his illness.

33. Haymarket Square was established in 1737 for the sale of wood, oats, and cattle. Known as the "belly of St. Petersburg," Haymarket Square became, by the mid-nineteenth century, the quarter for the lower classes of the city, as well as for prostitution and other dubious activities. Many of the old buildings in Haymarket Square, including the Church of the Assumption of the Mother of God, fell victim to urban planning in the Soviet era.

Haymarket Square was also the site where Raskolnikov in *Crime and Punishment* kissed the earth in a frenzied attempt to atone for the murder of the pawnbroker Alyona Ivanovna and her sister Lizaveta.

34. Andrei's claim is not true. As has been noted, he was not close to Fyodor and often did not see his brother for weeks on end.

35. Conceivably the individual is Senkovsky.

36. Dostoevsky is correct here: an incorrect interpretation of Psalm 32.

37. Helsingfors is the Swedish name for Helsinki. Mikhail was transferred to the city in 1847, but Fyodor never got to visit him there.

38. Dostoevsky is citing Vincenz Priessznitz, a German doctor and one of the founders of hydrotherapy, which became very popular in the 1830s.

39. Dostoevsky is referring to a book edition of *Poor Folk*.

40. Fyodor Mikhailovich Dostoevsky, son of Mikhail and Emiliya.

41. Carl von Roswald is the hero of George Sand's 1846 novel *Lucrezia Floriani*. He is also a partial prototype for the character of Ordynov in Dostoevsky's "The Landlady."

42. A reference to *The Double*.

43. Such an assertion is false.

44. Most likely Panaeva is referring to Belinsky's article "A Look at Russian Literature for 1846," which was published in January 1847.

45. The scene is unknown.

46. Again, Belinsky has in mind Maykov's "Something about Russian Literature in 1846."

47. By the "new criticism," Guber means Belinsky's reviews of Dostoevsky's first two works. Dostoevsky finished *The Double* on January 28, 1846.

48. Belinsky is referring to Dostoevsky's "Novel in Nine Letters," which was published in the January 1847 issue of *The Contemporary*.

49. Belinsky had written a similar missive to Botkin two days earlier.

50. Desperate for money, Dostoevsky was editing the proofs of an article on the Jesuits for the fifth volume of the *Reference Encyclopedia Dictionary*, which, edited by Albert Starchevsky, came out in May 1847.

51. Panaev is referring to the previously mentioned Alexandra Senyavina.

52. The book in question is Gogol's *Selected Passages from My Correspondence with Friends*, which glorified autocracy, serfdom, and Orthodoxy as God-given and sacred, and which caused Belinsky to call the author a "proponent of the knout, an apostle of ignorance, a champion of obscurantism, and a panegyrist of Tartar ways." See Belinskii, *Polnoe sobranie sochinenii*, vol. 10 (1956), 214.

53. Belinsky is quoting from Maykov's April 1847 article in *The Fatherland Notes*.

54. In the summer of 1847 Dostoevsky did not go to visit Mikhail; instead, Mikhail came to St. Petersburg.

55. Dostoevsky surely means two feuilletons a month, not a week.

56. The reference is probably to *Netochka Nezvanova*.

57. Mikhail Dostoevsky was twenty-seven years old at the time.

58. Mr. Imrek was a pen name for Konstantin Aksakov.

59. The work in question is *Russia in 1839* by the Marquis de Custine about his time in St. Petersburg, Moscow, and Yaroslavl. First published in 1841, his less than flattering account of Russia and Russians went through six printings and was read widely in England, France, and Germany.

Lost to obscurity for a time, Custine's work became a favorite text for disgruntled American diplomats who, stationed in Moscow during Stalin's rule, plundered the book for the writer's insights into the national despotism, for example, on Russians as "voluntary automata" who, among other things, surrendered to "the police of the imagination."

60. The Solovetsky Islands, located in the White Sea in northern Russia, are the site of the famous Solovetsky Monastery, which was founded in 1436 by the monk Zosima. Between 1926 and 1939 the monastery was converted into a prison and a labor camp, serving as a prototype for the camps of the gulag system. During World War II, the monastery housed young sailors in training. Beginning in the late 1980s, the Solovetsky Monastery, together with other churches in the locale, was permitted to conduct religious services and underwent rebuilding and restoration. In 1992 it was placed on the list of UNESCO World Heritage Sites, and today it is a place for pilgrimage and prayer.

61. Lake Ladoga, just to the northwest of St. Petersburg, hosts three religious institutions: the Valaam Monastery, thought to have been founded sometime in the twelfth century; the Konovsky Monastery, established around 1393; and the Alexander-Svirsky Monastery, which came into being in 1487.

62. Mount Athos, both a mountain and a peninsula in northeastern Greece, is home to some twenty monasteries under the jurisdiction of the Ecumenical Patriarch of Constantinople.

63. Dostoevsky is referring to Saint Peter, the patron saint of Moscow, who, in 1325, at the request of Grand Prince Ivan Kalita, transferred the metropolitan

cathedral-church from Vladimir to Moscow, thereby strengthening the political position of Moscow and establishing it as the spiritual capital of a fragmented Russia.

Dostoevsky is also referring to Saint Philip II, who was metropolitan of Moscow during the reign of Ivan the Terrible, and who, having dared openly to contradict royal authority, is alleged to have been murdered by the tsar.

64. The Archangel Cathedral is a Russian Orthodox church dedicated to the Archangel Michael. Located in the Kremlin in Moscow and constructed between 1505 and 1508, it was the main necropolis of the tsars until the relocation of the capital to St. Petersburg.

65. Not quite. The bell tower of Ivan the Great has existed since 1508, having been raised by Boris Godunov to its present height in 1600.

66. Dostoevsky has in mind such works as Grigorovich's "The Village," Herzen's *Who Is at Fault?*, and Goncharov's *A Common Story*.

67. Most likely Dostoevsky is thinking about Belinsky's "A Look at Russian Literature in 1846" and "A Look at Russian Literature in 1847"; as well as Maykov's "The Poetry of Koltsov" and "Something about Russian Literature in 1847."

68. At the end of 1846 and the beginning of 1847, the bookseller Alexander Smirdin had published collections of the writings of Vladislav Ozerov, Denis Fonvizin, and Mikhail Lomonosov.

69. A three-volume edition of the works of Krylov appeared in 1847.

70. Dostoevsky has in mind Bernadsky and Agin's album *One Hundred Drawings from the Writings of N. V. Gogol: "Dead Souls,"* which appeared in 1846.

71. Mikhail Nevakovich's album *Jumble* appeared four times a year from 1846 to 1849.

72. Pavlovsk is a town located about twenty miles south of St. Petersburg, and is the site of the Pavlovsk Palace, a major residence of the Russian imperial family.

73. Goncharov wrote *The Frigate Pallada* in 1854–57 and *Oblomov* in 1859. Dostoevsky published *Notes from the House of the Dead* in 1862 and *The Diary of A Writer* in two volumes, the first between 1873 and 1876 and the second between 1877 and 1881.

74. The reference is to Pyotr Karepin, who was the husband of Dostoevsky's sister Varvara, the financial guardian of the family after the death of the writer's father, Mikhail, and a man with whom Dostoevsky warred constantly over money, property, and other matters.

75. Mikhail is referring to a new and separate edition of *Poor Folk*.

76. Most likely the story in question is "Polzunkov."

77. At the time of his arrest in 1849, Dostoevsky owed Nekrasov 165 rubles. So it is reasonable to assume that Nekrasov agreed to the writer's present request for 150 silver rubles.

78. Most likely Dostoevsky is referring to "The Landlady."

79. Dostoevsky is correct here. Mikhail Dostoevsky retired in that month.

80. Dostoevsky is again referring to "The Landlady."

81. In 1848 there came into existence three large journals: *The Geographic News of the Russian Geographic Society*, *The Northern Survey*, and *The Moscow Miscellany*. As Kraevsky was an influential member of the Geographic Society, Dostoevsky was counting on his connections and assistance.

82. Mikhail visited his brother on September 27, 1847.
83. Mikhail Dostoevsky retired from service to the state on October 14, 1847.
84. Such an assertion is false. Andrei Dostoevsky did not even know who Petrashevsky was.
85. Dostoevskaya's story here is again pure fiction.
86. In truth, Pleschcheev was a year or two older.
87. Specifically in Dostoevsky's 1848 story, "The Honest Thief."

Source Notes

Part One

1846 and after. F. Dostoevskii, *Dnevnik pisatelia za 1873 god* (Berlin: Izdatel'stvo I. P. Ladyzhnikova, 1922), 216.
1846 and after. F. Dostoevskii, *Polnoe sobranie sochinenii v tridtsati tomakh*, vol. 27 (Moscow: Khudozhestvennaia literatura, 1984), 120.
1846 and after. Dostoevskii, *Polnoe sobranie sochinenii*, vol. 28, bk. 1 (1985), 296.
1846 and after. Dostoevskii, *Polnoe sobranie sochinenii*, vol. 18 (1978), 122.
1846 and after. S. Ianovskii, "Vospominaniia o Dostoevskom," *Russkii vestnik*, no. 4 (1884), 814–15.
1846 and after. N. Grech, *Zapiski o moei zhizni* (Moscow: Kniga, 1990), 91–92.
1846. P. Annenkov, "Molodost' I. S. Turgeneva, 1840–1856 g.," *Vestnik Evropy*, no. 2 (1884): 467.
1846. A. Dostoevskaya, "God kak zhizn'. Iz zapisnoi knizhki," *Literaturnaia gazeta* (April 16, 1986): 3.
January–March 1846. Dostoevskii, *Polnoe sobranie sochinenii*, vol. 28, bk. 1, 525.
January 1, 1846. V. Belinskii, *Polnoe sobranie sochinenii v tridnadtsati tomakh*, vol. 9 (Moscow: Akademiia nauk, 1955), 407–8.
January 2, 1846. Belinsky, *Polnoe sobranie sochinenii*, vol. 12 (1956), 254.
Before January 24, 1846. D. Grigorovich, *Vospominaniia* (Moscow: Zakharov, 2007), 73.
After January 24, 1846. I. Panaev, *Literaturnye vospominaniia* (Moscow: Pravda, 1988), 162.
After January 24, 1846. V. Sollogub, *Vospominaniia* (Moscow: Academia, 1931), 413–14.
January 26, 1846. Belinskii, *Polnoe sobranie sochinenii*, 261.
January 26, 1846. A. Grigoriev, "Peterburgskii sbornik, izdannyi N. Nekrasovym," *Illiustratsiia* (January 26, 1846): 59.
January 26, 1846. N. Kukol'nik, "Peterburgskii sbornik, izdannyi N. Nekrasovym," *Severnaia pchela* (January 26, 1846): 59.
January 30, 1846. V. Pletnev, *Perepiska Ia. K. Grota s P. A. Pletnevym*, vol. 2 (St. Petersburg: Tipografiia ministerstva putei soobshcheniia, 1896), 663–64.
January 30, 1846. L. Brandt, "Peterburgskii sbornik, izdannyi N. Nekrasovym," *Severnaia pchela* (January 30, 1846): 99.
Late January 1846. L. Lanskii, "Dostoevskii v neizdannoi perepiske sovremennikov (1837–1881)," in *Literaturnoe nasledstvo. F. M. Dostoevskii. Novye materialy i issledovaniia*, ed. V. Shcherbina et al. (Moscow: Nauka, 1973), 370.
Circa February 1846 and after. A. Dolinin, ed., *F. M. Dostoevskii: Pis'ma v chetyrekh tomakh*, vol. 2 (Moscow: Khudozhestvennaia literatura, 1930), 36.

SOURCE NOTES

Circa February 1846 and after. A. Dostoevskaia, *Vospominaniia* (Moscow: Khudozhestvennaia literatura, 1971), 159.
Circa February 1846 and after. Dostoevskii, *Dnevnik pisatelia za 1873 god*, 216.
Circa February 1846 and after. Vs. Soloviev, "Vospominaniia o F. M. Dostoevskom," *Istoricheskii vestnik*, no. 3 (1881): 608.
Circa February 1846 and after. Dostoevskii, *Dnevnik pisatelia za 1876 god* (Berlin: Izdatel'stvo I. P. Ladyzhnikova, 1922), 85.
Circa February 1846 and after. Dostoevskii, *Polnoe sobranie sochinenii*, vol. 11 (1974), 73.
Circa February 1846 and after. Dostoevskii, *Dnevnik pisatelia za 1873 god*, 222.
Circa February 1846 and after. Dostoevskii, *Dnevnik pisatelia za 1873 god*, 219.
Circa February 1846 and after. Dostoevskii, *Dnevnik pisatelia za 1876 god*, 163.
Circa February 1846 and after. F. Dostoevskii, "Zapisnaia tetrad', 1876–1877 gg.," in *Literaturnoe nasledstvo. Neizdannyi Dostoevskii. Zapisnye knizhki i tetradi, 1876–1877 gg.*, ed. V. Shcherbina et al., vol. 83 (Moscow: Nauka, 1971), 526.
Circa February 1846 and after. Dostoevskii, *Dnevnik pisatelia za 1873 god*, 218.
Circa February 1846 and after. Dostoevskii, *Dnevnik pisatelia za 1873 god*, 221–22.
Circa February 1846 and after. Dolinin, ed., *F. M. Dostoevskii. Pis'ma*, vol. 2, 149.
Circa February 1846 and after. Dostoevsky, *Polnoe sobranie sochinenii*, vol. 29, bk. 1 (1986), 145.
Circa February 1846 and after. Dostoevskii, *Polnoe sobranie sochinenii*, vol. 29, bk. 1, 208.
Circa February 1846 and after. Dostoevskii, *Polnoe sobranie sochinenii*, vol. 28, bk. 2 (1985), 259.
Circa February 1846 and after. Dostoevskii, *Dnevnik pisatelia za 1876 god*, 278.
Circa February 1846 and after. Dostoevskii, *Dnevnik pisatelia za 1877 god* (Berlin: Izdatel'stvo I. P. Ladyzhnikova, 1922), 310.
Circa February 1846 and after. Dostoevskii, "Zapisnaia tetrad'," 530.
Circa February 1846 and after. Dostoevskii, "Zapisnaia tetrad'," 530–31.
Circa February 1846 and after. Dostoevskii, "Zapisnaia tetrad', 1880–1881 gg.," 672.
Circa February 1846 and after. Dostoevskii, *Dnevnik pisatelia za 1873 god*, 412–13.
Circa February 1846 and after. Dostoevskii, *Dnevnik pisatelia za 1873 god*, 218–19.
Circa February 1846 and after. Dostoevskii, *Dnevnik pisatelia za 1873 god*, 219–20.
Circa February 1846 and after. Dostoevskii, *Dnevnik pisatelia za 1873 god*, 220.
Circa February 1846 and after. Dolinin, *Dostoevskii, Pis'ma*, vol. 2, 364.
Circa February 1846 and after. Dostoevskii, *Polnoe sobranie sochinenii*, vol. 11 (1974), 73.
Circa February 1846 and after. Dostoevskii, *Polnoe sobranie sochinenii*, vol. 14 (1976), 500.
Circa February 1846 and after. Dostoevskii, *Dnevnik pisatelia za 1873 god*, 220–21.
Circa February 1846 and after. Dostoevskaia, *Vospominaniia*, 159.
Circa February 1846 and after. Dostoevskii, *Dnevnik pisatelia za 1873 god*, 221.
Circa February 1846 and after. Dolinin, *Dostoevskii, Pis'ma*, vol. 2, 364.
Circa February 1846 and after. Dostoevskii, *Polnoe sobranie sochinenii*, vol. 29, bk. 1, 260.
Circa February 1846 and after. Dolinin, *Dostoevskii. Pis'ma*, vol. 2, 364–65.
Circa February 1846 and after. Dostoevsky, *Polnoe sobranie sochinenii*, vol. 29, bk. 1, 146.
Circa February 1846 and after. Dostoevskii, *Polnoe sobranie sochinenii*, vol. 18 (1978), 127.
Circa February 1846 and after. Dostoevskii, *Polnoe sobranie sochinenii*, vol. 3 (1972), 193.
Circa February 1846 and after. Ianovskii, "Vospominaniia," 817.

SOURCE NOTES   235

Circa February 1846 and after. Turgenev, *Polnoe sobranie sochinenii. Sochineniia*, vol. 14 (1967), 52.
Circa February 1846 and after. A. Panaeva, *Vospominaniia* (Moscow: Gosudarstvennoe izdatel'stvo khudozhestvennoi literatury, 1956), 145.
Circa February 1846 and after. Ianovskii, "Vospominaniia," 817.
Circa February 1846 and after. P. Annenkov, *Literaturnye vospominaniia* (Moscow: Pravda, 1989), 259–60.
Circa February 1846 and after. Dostoevskii, *Polnoe sobranie sochinenii*, vol. 27 (1984), 198.
Circa February 1846 and after. Panaeva, *Vospominaniia*, 144–45.
Circa February 1846 and after. Dostoevskaia, *Vospominaniia*, 159.
Circa February 1846 and after. Dostoevskii, *Dnevnik pisatelia za 1873 god*, 39.
Circa February 1846 and after. Dostoevskaia, *Vospominaniia*, 60.
Circa February 1846 and after. Dostoevskaia, *Vospominaniia*, 316.
Circa February 1846 and after. L. Dostoevskaia, *Dostoevskii v izobrazhenii svoei docheri* (St. Petersburg: Andreev i sinov'ia, 1992), 45.
Circa February 1846 and after. Ianovskii, "Vospominaniia," 814.
Circa February 1846 and after. Dostoevskaia, *Vospominaniia*, 159.
Circa February 1846 and after. Dostoevskaia, *Dostoevskii*, 46.
Circa February 1846 and after. Grigorovich, *Vospominaniia*, 84–85.
Circa February 1846 and after. Panaeva, *Vospominaniia*, 144.
Circa February 1846 and after. I. Panaev, "Vospominaniia o Belinskom," *Sovremennik*, no. 1 (1860): 369.
Circa February 1846 and after. Turgenev, *Polnoe sobranie sochinenii*, vol. 14, 52.
Circa February 1846 and after. I. Panaev, "Zametki novogo poeta," *Sovremennik*, no. 12 (December 1855): 238–39.
Circa February 1846 and after. N. Nekrasov, "Kamennoe serdtse," in *Tonkii chelovek i drugie neizdannye proizvedeniia* (Moscow: Federatsiia, 1928), 231–38.
Circa February 1846 and after. Nekrasov, "Kamennoe serdtse," 238–40
Circa February 1846 and after. Nekrasov, "Kamennoe serdtse," 240–44.
Circa February 1846 and after. Nekrasov, "Kamennoe serdtse," 244–48.
Circa February 1846 and after. Nekrasov, "Kamennoe serdtse," 248–51.
Circa February 1846 and after. Nekrasov, "Kamennoe serdtse," 251–55.
Circa February 1846 and after. Nekrasov, "Kamennoe serdtse," 255–60.
Circa February 1846 and after. Nekrasov, "Kamennoe serdtse," 260–62.
Circa February 1846 and after. Nekrasov, "Kamennoe serdtse," 262–68.
Circa February 1846. Panaeva, *Vospominaniia*, 177–78.
Circa February 1846. I. Nikol'skii, *Turgenev i Dostoevskii. Istoriia odnoi vrazhdy* (Sofia: Rossisko-Bolgarskoe Knigoizdatel'stvo, 1921), 5–6.
Circa February 1846. D. Grigorovich, "Iz zapisnoi knizhki D. V. Grigorovicha," *Ezhemesiachnye literaturnye prilozheniia k "Nive,"* no. 11 (1901): 393–94.
Circa February 1846. Grigorovich, *Vospominaniia*, 139.
Circa February 1846. A. Suvorin, "Nabroski i melochi," *Novoe vremia* (May 18, 1880): 4.
Circa February 1846. M. Stasiulevich and M. Lemke, eds., *M. Stasiulevich i ego sovremenniki v ikh perepiske*, vol. 3 (St. Petersburg: M. Stasiulevich, 1912), 388.
Circa February 1846. N. Nekrasov, *Polnoe sobranie sochinenii i pisem v piatnadtsati tomakh*, vol. 4 (Leningrad: Nauka, 1982), 39.

Circa February 1846. A. Dolinin, ed., *F. M. Dostoevskii. Stat'i i materialy*, vol. 2 (Leningrad: Mysl', 1924), 387.
Circa February 1846. D. Grigorovich, "Otryvki iz zapisnoi knizhki D.V. Grigorovicha," *Niva*, no. 11 (1901): 393.
Circa February 1846. Dostoevskaia, *Dostoevskii*, 46.

Part Two

February 1846. Lanskii, "Dostoevskii," 370.
February 1846. Dostoevskaya, *Dostoevskii*, 47.
February 1, 1846. Dolinin, *Dostoevskii. Pis'ma*, vol. 1, 86–87.
February 1, 1846. Dostoevskii, *Dnevnik pistelia za 1877 god*, 456.
February 1, 1846. Belinskii, *Polnoe sobranie sochinenii*, vol. 9, 475–76.
February 1, 1846. Belinskii, *Polnoe sobranie sochinenii*, vol. 9, 493.
February 1, 1846. P. Pletnev, "Novye sochineniia," *Sovremennik*, no. 2 (1846), 273.
February 1, 1846. F. Bulgarin, "Zhurnal'naia vsiakaia vsiachina," *Severnaia pchela*, no. 27 (February 1, 1846): 107.
February 1, 1846. A. Grigoriev, *Literaturnaia kritika* (Moscow: Khudozhestvennia literatura, 1967), 459.
February 5, 1846. Ia. Grot, *Sochineniia i perepiska P.A. Pletneva*, vol. 3 (St. Petersburg: Tipografiia Imperatorskoi Akademii nauk, 1885), 570.
February 6, 1846. Belinskii, *Polnoe sobranie sochinenii*, vol. 12, 261.
February 6, 1846. K. Grot, ed., *Perepiska Ia. K. Grota s P. A. Pletnevym*, vol. 2 (St. Petersburg: Tipografiia Ministerstva putei soobshcheniia, 1896), 668–69.
February 9, 1846. Grot, ed., *Perepiska*, 671.
February 9, 1846. A. Grigoriev, "Novye knigi. Peterburgskii sbornik, izdannyi N. Nekrasovym," *Vedomosti Sankt-Peterburgskoi gorodskoi politsii*, no. 39 (February 9, 1846): 2.
February 10, 1846. Bez podpisi, "Peterburgskii sbornik, izdannyi N. Nekrasovym," *Russkii invalid* (February 10, 1846): 137–38.
February 12, 1846. Bez podipisi, "Peterburgskii sbornik, izdannyi N. Nekrasovym," *Russkii invalid* (February 12, 1846): 137.
February 15, 1846. Lanskii, "Dostoevskii," 370.
February 16, 1846. N. Barsukov, *Zhizn' i trudy M. P. Pogodina*, kn. 8 (St. Petersburg: Tipografiia M.M. Stasiulevicha, 1894), 349.
February 18, 1846. N. Iazykov, "Pis'ma N. M. Iaykova k N. V. Gogoliu," *Russkaia starina*, no. 12 (1896): 640–41.
February 19, 1846. Belinskii, *Polnoe sobranie sochinenii*, vol. 12, 265.
February 28, 1846. L. Brandt, "Russkaia literatura. Zhurnalistika," *Severnaia pchela* (February 18, 1846): 187.
February 28, 1846. L. Brandt, "Russkaia literatura. Zhurnalistika," *Severnaia pchela* (February 28, 1846): 187.
February 28, 1846. Bez podpisi, "Smes'. Literaturnye izvestiia i zametki," *Finskii vestnik*, vol. 8, pt. 5 (1846): 4.
March 1, 1846. Belinskii, *Polnoe sobranie sochinenii*, vol. 9, 543, 549, and 550–51.
March 1, 1846. Belinskii, *Polnoe sobranie sochinenii*, vol. 9, 551–52.
March 1, 1846. Belinskii, *Polnoe sobranie sochinenii*, vol. 9, 552–54.
March 1, 1846. Belinskii, *Polnoe sobranie sochinenii*, vol. 9, 554–55, and 563.

March 1, 1846. Belinskii, *Polnoe sobranie sochinenii*, vol. 9, 563–65.
March 1, 1846. Belinskii, *Polnoe sobranie sochinenii*, vol. 9, 565–66.
March 1, 1846. A. Nikitenko, "Peterburgskii sbornik, izdannyi N. Nekrasovm," *Biblioteka dlia chteniia*, no. 3, otd. 5 (1846), 18, 21, 26, and 30.
March 1, 1846. O. Senkovsky, "Literaturnaia letopis'," *Biblioteka dlia chteniia*, no. 3 (March 1846): 2–3.
March 1, 1846. L. Brandt, "Zhurnalistika," *Severnaia pchela* (March 1, 1846): 191.
March 1, 1846. L. Brandt, "Zhurnalistika," *Severnaia pchela* (March 1, 1846): 191.
March 1, 1846. A. Studitskii, "Russkie literaturnye zhurnaly za fevral' 1846-go goda," *Moskvitianin*, no. 3 (1846): 194.
March 3, 1846. S. Shevyrev, "Peterburgskii sbornik, izdannyi N. Nekrasovym," *Moskvitianin*, no. 2 (1846): 163–70.
March 3, 1846. Shevyrev, "Peterburgskii sbornik," 172–74.
March 4, 1846. K. Grot, "K perepiske N. V. Gogolia s P. A. Pletnevym. Neizdannye pis'ma 1832–1846 gg.," *Izvestiia otdeleniia russkogo iazyka i slovesnosti imperatorskoi Akademii nauk* 5, no. 1 (1900): 279.
March 9, 1846. F. Bulgarin, "Zhurnal'naia vsiakaia viachina," *Severnaia pchela*, no. 55 (March 9, 1846): 218.
March 18–21, 1846. V. Shenrok, "N. V. Gogol' i Viel'gorskie v ikh perepiske," *Vestnik Evropy*, no. 11 (1889): 105.
Circa early spring 1846. Grigorovich, *Vospominaniia*, 76.
April–May 1846 and after. Dostoevskii, *Polnoe sobranie sochinenii*, vol. 28, bk. 1, 224.
April–May 1846 and after. Dostoevskii, *Polnoe sobranie sochinenii*, vol. 28, bk. 1, 296.
April–early May 1846 and after. Ianovskii, "Vospominaniia," 796–99.
April–early May 1846 and after. Ianovskii, "Vospominaniia," 805–6.
April–early May 1846 and after. Dolinin, *F. M. Dostoevskii. Stat'i i materialy*, 380–81.
April 1, 1846. Dolinin, *F. M. Dostoevskii. Pis'ma*, vol. 1, 88.
April 1, 1846. Belinskii, *Polnoe sobranie sochinenii*, vol. 9 (1955), 612 and 650.
April 15, 1846. F. Bulgarin, "Russkaia literatura," *Severnaia pchela*, no. 81 (April 15, 1846): 522.
April 26, 1846. Dolinin, *F. M. Dostoevskii. Pis'ma*, vol. 1, 90–92.
April 30, 1846. A. Grigoriev, "Bibliograficheskaia khronika," *Finskii vestnik*, no. 9 (1846): 21 and 24–30.
May 1, 1846. Bez podpisi, "Moskovskaia letopis. Zhizn' v Moskve v aprele 1846 goda," *Moskvitianin*, no. 5 (1846): 212.
May 14, 1846. N. Gogol', *Polnoe sobranie sochinenii v semnadtsati tomakh*, vol. 13 (Moscow: Izdatel'stvo Moskovskoi Patriarchii, 2009), 319.
Circa mid-May 1846. I. Iakubovich, *Letopis' zhizni i tvorchestva F. M. Dostoevskogo v trekh tomakh*, vol. 1 (St. Petersburg: Gumanitarnoe agentstvo "Akademicheskii proekt," 1993), 117.
May 16, 1846. Dolinin, *F. M. Dostoevskii. Pis'ma*, 92–93.
After May 16, 1846. Dolinin, *F. M. Dostoevskii. Pis'ma*, 569.
After May 16, 1846. Dolinin, *F. M. Dostoevskii. Pis'ma*, 313–14.
May 24, 1846. Dostoevskii, *Polnoe sobranie sochinenii*, vol. 18, 138.
May 24, 1846. Dostoevskii, *Polnoe sobranie sochinenii*, vol. 28, 124.
June 14, 1846. Belinskii, *Polnoe sobranie sochinenii*, vol. 12, 287.
June 15, 1846. Bez podpisi, "Novosti zagranichnye," *Severnaia pchela*, no. 133 (June 15, 1846): 529.

June 24, 1846. N. Iazykov, "Pis'ma N. M. Iazykova k N. V. Gogoliu," *Russkaia starina*, no. 12 (1896): 644.
Circa July 1846 and after. M. Alekseev, ed., *Literaturnyi arkhiv. Materialy po istorii literatury i obshchestvennogo dvizheniia*, vol. 6 (Moscow: Akademiia nauk, 1961), 305.
Circa July 1846 and after. S. Derkach, "I. A. Goncharov i kruzhok Maikovykh," *Uchenye zapiski. Seriia filologicheskikh naukh* 355, no. 76 (1971): 21.
Circa July 1846 and after. A. Skabichevskii, *Literaturnye vospominaniia* (Moscow: Zemlia i fabrika, 1928), 113–15.
Circa July 1846 and after. A. Starchevskii, "Odin iz zabytkh zhurnalistov," *Istoricheskii vestinik*. no. 3 (1886): 374–76.
Circa July 1846 and after. Dolinin, *F. M. Dostoveskii. Stat'i i materialy*, 384.
July 1846. P. Bilyarskii, "Obozrenie russkikh gazet i zhurnalov za pervoe trekhmesiachie 1846 goda," *Zhurnal ministerstva narodnogo prosveshcheniia*, no. 7 (1846): 104.
July 1, 1846. V. Maykov, "Peterburgskie vershiny, opisannye Ia. Butkovym," *Otechestvennye zapiski*, no. 7 (1846): 12.
July 12, 1846. Belinskii, *Polnoe sobranie sochinenii*, vol. 12, 300–301.
August 15–18, 1846. F. Loeve, "'Die armen Leute,' Roman (In Briefen) von F. M. Dostojewski," *Sankt-Peterburgische Zeitung* (August 15–18, 1846): 737–51.
Early September 1846. K. Trutovskii, "Vospominaniia o Feodore Mikhailoviche Dostoevskom," *Russkoe obozrenie*, no. 1 (1893): 216.
September 1, 1846. V. Maykov, "Kratkoe nachertanie istorii russkoi literatury," *Otechestvennye zapiski*, no. 9 (1846): 10.
September 5, 1846. Dolinin, *F. M. Dostoevskii. Pis'ma*, vol. 1, 93–94.
September 11, 1846. Grot, ed., *Perepiska*, 882.
September 17, 1846. Dolinin, *F. M. Dostoevskii. Pis'ma*, 94–96.
September 17, 1846, and after. Grigorovich, *Vospominaniia*, 76–77.
September 17, 1846, and after. Grigorovich, *Vospominaniia*, 77–78.
September 17, 1846, and after. N. Piksanov, *Iz arkhiva F.M. Dostoevskogo. Pis'ma russkikh pisatelei* (Moscow: Gosizdat, 1923), 30.
September 17, 1846, and after. Dolinin, *F. M. Dostoevskii. Stat'i i materialy*, 382–83.
September 17, 1846, and after. V. Bervi-Flerovskii, "Petrashevskii," in *Sorokovye gody XIX veka: v memuarakh sovremennikov, dokumentakh, i khudozhestvennyikh proizvedeniiakh* (Moscow: Khudozhestvannia literatura, 1959), 191.
September 17, 1846, and after. V. Bervi-Flerovskii, "Vospominaniia," *Golos minuvshego*, no. 3 (1915): 143.
September 17, 1846, and after. V. Enisherlov, "Sem'ia moei materi," *Prometei* 13 (1983): 260.
September 17, 1846, and after. R. Poddubnaia, "Beketovskii krug v ideinykh iskaniiakh Dostoevskogo 1840 godov," *Osvobidetel'noe dvizhenie v Rossii* (Saratov) 8 (1978): 30.
Between 21 and 26, 1846. N. Nekrasov, *Polnoe sobranie sochinenii*, vol. 14, bk. 1 (1998), 58.

Part Three

October 1, 1846. E. Liatskii, ed., *Belinskii. Pis'ma*, vol. 3 (St. Petersburg: Tipografiia M. M. Stasiulevicha, 1914), 362.

October 5–8, 1846. A. Herzen, *Sobranie sochinenii v tridtsati tomakh*, vol. 22 (Moscow: Izdatel'stvo Akademiia nauk, 1961), 259.
October 7, 1846. Dolinin, *F. M. Dostoevskii. Pis'ma*, 96–98.
October 14, 1846. A. Pleshcheev, "Peterburgskaia khronika," *Russkii invalid* (October 13, 1846): 908.
Before October 16, 1846. Panaeva, *Vospominaniia*, 144.
Before October 16, 1846. Panaeva, *Vospominaniia*, 145.
Before October 16, 1846. A. Orlova, "Iz vospomaniii o semeinoi zhizni V. G. Belinskogo," in *V pol'zu golodaiushchikh. Lepta Belinskogo* (Moscow: Tipografiia D.I. In Inozemtseva, 1892), 30.
Circa October 16, 1846. I. Pavlovsky, *Souvenirs sur Tourgueneff* (Paris: A. Savine, 1887), 38–39.
Circa October 16, 1846, and after. Panaeva, *Vospominaniia*, 145–46.
After October 16, 1846. Panaeva, *Vospominaniia*, 146.
After October 16, 1846. Grigorovich, *Vospominaniia*, 90.
After October 16, 1846. Dostoevskaya, *Dostoevskii*, 46–47.
After October 16, 1846. Dostoevskii, *Polnoe sobranie sochinenii*, vol. 2 (1972), 152.
October 17, 1846. Dolinin, *F. M. Dostoevski. Pis'ma*, 98–99.
October 18, 1846. Dostoevskii, *Polnoe sobranie sochinenii*, vol. 28, bk. 1, 130.
Late October 1846. Dolinin, *F. M. Dostoevskii. Pis'ma*, 99–102.
November 1, 1846. V. Maykov, "Stikhotvoreniia Kol'tsova," *Otechestvennye zapiski*, no. 11 (1846): 21.
November 9, 1846. F. Bulgarin, "Pis'ma vechnostranstvuiushchago zhida k F. B.," *Severnaia pchela*, no. 254 (November 9, 1846): 1015.
November 17, 1846. V. Kniazhin, ed., *Apollon Aleksandrovich Grigoriev. Materialy dlia biografii* (Petersburg: Izdanie Pushkinskogo Doma pri Akademii Nauk, 1917), 115–16.
November 23, 1846. F. Bulgarin, "Medintsinskaya literatura," *Severnaia pchela*, no. 265 (November 23, 1846): 1059.
November 26, 1846. Dolinin, *F. M. Dostoevskii. Pis'ma*, 102–3.
December 17, 1846. Dolinin, *F. M. Dostoevskii. Pis'ma*, 103–5.
Late 1846 and after. Ianovskii, "Vospominaniia," 799.
Late 1846 and after. Ianovskii, "Vospominaniia," 799–800.
Late 1846 and after. Ianovskii, "Vospominaniia," 802.
Late 1846 and after. Dolinin, *F. M. Dostoevskii. Pis'ma*, 394.
Late 1846 and after. S. Ianovskii, "Bolezn' F. M. Dostoevskogo," *Novoe vremia* (February 24, 1881): 1–2.
Late 1846 and after. Dolinin, *F. M. Dostoevskii, Pis'ma*, vol. 3, 23.
Late 1846 and after. Dostoevskaia, *Dostoevskii*, 49.
Late 1846 and after. G. Galagan, "Konchina i pokhorony F. M. Dostoevskogo (V pis'makh E. A. i M. A. Rykachevykh), in *Dostoevskii. Materialy i issledovaniia*, ed. V. Bazanov, vol. 1 (Leningrad: Nauka, 1974), 303.
Late 1846 and after. A. Dostoevskii, "O F. M. Dostoevskom. Pis'mo k izdatel'iu," *Novoe vremia* (February 8, 1881): 2.
Late 1846 and after. Ianovskii, "Vospominaniia," 802.
Late 1846 and after. Ianovskii, "Vospominaniia," 803.
Late 1846 and after. Ianovskii, "Vospominaniia," 812.

SOURCE NOTES

Late 1846 and after. Dolinin, *F. M. Dostoevskii. Pis'ma*, 395.
Late 1846 and after. Dolinin, *F. M. Dostoevskii. Stat'i i materialy*, 380–81.
Late 1846 and after. Dolinin, *F. M. Dostoevskii. Stat'i i materialy*, 381.
Late 1846 and after. Ianovskii, "Vospominaniia," 813–14.
Late 1846 and after. Dolinin, *F. M. Dostoevskii. Stat'i i materialy*, 393.
Late 1846 and after. Dolinin, *F. M. Dostoevskii. Stat'i i materialy*, 393–94.
Late 1846 and after. Ianovskii, "Vospominaniia," 802.
Circa 1847. Soloviev, "Vospominaniia," 609.
Circa 1847. Dostoevskii, *Polnoe sobranie sochinenii*, vol. 3 (1972), 208.
Circa 1847. Dostoevskaia, *Dostoevskii*, 49.
Circa 1847. Dolinin, *F. M. Dostoevskii. Pis'ma*, 257.
Circa 1847. Grigorovich, *Vospominaniia*, 75–76.
January–February 1847. Dolinin, *F. M. Dostoevskii. Pis'ma*, 105–8.
January 1847 and after. Dostoevskaya, *Dostoevskii*, 48.
January 1847 and after. Panaeva, *Vospominaniia*, 175.
After January–February 1847. Dostoevskii, *Polnoe sobranie sochinenii*, vol. 18, 70–71.
January 1, 1847. Belinskii, *Polnoe sobranie sochinenii*, vol. 10 (1956), 39–40.
January 1, 1847. Belinskii, *Polnoe sobranie sochinenii*, vol. 10, 40–41.
January 1, 1847. Belinskii, *Polnoe sobranie sochinenii*, vol. 10, 41–42.
January 1, 1847. V. Maikov, "Nechto o russkoi literature v 1846 godu," in V. Maikov, *Litereraturnaia kritika. Stat'i, retsenzii* (Leningrad: Khudozhestvennaia literatura, 1985), 179–83.
January 5, 1847. E. Guber, "Russkaia literatura v 1846 godu," *Sankt-Peterburgskie vedomosti* (January 5, 1847): 2.
February 1, 1847. Belinskii, *Polnoe sobranie sochinenii*, vol. 10, 98.
February 19, 1847. Belinskii, *Polnoe sobranie sochinenii*, vol. 12, 335–36.
February 21, 1847. K. Aksakov, "Peterburgskii sbornik, izdannyi Nekrasovym," in *Moskovskii literaturnyi i uchenyi sbornik* (Moscow: Tipografiia Semena, 1847), 29–36.
Circa March 1847 and after. Dostoevskii, *Polnoe sobranie sochinenii*, vol. 18, 138.
March 5, 1847. A. Grigoriev, "Obozrenie zhurnal'nykh iavlenii za ianvar' i fevral' tekushchago goda," *Moskovskii gorodskoi listok* (March 5, 1847): 2.
March 5, 1847. I. Goncharov, "Neizdannye pis'ma I. A. Goncharova," *Krasnyi arkhiv*, no. 2 (February 1923): 257.
March 17, 1847. A. Grigoriev, "Gogol i ego poslednaia kniga," *Moskovskii gorodskoi listok* (March 17, 1847): 250.
March 27, 1847. V. Botkin, *Literaturnaya mysl'. Al'manakh*, vol. 2 (Petrograd: Mysl', 1923), 190.
April–June 1847. Dolinin, *F. M. Dostoevskii. Pis'ma*, 113.
April–mid-May 1847. Dolinin, *F. M. Dostoevskii. Pis'ma*, 112.
April 1, 1847. I. Panaev, "Eshche neskol'ko stikhotvoreniia novogo poeta," *Sovremennik*, no. 4, otd. 4 (1847): 154–55.
April 12, 1847. F. Bulgarin, "Zhurnal'naia vsiakina vsiachina," *Severnaia pchela*, no. 84 (April 12, 1847): 322.
April 13, 1847. Dostoevskii, *Polnoe sobranie sochinenii*, vol. 18, 113–14.
April 21, 1847. L. Brandt, "Russkaia literatura," *Severnaia pchela*, no. 88 (April 21, 1847): 550–51.

SOURCE NOTES 241

April 27, 1847. F. Dostoevskii, *Polnoe sobranie khudozhestyennykh proizvedenii v tridnadtasti tomakh*, vol. 13 (Leningrad: Gosudarstevennoe izdatel'stvo, 1930), 9.
April 27, 1847. Dostoevskii, *Polnoe sobranie khudozhestyennykh proizvedenii*, 11.
April 27, 1847. Dostoevskii, *Polnoe sobranie khudozhestyennykh proizvedenii*, 15.
May 1847. Lanskii, "Dostoevskii," 372.
May 1, 1847. Belinskii, *Polnoe sobranie sochinenii*, vol. 10, 180 and 186.
Circa May 7, 1847. Dolinin, *F. M. Dostoevskii. Pis'ma*, 108–9.
May 30, 1847. A. Grigoriev, "Obozrenie za aprel'," *Moskovskii gorodskoi listok* (May 30, 1847): 465.
June 1847. Belinskii, *Polnoe sobranie sochinenii*, vol. 10, 206.
June 1, 1847. Dostoevskii, *Polnoe sobranie khudozhestyennykh proizvedenii*, 21–23.
June 1, 1847. Dostoevskii, *Polnoe sobranie khudozhestyennykh proizvedenii*, 23.
June 1, 1847. Dostoevskii, *Polnoe sobranie khudozhestyennykh proizvedenii*, 24–26.
June 13, 1847. Lanskii, "Dostoevskii," 372.
June 15, 1847. Dostoevskii, *Polnoe sobranie khudozhestyennykh proizvedenii*, 27–31.
June 17, 1847. A. Grigoriev, "Moskovskii literaturnyi i uchenyi sbornik na 1847 g.," *Moskovskii gorodskoi listok* (June 17, 1847): 524.
Summer 1847. M. Yazykov, "Pis'mo k redaktsiiu," *Novoe vremia* (March 2, 1881): 2.
July 7, 1847. Ianovskii, "Bolezn' F. M. Dostoevskogo," 1–2.
July 7, 1847. Ianovskii, "Vospominaniia," 800–801.
Mid-July 1847. Ianovskii, "Vospominaniia," 801–2.
After July 15, 1847. Dolinin, *F. M. Dostoevskii. Stat'i i materialy*, 383–84.
After July 15, 1847. Grigorovich, *Vospominaniia*, 100.
After July 15, 1847. Ianovskii, "Vospominaniia," 814.
After July 15, 1847. Dostoevskaia, *Vospominaniia*, 60.
July 25, 1847. Nekrasov, *Polnoe sobranie sochinenii*, vol. 14, bk. 1 (1998), 75.
August 1847. I. Goncharov, "V. N. Maikov (Nekrolog)," *Otechestvennye zapiski*, no. 8 (1847): 104–8.
August 15, 1847. Alexei Pleshcheev, "Fel'ton, Peterburgskaia khronika," *Russkii invalid*, no. 181 (August 15, 1847): 2.
August 16, 1847. M. Dostoevskii, "Pis'ma M. M. Dostoevskogo k F. M. Dostoevskomu," in *Iskusstvo*, vol. 3, kn. 1 (1927), 107–8.
Late August–early September 1847. F. Dostoevskii, *Polnoe sobranie sochinenii*, vol. 28, bk. 1, 142–43.
September 9, 1847. Dolinin, *F. M. Dostoevskii. Pis'ma*, vol. 1, 110–12.
September 13, 1847. Dostoevskii, "Pis'ma M. M. Dostoevskogo," 108–9.
Fall 1847 and after. Dostoevskii, *Polnoe sobranie sochinenii*, vol. 18, 139–40.
Fall 1847 and after. Dostoevskaya, *Dostoevskii*, 53.
Fall 1847 and after. Dostoevskaya, *Dostoevskii*, 53.
Circa early October 1847. Ianovskii, "Vospominaniia," 811.
October 1847 and after. Dosteovskaia, *Dostoevskii*, 49.
October 1, 1847. M. Volotskoi, *Khronika roda Dostoevskogo, 1506–1933* (Moscow: Sever, 1933), 173.
November 4–8, 1847. Belinskii, *Polnoe sobranie sochinenii*, vol. 12, 421.
November 20–December 2, 1847. Belinskii, *Polnoe sobranie sochinenii*, vol. 12, 430.

Index

Aksakov, Konstantin, 207; on *The Double*, 172, 181, 190; pen name for, 229n58; on *Poor Folk*, 171, 181, 190
Alexander III (tsar of Russia), 207; Dostoevsky's letter to, 48
Alexandra Fyodorovna (empress of Russia), 86, 125, 207
Annenkov, Pavel, 207; on Belinsky, 29, 50–51, 218n29; on Feuerbach, 218n32; on literary contributions in 1846, 33, 83
Anton Goremyka (Grigorovich), 17, 33
anxiety: Dostoevsky's, 4, 5, 34, 62, 90, 112, 117, 133, 154, 155, 159, 160, 203; of Dostoevsky's characters, 138, 202
atheism, Belinsky's, 45, 46–47, 217n24

Babikov, Konstantin, 207; article commissioned by, 216n16
Balzac, Honoré de, 207; appeal to Dostoevsky, 34; Dostoevsky compared to, 1, 7, 8; publication in Russia, 222n14; Russian counterpart to, search for, 3
Beketov, Alexei, 87, 110, 134, 207
Beketov, Andrei, 87, 207
Beketov, Nikolai, 87, 136, 207
Beketovs, 87–88, 136; Dostoevsky's friendship with, 88, 136, 151, 152, 204; gatherings at, 20, 21, 87, 110, 133, 134–35
Belinskaya, Maria, 207; relations with Dostoevsky, 121, 163; relations with husband, 30; trip to Revel, 118–19, 120, 126–27, 225n51
Belinsky, Grigory Nikiforovich, 2, 207
Belinsky, Vissarion, 207; beliefs of, 29–30, 42–47, 217n20, 217n24; conflicting selves of, 30–31; and *The Contemporary* (journal), 2, 30, 141, 222n6, 224n38; criticism of Gogol, 229n52; death of, 29; defense of Dostoevsky, 142–43; disappointment with Dostoevsky, 7–8, 13–15, 171; *Dmitri Kalinin*, 2; Dostoevsky's article on, 39–40, 216n16; Dostoevsky's conflicted relationship with, xv, 5, 31–32, 40–51, 53, 151, 152; on Dostoevsky's talent, 96, 97, 103, 104, 117, 164, 179; on *The Double*, 13–14, 17, 50–51, 91, 96–97, 101–4, 163, 164–66, 181; efforts to remake Dostoevsky, 5, 6, 13, 31, 50–51, 103, 104; family background of, 1–2; and *The Fatherland Notes* (journal), 2, 30, 116, 222n17, 224n38; goals for literature and life, 2–3; illness of, 29, 30, 224n39; intensity of, 40–41, 46, 220n45; on "The Landlady," 202; letters to Turgenev, 30, 171; and *Leviathan* (almanac), 34, 116, 216n9, 224n40; limitations of, 46, 48–49, 54, 217n25; literary career of, 2, 29; Maykov (Valerian) as successor to, 21, 215n3, 222n6; on "Mr. Prokharchin," 14, 163, 166; on "A Novel in Nine Letters," 14, 171; on *The Petersburg Miscellany*, 35; on *Poor Folk*, critical analysis of, 13, 97–101, 164, 165; on *Poor Folk*, enthusiasm over, 1, 3, 34, 49–50, 54, 57–62, 65–68, 76–77, 89, 91, 94, 95–96; on Pushkin, 48–49, 100, 170, 219n38, 219n40, 220n41; on "Shaved Sideburns," 92; Western thinkers influencing, 29, 47–48; wife of, 30
Belinsky circle: attacks on/lampoons of Dostoevsky, 6–9, 11, 53–57, 82–83, 88, 142–43, 174–76, 205; Dostoevsky's break with, 11, 26, 53–54, 85, 143–45, 150–51, 163–64, 203; gossip and slander in, 8–11, 73–76, 144, 171; initial praise for Dostoevsky, 7, 205; literary sympathizers of, 9–10, 68–73, 77–78, 79–81; Maykovs' gatherings compared to, 87; Nekrasov's *The Stone Heart* as description of, 10–11, 68–81
Bernardsky, Yevstafy, 150, 184, 207, 227n21, 227n22

244 INDEX

Bervi-Flerovsky, Vasily, 136, 207
Bilyarsky, Pyotr, 126, 207
Blanc, Louis, 29, 207
Blok, Alexander, 87, 207
booksellers, Dostoevsky's relations with, 6, 16, 22, 140, 147–48
Botkin, Vasily, 30, 173, 202, 207, 217n24, 221n54
Brandt, Leopold, 208; on Dostoevsky's works, 36–39, 95, 106–7; on Goncharov, 177
"The Bronze Horseman" (Pushkin), 2
The Brothers Karamazov (Dostoevsky), xi; characters in, commonalities with author, 27; reference to Belinsky in, 46; seeds for, in early works, 21
Bulgarin, Faddei, 208, 222n13; criticism of contemporary writers, 117, 149–50, 176; criticism of Dostoevsky's work, 91–92, 110, 149
Butkov, Yakov, 156, 180, 201, 204, 208
Byron, George Gordon (Lord), 208; Dostoevsky compared to, 4; writing process of, 66

Cabet, Étienne, 29, 47, 208, 218n29
"The Carriage" (Gogol), 49, 219n39
Catherine the Great (empress of Russia), 183, 208
censorship: Belinsky on, 6, 220n45; Dostoevsky on, 39, 133, 148
The Chalice (anthology), 216n16
characters, in nineteenth-century Russian literature, 3
characters, in Dostoevsky's fiction: Belinsky circle members compared to, 7, 10; commonalities with author, xiii, xiv, 4, 5, 11, 15, 26, 27, 171, 205, 228n32; criticism of, 11–12; development of, xiv, 139; early, 137, 138–39; Gogol's characters compared to, 97, 109, 137; psychology of, exploration of, 6, 163, 167, 168
circles: literary, 8; social, Dostoevsky on, 177–78. *See also* Belinsky circle; gatherings
A Common Story (Goncharov), 33, 87, 126, 173; Dostoevsky on, 176–77
communism, Belinsky as proponent of, 29, 31–32, 44
The Contemporary (journal): Belinsky's criticism of Dostoevsky's works in, 163; Belinsky's move to, 2, 30, 141, 152, 222n6, 224n38; Dostoevsky's dealings with, 141, 145, 146, 150, 152, 229n48; Gogol's article in, 131; Goncharov's *An Ordinary Story* in, 176; Nekrasov as publisher of, 2, 141, 150, 224n38; rivalry with *The Fatherland Notes*, 146, 150, 152, 179
Crime and Punishment (Dostoevsky), xi, 139, 228n33
"Cult" (Leroux), 218n30
Custine, Marquis de: *Russia in 1839*, 181–82, 229n59

dance, Dostoevsky's love of, 193
deadlines, writing for: Belinsky's complaints about, 30; Dostoevsky's complaints about, 6, 33
Dead Souls (Gogol), 5; Belinsky's views on, 32; Dostoevsky's works compared to, 5, 7, 11, 14, 131; illustrations for, 150, 184, 227n21, 227n22
death: Belinsky's fear of, 30; Dostoevsky's fear of, 18, 131, 159
debt(s), Dostoevsky's, 16, 26, 162; to brother Mikhail, 142, 145, 148; to Kraevsky, 33, 118, 119, 141, 150, 151, 152, 162, 171, 179, 199, 227n25; to Maykovs, 179; to Nekrasov, 150, 162, 197–98, 199, 230n77
Decembrists, 1
democracy, proponents of, 2, 11
depression, Dostoevsky's, 115, 131, 159–60, 161, 162, 203
Devils (Dostoevsky), xi; characters in, 7, 27, 139; "Notes" on, 40–41, 46
Diary of a Madman (Gogol), 223n24; Dostoevsky's works compared to, 11, 92, 97, 160; hero of, 223n28
Diary of a Writer (Dostoevsky). See *A Writer's Diary*
Dickens, Charles: Dostoevsky compared to, 1, 7, 8, 137; Russian counterpart to, search for, 3
Ditmar, Emiliya. See Dostoevskaya, Emiliya
Dmitri Donskoi (grand prince of Moscow), 182, 183
Dmitri Kalinin (Belinsky), 2
Dostoevskaya, Anna (wife): on Dostoevsky's relationship with Belinsky, 40, 47, 53; on Dostoevsky's relationship with Maykov (Apollon), 194; on Dostoevsky's relationship with Nekrasov, 52; marriage of, 225n59; memoirs of, 34, 40, 47, 52, 53; Yanovsky's letters to, 83–84, 114, 126, 135, 154, 157–58, 193

Dostoevskaya, Emiliya (sister-in-law), 202, 208; Belinskaya's visit to Revel and, 118, 120, 121; Dostoevsky's relationship with, 17, 27, 146, 151, 152, 162, 180

Dostoevskaya, Lyubov (daughter): on *The Double*, 163; on father's epilepsy, 155, 160, 215n1; on father's shyness with women, 84; on father's visits to Vielgroskys, 86; on Petrashevsky circle, 200–201; on *Poor Folk*, 88, 163; on response to *Poor Folk*, 52, 53

Dostoevskaya, Maria (mother), 15

Dostoevskaya-Ivanova, Vera (sister): marriage of, 39, 90, 117, 223n19; relationship with brother, 34, 78, 117

Dostoevskaya-Karepina, Varvara (sister), 34, 185

Dostoevsky, Andrei (brother), 202; on Fyodor's illnesses, 155–56; relationship with Fyodor, 122, 146, 155, 228n34; on sister Vera's husband, 223n19

Dostoevsky, Fyodor: alienation from friends and family, 16, 26, 39, 203, 204; anxiety and paranoia of, 4, 5, 34, 62, 90, 112, 117, 133, 154, 155, 159, 160, 203; childhood of, xiii, 4, 15; commitment to truth, 157–58; conflicting selves of, xiv, 8, 27, 204; conservatism of later years, 31; depression of, 115, 131, 159–60, 161, 162, 203; discomfort in public, 3–4, 5, 35, 52, 62–65, 83–84, 174; education of, 4, 18; existing studies of, shortcomings of, xii; faith and patriotism of, 16, 20, 46, 47, 153, 158, 227n30; fascination with dreamers, 23–26, 188–90; financial difficulties of, 16, 26, 116, 118, 120–21, 132, 140–42, 145–48, 158–59, 161–62, 173, 179, 197–99, 229n50; generosity of, 158–59; high hopes regarding, 1, 3, 5, 7, 107; hypochondria of, 18, 19, 33, 90, 111, 112–13, 131, 141, 154–55; independent streak of, 6, 22, 96, 204; indifference to sociopolitical issues, 6, 20; insecurity as writer, 5, 15, 16–17, 62, 63–64, 203, 204; love of music, 20, 52, 86; personal and professional crises in 1846–1847, xiii–xiv, 27–28; physical appearance of, 3, 8, 35, 83, 111, 114; pride and arrogance of, 4–5, 8, 15, 25–26, 50, 51, 53, 54, 55–56, 62, 66, 89–90, 115, 133, 162–63, 174–75, 204; rivals of, 15, 17, 53, 116, 176–77; uneven path to greatness, xi–xiv, 203, 206. *See also specific titles of works*

Dostoevsky, Mikhail (brother): Belinskaya's trip to Revel and, 118–19, 120, 126–27, 225n51; business plans with Fyodor, 147–48, 196–97, 199; children of, 151, 153, 202, 225n52; financial support for Fyodor, 142, 145; letters to, 88–90, 114–19, 120–21, 131–34, 140–42, 145–49, 150–53, 160, 161–63, 179–80, 198–99; move to St. Petersburg, 200, 201–2; relationship with Fyodor, 17, 26–27, 88–90, 117, 132, 150, 151, 202, 204; retirement plans of, 196–97, 198, 200; self-projection on, 26–27, 133–34, 151–52, 161; translations by, 22, 116–17, 180, 199, 225n45

Dostoevsky, Mikhail (father), 6, 15

The Double (Dostoevsky): Aksakov on, 172, 181, 190; author's doubts about, 5, 16–17, 90–91, 116; author's hopes for, 5, 89–90, 160, 162–63; Belinsky's response to, 13–14, 17, 50–51, 91, 96–97, 101–4, 163, 164–66, 181; Brandt's review of, 95; compared to *Poor Folk*, Lyubov Dostoevskaya on, 163; failure of, xiii, 12, 203, 204; Grigoriev on, 119, 149, 173; hero of, 137, 138–39; indifference to sociopolitical issues in, 6; Maykov's praise for, 21, 88, 126, 168–69; parody of, 181; planned publication in book form, 22, 147, 148, 150, 226n13, 227n20; process of writing, 89; publication in *The Fatherland Notes* (journal), 89–90, 220n49; reviewers' condemnation of, 12, 95, 109, 115–16, 126, 137–38, 162, 163, 164–66, 167, 170; seeds for later works in, 21, 138, 139, 205

dreamers, Dostoevsky's fascination with, 23–26, 188–90

Druzhinin, Alexander, 17, 208, 221n54

Dumas, Alexander, 14, 149, 223n31

editing work, Dostoevsky and, 173–74
editors, Dostoevsky's relations with, 6, 16, 26
education, Dostoevsky's, 4, 18
envy, of Dostoevsky's fellow writers, 7, 53, 91, 144–45
epilepsy (falling sickness): causes and treatment of, 227n31; warning symptom of, 228n32
epilepsy, Dostoevsky's: brother Alexei on, 155–56; daughter Lyubov on, 155, 160, 215n1; doubts about, 18–20; Grigorovich on, 215n1; Nekrasov on, 62, 215n2; Yanovsky on, 18–19, 20, 154–55, 191–92; Yazykov on, 19, 190–91

246 INDEX

The Essence of Christianity (Feuerbach), 218n32
Eugene Onegin (Pushkin): Belinsky on, 32, 100; heroine of, 100, 223n29; *Poor Folk* compared to, 7; process of writing, 66

faith: Belinsky's rejection of, 45, 46–47, 217n24; Dostoevsky's, 16, 20, 46, 47, 153, 158, 227n30; Yanovsky's, 18
falling sickness. *See* epilepsy
The Fatherland Notes (journal), 222n17; Belinsky and, 2, 30, 116, 222n17, 224n38; criticism of, 33, 106; Dostoevsky (Fyodor) and, 148, 149, 150, 152; Dostoevsky (Mikhail) and, 225n45; Maykov (Valerian) as lead critic for, 133, 164, 222n6; publication of *Netochka Nezvanova* in, 152, 227n24; publication of *The Double* in, 89–90, 220n49; rivalry with *The Contemporary*, 146, 150, 152, 179
Feuerbach, Ludwig von, 29, 47, 86, 209, 218n32
feuilleton-style journalism, Dostoevsky and, 22–25, 179
financial difficulties, Dostoevsky's, 16, 26, 116, 118, 120–21, 132, 140–42, 145–48, 158–59, 161–62, 173, 179, 197–99, 229n50. *See also* debt(s)
Fourier, Charles, 29, 87, 136, 200, 209, 226n73
French literature: Dostoevsky's work compared to, 13, 101; Gogol's work compared to, 88
French socialists, influence on Belinsky, 29, 44, 47, 48, 218n29, 218n31
friend(s)/friendship, Dostoevsky's: alienation from, 16, 53; with Beketovs, 88, 136, 151, 152, 204; with Belinsky, conflicted nature of, xv, 5, 31–32, 40–51, 53, 121; with brother Mikhail, 17, 26–27, 117, 132, 150, 151, 202, 204; insincere, betrayals by, 7–8, 53–54, 88, 144–45; with Maykovs, 26, 87, 88, 126, 135, 179, 193, 194, 204; with Pleshcheev, 88, 123, 157, 204; with Vielgorskys, 85, 204; with Yanovsky, 17–20, 111–14, 120, 153, 155, 156–57, 201, 204. *See also* gatherings
The Frigate Pallada (Goncharov), 193, 230n73

Gall, Franz Joseph, 113, 209, 224n36
The Gambler (Dostoevsky), 139
gatherings: at Beketovs, 20, 21, 87, 110, 133, 134–35; Dostoevsky as host for, 20–21,

156, 201; Dostoevsky's discomfort at, 3–4, 5, 35, 52, 62–65, 83–84, 174; at Maykovs, 20, 21, 87, 123, 125–26, 135, 193; at Vielgorskys, 20, 21, 83–84, 86
generosity, Dostoevsky's, 158–59
A Gentle Creature (Dostoevsky), 12
German literature, Dostoevsky's work compared to, 8, 119, 137
German national character, Dostoevsky on, 23, 185, 187–88
German philosophers, influence on Belinsky, 29, 42, 47–48
Godunov, Boris (tsar of Russia), 182–83, 209
Goegg-Pouchoulin, Maria, 42, 209, 217n21
Goethe, Johann Wolfgang von, 209; Dostoevsky (Fyodor) compared to, 127; Dostoevsky's (Mikhail) translation of, 116–17, 225n45
Gogol, Nikolai, 209; Belinsky on, 48, 49, 219n37, 219n39; "The Carriage," 49, 219n39; characters of, 3; *Dead Souls*, 5, 7, 11, 14, 32, 131, 150, 184, 227n21, 227n22; death of, 149, 227n16; depiction of social reality in, 167–68; *Diary of a Madman*, 11, 92, 97, 160, 223n24, 223n28; Dostoevsky compared to, 1, 4, 5, 8, 11, 12, 14, 15, 21, 36, 54, 66, 88, 89–90, 92, 96, 97, 122–23, 137, 149, 165, 166, 177; influence on Dostoevsky, claims regarding, 11, 96, 97, 109, 131, 144, 160, 163, 167, 172, 180; *The Inspector General*, 165; Lermontov compared to, 149; letters to, 94, 110, 122–23, 149; Loeve on, 127, 130; "Nevsky Prospekt," 2, 223n25; "The Nose," xi, 2; "The Overcoat," xi, 160, 180, 223n28; path to greatness, xi, xii, 26, 203; on *Poor Folk*, 120; retreat from fiction, 3, 131, 176, 227n16; *Selected Passages from Correspondence to Friends*, 3, 178, 225n67, 229n52; at Vielgorskys' gatherings, 86; writing process of, 66
Goncharov, Ivan, 209; *A Common Story*, 33, 87, 126, 173, 176–77; as Dostoevsky's rival, 15, 17, 116; *The Frigate Pallada*, 193, 230n73; literary debut of, 224n42; at Maykovs' gatherings, 87, 123, 126, 135; obituary for Maykov (Valerian), 194–95; *Oblomov*, 193, 230n73; *The Precipice*, 124
Grech, Nikolai, 33, 209
Grigoriev, Apollon, 209; on Belinsky, 42, 217n20; on *The Double*, 119, 149, 173; on

"Mr. Prokharchin," 180; on "A Novel in Nine Letters," 173; on *Poor Folk*, 35–36, 92, 93, 173, 190
Grigorovich, Dmitri, 204, 209; *Anton Goremyka*, 17, 33; at Beketovs' gatherings, 110, 133, 134–35; on Gogol's influence on Dostoevsky, 160; on Maykovs' gatherings, 193; memoirs of, 34, 53–54, 83, 84; and rumors about Dostoevsky, 6, 8, 53–54, 83, 144, 215n1, 226n7; *The Village*, 17, 133, 152–53, 226n70, 227n28
Grot, Yakov, 36, 92, 132, 209
Guber, Eduard, 169–70, 209

Haymarket Square, St. Petersburg, 228n33; as trigger for Dostoevsky's epilepsy, 19, 155
Hegel, Georg, 29, 209
A Hero of Our Time (Lermontov), 7, 149
Herzen, Alexander, 209; Belinsky's letters to, 30, 34, 35, 92, 94, 217n24; as Dostoevsky's rival, 15, 17, 116, 140; socialist ideas and, 218n32; works of, 17, 224n42
Hoffmann, E. T. A., 209; Dostoevsky compared to, 8, 119, 137
Hugo, Victor, 209; Dostoevsky compared to, 1, 7, 8, 149–50; publication in Russia, 222n14; Russian counterpart to, search for, 3
hydrotherapy, 162, 228n38
hypochondria, Dostoevsky's, 18, 19, 33, 90, 111, 112–13, 131, 141, 154–55

The Idiot (Dostoevsky), xi; characters in, 3, 139; seeds for, in early works, 21
illnesses, Dostoevsky's, 16, 26; Belinsky on, 50, 142–43; brother Andrei on, 155–56; impact on literary activities, 32; self-reported, 19, 33, 90, 111, 117–18, 131, 159–60, 162, 173, 180; Yanovsky on, 18, 26, 112–13, 153–55, 191–92; Yazykov on, 19, 190–91. *See also* anxiety; depression; epilepsy; hypochondria
Illustration (newspaper), 89, 222n12
The Inspector General (Gogol), 165
The Insulted and Injured (Dostoevsky), 49, 159–60
Ivan IV the Terrible (Grand Prince of Moscow), 182, 183, 209
Ivanov, Alexander Pavlovich, 39, 209, 223n19
Izmailov, Alexander, 86, 209, 225n63

journalism: Belinsky's repugnance for, 30; Dostoevsky's work in, 22–25, 39–40, 179. *See also specific journals*

Karepin, Pyotr, 198, 209
Katkov, Mikhail, 33, 111, 210
Khanykov, Nikolai, 87, 210
"Khor and Kalinych" (Turgenev), 17
Kraevsky, Andrei, 210; Belinsky's work for, 30, 224n38; Dostoevsky's indebtedness to, 33, 118, 119, 141, 150, 151, 152, 162, 171, 179, 199, 227n25; Dostoevsky's works published by, 132, 146, 152, 202
Krylov, Ivan, 184, 210; Loeve on, 127, 130
Kukolnik, Nikolai, 210, 222n12; review of *Poor Folk*, 36
Kvitka-Osnovyanenko, Hryhory, 210; Dostoevsky compared to, 11, 12, 36; *Mr. Kholyavsky*, 148, 226n15

Lamennais, Robert de, 29, 210
"The Landlady" (Dostoevsky): author's doubts about, 5; failure of, xiii, 12, 26, 137–38, 202, 203, 204; hero of, 137, 138–39, 228n41; indifference to sociopolitical issues in, 6; publication of, 226n10; significance for later works, 138, 139, 205; writing of, 163, 198
Lermontov, Mikhail, 201; Dostoevsky compared to, 1, 7, 11, 14, 132; Gogol compared to, 149; *A Hero of Our Time*, 7, 149
Leroux, Pierre, 29, 47, 210; "Cult," 218n30
Leviathan (almanac), 34, 116, 140, 216n9, 224n40, 226n1
liberalism, proponents of, 2, 11, 31, 42, 43
The Library for Reading (journal), 89, 152, 222n14
literary circles, 8. *See also* Belinsky circle
literary criticism: Dostoevsky on, 184; impact on writers, Belinsky on, 170–71
Lkhovsky, Ivan, 19, 210
Loeve, Ferdinand, 127–31, 210

Main Engineering Academy, St. Petersburg, 3, 18, 20, 87, 221n55
Maykov, Apollon, 19, 86, 123–24, 210; Dostoevsky's letters to, 39–40, 42–43, 49; friendship with Dostoevsky, 88, 194; Pleshcheev's letter to, 123; Yanovsky's letter to, 154
Maykov, Konstantin, 125, 210
Maykov, Leonid, 86, 124, 125, 210
Maykov, Nikolai, 86, 123, 124–25, 135, 210

Maykov, Valerian, 86, 124, 125, 194–96, 210; as Belinsky's successor, 21, 215n3, 222n6; as critic, 164, 195; death of, 21, 135, 164; on *The Double*, 21, 88, 126, 168–69; insights into Dostoevsky's early work, 21, 88, 131, 133, 166–69, 204; on masters of Russian literature, 149; on *Poor Folk*, 166–67, 168; wife of, 86, 125, 225n62

Maykov, Vladimir, 124, 125, 210

Maykova, Natalya, 86, 125, 210, 225n62

Maykova, Yevgenya, 86, 114, 124, 125, 135, 211

Maykovs, 86–87, 123–26; gatherings at, 20, 21, 87, 123, 125–26, 135, 193; support for Dostoevsky, 26, 87, 179, 204

medicine, Dostoevsky's interest in, 20, 113

Melgunov, Nikolai, 88, 94, 211

Miller, Orest, 120, 211

money management, Dostoevsky's difficulty with, 158–59. *See also* financial difficulties

Mr. Kholyavsky (Kvitka-Osnovyanenko), 148, 226n15

"Mr. Prokharchin" (Dostoevsky): author's doubts about, 5; Belinsky's review of, 14, 163, 166; censorship of, 133; echoes of previous works in, 224n41; failure of, xiii, 12, 203, 204; hero of, 137, 138–39, 228n32; indifference to sociopolitical issues in, 6; Maykov (Valerian) on, 169; presented at Maykovs' gatherings, 87; publication of, 132; reviewers' condemnation of, 137–38, 170, 180, 226n9; significance for later works, 138, 139, 205; writing process for, 119, 163, 225n49; Yanovsky on, 193

The Muscovite (journal), 223n26

music, Dostoevsky's love of, 20, 52, 86, 152

Natural school in Russian literature, 173, 223n20

Nechaev, Sergei, 48, 211

Nekrasov, Nikolai, 211; attacks on/lampoons of Dostoevsky, 6, 9, 82–83; Belinsky's difficulties with, 30; and *The Contemporary* (journal), 2, 141, 224n38; Dostoevsky on character of, 52; Dostoevsky's clashes with, 5, 81–82, 150–51, 152, 164; Dostoevsky's indebtedness to, 150, 162, 197–98, 199, 230n77; Dostoevsky's works published in journal of, 52, 53, 140, 220n49; efforts to remake Dostoevsky, 5, 6; excitement over Dostoevsky's *Poor Folk*, 1, 3; family background of, 2; and *Illustrated Almanac*, 194; literary career of, 2–3; at Maykovs' gatherings, 135; and Natural school in Russian literature, 223n20; "On the Road," 92, 94, 223n21; and Panaeva, 225n66; "The Petersburg Corners," 150; *The Stone Heart*, 10–11, 57–81, 215n2, 221n54; translations for, 116

Netochka Nezvanova (Dostoevsky): characters in, 7, 86, 144–45, 162; process of writing, 22, 141, 147; publication of, 26, 152, 179, 227n24

Nevakovich, Mikhail, 184, 211, 230n71

"Nevsky Prospekt" (Gogol), 2, 223n25

Nicholas I (tsar of Russia), 1, 125

Nikitenko, Alexander, on *Poor Folk*, 104–5

The Northern Bee (newspaper), 89, 106, 117, 222n13

"The Nose" (Gogol), xi, 2

Notes from the House of the Dead (Dostoevsky), 193, 230n73

Notes from the Underground (Dostoevsky), xi, xii, 27, 139

"A Novel in Nine Letters" (Dostoevsky): author's doubts about, 5; Belinsky on, 14, 171; failure of, xiii, 12, 137–38, 203, 204; Grigoriev on, 173; indifference to sociopolitical issues in, 6; publication of, 229n48; significance for later works, 138, 139, 205

Oblomov (Goncharov), 193, 230n73

Odoevsky, Vladimir, 89, 211

"On the Road" (Nekrasov), 92, 94, 223n21

Orlova, Agrafena, 126, 143, 211, 225n51

Orlova, Maria, 30. *See also* Belinskaya, Maria

"The Overcoat" (Gogol), xi, 160, 180, 223n28

Panaev, Ivan, 211; attacks on/lampoons of Dostoevsky, 6, 8, 9, 55–57, 82–83, 174–76; on Belinsky's anthology (*Leviathan*), 140; Belinsky's difficulties with, 30; and *The Contemporary* (journal), 141; Dostoevsky compared to, 204; Dostoevsky's clashes with, 5, 164; on *Poor Folk*, 54

Panaeva, Avdotya, 211; Dostoevsky's feelings for, 90; on Dostoevsky's pride and arrogance, 54, 81–83; on Dostoevsky's relations with Belinsky, 50, 51; on Dostoevsky's withdrawal from Belinsky circle, 143–44, 163–64; and Nekrasov, 225n66

patriotism: Dostoevsky's, 20, 48, 153, 227n30; Yanovsky's, 18
Pavlov, Nikolai, 88, 211
Pavlovsky, Isaak, 143, 211
"The Petersburg Chronicle" (Dostoevsky), 22–25, 26; excerpts from, 176–78, 181–90
"The Petersburg Corners" (Nekrasov), 150
The Petersburg Miscellany (anthology): Nekrasov and, 2; pictorial advertisement for, 106–7; publication of *Poor Folk* in, 35, 91, 106–7, 133, 216n8, 220n49
Petersburg tradition, in Russian literature, 2
Peter the Great (emperor of Russia): architecture associated with, 183; Belinsky on, 30; Dostoevsky on, 22, 187; and Table of Ranks, 109, 224n35
Petrashevsky, Mikhail: Dostoevsky (Andrei) and, 200–201, 231n84; Dostoevsky (Fyodor) and, 6, 121–22, 172; Dostoevsky (Mikhail) and, 200; Maykov (Valerian) and, 86; and *Pocket Dictionary of Foreign Words*, 222n7; as proponent of Fourier, 136
Petrashevsky affair, Dostoevsky's involvement in, xiv, 9, 21, 154, 201, 205
phrenology, 113, 224n36
physical appearance, Dostoevsky's, 3, 8, 35, 83, 111, 114
Pleshcheev, Alexei, 87, 211; Dostoevsky's critique of work of, 201; on Dostoevsky's talent, 21, 142; friendship with Dostoevsky, 88, 123, 157, 204; on Maykov (Valerian), 195–96
Pletnyov, Pyotr, 211; letter to Gogol, 110; on *Poor Folk*, 36, 91, 92, 122, 132
Pocket Dictionary of Foreign Words, 86, 222n7
Pogodin, Mikhail, 88, 94, 211, 223n26
Poor Folk (Dostoevsky): Aksakov on, 171, 181, 190; Belinsky's critical analysis of, 13, 97–101, 164, 165; Belinsky's excitement over, 1, 3, 34, 49–50, 54, 57–62, 65–68, 76–77, 89, 91, 94, 95–96; criticism of, 11–12, 13, 35–39, 89, 91–101, 104–9, 119–20, 122–23, 164, 167, 170, 171, 190; Dostoevskaya (Lyubov) on, 88, 163; enthusiastic reception of, xi, 1, 3, 7, 34–35, 52, 57–61, 88, 89, 93–94, 111, 170, 204; envy over success of, 7, 53, 91; failure of writings immediately following, xiii, 6, 7–8, 11–15, 203, 204; Gogol's comments on, 120; Gogol's influence on, claims regarding, 88, 93, 109, 144, 160; Grigoriev on, 35–36, 92, 93, 173, 190; Guber on, 170; Loeve's analysis of, 127–31; parodies of, 53; pictorial advertisement for, 106–7; process of writing, 66, 221n56; psychological analysis in, Maykov on, 168; publication in book form, plans for, 22, 140, 147–48, 150, 162, 197, 199, 226n13, 227n20; publication in *The Petersburg Miscellany*, 35, 91, 106–7, 133, 216n8, 220n49; seeds for later works in, 21; Shevyryov's analysis of, 107–9; success of, impact on author, xiii–xiv, 1, 3, 4–5, 7, 15
Poretsky, Alexander, 19, 211
The Precipice (Goncharov), 124
pride and arrogance, Dostoevsky's, 4–5, 8, 15, 25–26, 50, 51, 53, 54, 55–56, 62, 66, 89–90, 115, 133, 162–63, 174–75, 204
Priessznitz, Vincenz, 162, 211, 228n38
progressivism: efforts to mold Dostoevsky in guise of, 5; proponents of, 2, 87, 123
Proudhon, Pierre-Joseph, 29, 47, 211
psychological analysis, in Dostoevsky's works, 6, 163; Maykov on, 167, 168
publishers, Dostoevsky's relations with, 6, 16, 26
Pushkin, Alexander, 211; Belinsky on, 48–49, 100, 170, 219n38, 219n40, 220n41; "The Bronze Horseman," 2; characters of, 3; critical reception of works of, 170; death of, 3; Dostoevsky compared to, 1, 4, 14, 66, 89, 96, 137, 149–50; *Eugene Onegin*, 7, 32, 66, 100, 219n40, 223n29; Loeve on, 127, 130; path to greatness, xi, xii, 203, 206; *The Tales of Belkin*, 48, 219n38; writing process of, 66
Pyat, Felix, 48, 211, 219n34

railways, construction of, 40–41
A Raw Youth (Dostoevsky), 139
realism, in Russian literature, 204; Belinsky as proponent of, 29, 45; Dostoevsky and, 3, 12, 204, 205; Natural School and, 223n20
Reference Encyclopedia Dictionary, 173, 229n50
religion: Belinsky on, 45, 46–47, 217n24; Dostoevsky and, 16, 20, 46, 47, 113, 153, 158, 227n30; Feuerbach on, 218n32; Leroux on, 218n30; Strauss on, 219n33; Yanovsky and, 18
Renan, Ernest, 45, 217n23

Revel (Tallinn), Estonia, 225n46; Belinskaya's trip to, 118–19, 120, 126–27, 225n51; Dostoevsky's visits to, 27, 118, 122, 152, 227n27
Rubinstein, Anton, 225n52
Russia in 1839 (Custine), 181–82, 229n59
Russian history and nationality, Dostoevsky on, 22–23, 182–84
Russian literature: contemporary, Dostoevsky on, 184–85; Dostoevsky held as hope for, 1, 3, 7, 107; Dostoevsky's place in, Belinsky on, 97; Dostoevsky's place in, Loeve on, 127, 130–31; Guber on, 169–70; Natural school in, 173, 223n20; progressivism in, proponents of, 2, 87, 123; versus western European literature, 2–3; women in, portrayal of, 100
Russian national character: Dostoevsky on, 23, 177, 185–89; Shevyryov on, 109
Rykacheva, Yevgenya, 155, 212

Saint-Simon, Henri de, 29, 212
Saltykov-Shchedrin, Mikhail, 212, 218n31
Sand, George, 212; Belinsky on, 47, 218n28; *Lucrezia Floriani*, 162, 228n41; publication in Russia, 222n14
Schelling, Friedrich, 29, 212
Schiller, Friedrich, 29, 212; Dostoevsky's (Mikhail) translation of, 199
Scribe, Eugène, 212, 222n14
Selected Passages from Correspondence to Friends (Gogol), 3, 178, 225n67, 229n52
Senkovsky, Osip, 212, 222n14; on *Poor Folk*, 105–6
Senyavina, Alexandra, 84, 175, 212, 229n51
"Shaved Sideburns" (Dostoevsky), 116, 133, 142, 224n41; Belinsky on, 92; efforts to publish, 145–46
Shevyryov, Stepan, 18, 212, 223n26; on *The Double*, 109; on *Poor Folk*, 107–9
Siberia, exile in, xiv, 9, 156, 205
siblings, Dostoevsky's relationship with, 16; with Andrei, 122, 146, 155, 228n34; with Mikhail, 17, 26–27, 117; with Varvara, 34, 185; with Vera, 34, 117, 178, 223n19
Skabichevsky, Alexander, 123–24, 212
Slavophiles: Belinsky and, 42, 43–44, 217n20; versus Westernizers, 6, 23
Smirdin, Alexander, 184, 212, 230n68
social gatherings. *See* gatherings

socialism: Belinsky as champion of, 29, 31–32, 45, 47; discussions of, 87; Maykov (Valerian) as champion of, 86
sociopolitical issues: Belinsky's views on, 29–30, 31–32; Dostoevsky's indifference regarding, 6, 20; in Gogol's works, 167–68
Socrates, Dostoevsky compared to, 18, 114
Sollogub, Vladimir, 85, 212; on *Poor Folk*, 34–35, 89
Solovyov, Vsevelod, 40, 159, 212
Starchevsky, Albert, 212; Dostoevsky's work for, 173–74, 229n50; on Maykovs, 124–26
The Stone Heart (Nekrasov), 10–11, 57–81, 215n2, 221n54
St. Petersburg: Dostoevsky on, 23, 181, 183. *See also under* Petersburg
Strakhov, Nikolai, 212; Dostoevsky's letters to, 43, 45–46, 48–49
Strauss, David, 29, 48, 212, 219n33
Sue, Eugène, 14, 149, 223n31, 224n42
Surovin, Alexei, 83, 213

"A Tale about Destroyed Offices" (Dostoevsky), 116, 224n41
talent, Dostoevsky's: Belinsky on, 96, 97, 103, 104, 117, 164, 179; Brandt on, 106; Gogol on, 120; Guber on, 170; impact of criticism on, debate regarding, 170–71; Pleshcheev on, 142; questioning of, 179; Senkovsky on, 106; Shevyryov on, 109
The Tales of Belkin (Pushkin), 48, 219n38
Tolstoy, Leo, xi, xii, 203, 206, 213
truth, Dostoevsky's commitment to, 157–58
Trutovsky, Konstantin, 131, 132, 213
Tseidler, Pyotr, 19, 213
Turgenev, Ivan, 213; attacks on/lampoons of Dostoevsky, 6, 9, 82–83, 142, 143; on Belinsky, 46, 49–50, 54, 217n25, 220n45; Belinsky's criticism of, 49; Belinsky's letters to, 30, 171; Dostoevsky's clashes with, 5, 8, 53–54, 142–43, 144; on Grigorovich, 226n7; "Khor and Kalinych," 17; and Natural school in Russian literature, 223n20; path to greatness, xi, xii, 203, 206

Vielgorskaya, Anna, 213; correspondence with Gogol, 110, 120
Vielgorskaya, Luiza, 85–86, 213

Vielgorsky, Mikhail, 85, 86, 213
Vielgorskys, 85–86; gatherings at salon of, 20, 21, 83–84, 86; as haven for Dostoevsky, 85, 204
The Village (Grigorovich), 17, 133, 152–53, 226n70, 227n28
The Village of Shepanchikovo and Its Inhabitants (Dostoevsky), 224n41

Westernizer(s): Belinsky as, 23, 30, 31, 42; Dostoevsky on, 44; *The Fatherland Notes* (journal) and, 222n17; influence on Dostoevsky, 23; versus Slavophiles, 6, 23
women: Dostoevsky's attitude toward, 8, 16, 33, 55, 84, 90, 175, 193; portrayal in Russian literature, Belinsky on, 100
women's movement, Belinsky and, 42, 220n43
A Writer's Diary (Dostoevsky), 6, 193, 230n73; on Belinsky, 16, 40, 41–42, 43, 44–45, 46–47, 51; on *The Double*, 90–91; on Nekrasov, 52
writing style, Dostoevsky's: Aksakov's parody of, 181; Belinsky's criticism of, 13, 14, 51, 164, 165; long-windedness of, criticism of, 51, 89, 104, 164, 165, 167, 169, 170

Yanovsky, Stepan, 17–20; commonalities with Dostoevsky, 17–18; on Dostoevsky's attitude toward women, 33, 193; on Dostoevsky's commitment to truth, 157–58; on Dostoevsky's epilepsy, 18–19, 20; on Dostoevsky's generosity, 158–59; on Dostoevsky's goals, 120; on Dostoevsky's interest in music and dance, 52, 193; friendship with Dostoevsky, 17–20, 111–14, 120, 153, 155, 156–57, 201, 204; introduction to Dostoevsky, 111; letters to Anna Dostoevskaya, 83–84, 114, 126, 135, 154, 157–58, 193; on Maykovs, 135; medical treatment of Dostoevsky, 18, 26, 112–13, 153–55, 191–92
Yazykov, Mikhail: on Dostoevsky's epilepsy, 19, 190–91; Dostoevsky's plans to publish with, 141; at Maykovs' gatherings, 135; on *Poor Folk*, 94, 122–23

www.ingramcontent.com/pod-product-compliance
Lightning Source LLC
Chambersburg PA
CBHW020834160426
43192CB00007B/643